VALUES IN HIGHER EDUCATION

VALUES IN HIGHER EDUCATION

Edited by Simon Robinson and
Clement Katulushi

Aureus & The University of Leeds

First published in 2005 by
Aureus Publishing Limited on behalf of the University of Leeds

ISBN 1-899750-13-4

A catalogue record for this book is available from the British Library

Typeset by Andrew Buckley, Clunton, Shropshire

Printed and bound in Great Britain

Aureus Publishing Limited
Castle Court
Castle-upon-Alun
St Bride's Major
Vale of Glamorgan
CF32 0TN
Tel: 01656 880033
International Tel/Fax: (+044) 1656 880033
E-mail: sales@aureus.co.uk
Website: *www.aureus.co.uk*

Contents

CONCLUSION

Preface

Melvyn Bragg

In some ways modern universities threaten to return to their origins in the Middle Ages. Then they were primarily engines for the furthering of the authority of the almost unimaginably powerful Roman Catholic Church. They were also the source of the law of the land – an equally utilitarian function.

Now the purpose of universities, in the minds of many politicians and powerbrokers, is as the engine of economic growth, involved in all the material advancements of the hitherto unimaginably far reaching consequences of successive technological revolutions. China aims to build ten universities over the next ten years. Each one to be as well-endowed, and as effective, as Harvard. Leaders the world over are being advised that in the accelerated Age of Information, the university is king.

But 'uneasy lies the head…' In this country the project is to put 50 per cent of 18–30 year olds through modern universities. This means encouraging mature as well as traditional students to come to universities. In the late fifties when I went to university, the figure, of mostly traditional students, was about seven per cent. The strain of this inflation (now quite near realisation) is inevitable and evident. And so more universities have been created – mostly from Polytechnics. Sixth forms have also expanded greatly, and so have the expectations of higher education. But investment has not kept pace, and teachers, lecturers and post-graduate students have suffered a comparative and demoralising slip in professional regard, and in the salary league, at the same time as they have borne much of the burden of this violent growth.

I am on the side of growth, and from my perspective as Chancellor of the University of Leeds I see its advantages on all sides. I also see its problems.

Some talk of 'crisis'. But then 'crisis', like 'chaos', has become a cheapened word. There is however a serious resource problem, one which leads into several levels of debate on underlying values.

The current form of attack is to raise tuition fees. This has set off an acrimonious debate. Broadly there are those who believe that university education should be as freely available as primary and secondary education. Those at the other extreme believe that for the chosen 50 per cent to be subsidised through the third stage of education out of the pockets of those who will not receive the proven life and income benefits for such an education is socially and morally unacceptable. And – because this debate has brought in many players – there are those, fed up with what they see as the bureaucratic and political stupidity of the arguments, who want to cut loose from government altogether and set up their university shop independently, USA-style.

I receive letters from students saying that the debt from tuition fees is too great to bear. Yet I read the speeches and see the legislation of politicians showing an extraordinary care taken to cushion the worst off and to enable the better off to repay their debts inside a flexible and tolerant system.

There are those who ask why should the other 50 per cent of 18–30 year olds get no help solely because they do not shine in that rather narrow band of achievement called 'academic excellence'. This is an argument which needs to be considered. Yet there are others who claim that the country should be very grateful that an 18-year-old is devoting such a long time to train as a doctor. Then there is Philip Green, one our greatest entrepreneurs, who deeply questions the value for the nation of so many young people using – he might say wasting – their best years in academia and not in a university of hard knocks. He has a popular following, with many people arguing that we get far too many graduates but we cannot find enough skilled plumbers, electricians or practical engineers, those who drive the manufacturing economy. Historians can point to the track record of those who did not go to university to underpin this argument. And in the arts, the sciences, politics, and in the study of war and commerce, there is a list every bit as distinguished of those who did not as those who did go to university.

So universities at the moment are central to the national debate. They are the water-cooler around which is gathered arguments about the society we want to be. For many people universities are seen as the 'Open Sesame' to the riches of the future. I tend to agree with that and it may be true. In certain proven areas, as we can see over a whole range of medical studies, to take but one instance at the University of Leeds, they certainly are. But questions remain, about purpose and values, and it is very timely that representatives from different disciplines address them within these covers. There was never a better time for 'jaw-jaw' on this subject than now.

Introduction

[The university] is a place where those who hate ignorance may strive to know; where those who perceive truth may strive to make others see; where seekers and learners alike, banded together in the search for knowledge, will honour thought in all its finer ways, will welcome thinkers in distress or in exile, will uphold ever the dignity of thought and learning and will exact standards on these things. (John Masefield)

R on Dearing, in the foreword of his 1997 report, quotes Masefield with approval, as summing up the values 'which characterise higher education and which are fundamental to any understanding of it'. There are many universities in tight corners who might not recognise in this quote the reality of their life in HE. Nonetheless, it has a fine feeling and Dearing later begins to unpack such values through suggesting the four basic aims of the university:

• To develop individuals' potential to be well equipped for work and to contribute to society.

• To increase knowledge and understanding – for their own sake and for the economy.

• To serve the needs of the economy at all levels.

• To shape a democratic, civilised and inclusive society.[1]

This series of purposes and values takes us very quickly in a complex debate, and our book tries to capture something of that depth and complexity.

Much of the discussion in this book comes from debates held at the University of Leeds, and involves many who have clear connection to the university. Rowan Williams, for instance, spent some years teaching at Mirfield Theological College before moving to Cambridge, and Peter Scott is a former Pro-Vice-Chancellor at Leeds. It is fitting that on its 100th anniversary the University of Leeds should be leading a reflection on the

1

purpose and values of higher education. Other contributors remind us of the global and diverse nature of modern higher education. Universities which have grown out of apparently local and civic interest are now inescapably global and must deliver education in many different ways.

This book is about the continuing development of higher education and how this occurs in relation to ever changing stakeholders and needs. The purpose of universities in the thirteenth century was to do with teaching and preparation for the professions of the law and the clergy. Now universities seek to serve the interests of a much wider number of professions, the nation in economic terms, and the nation in terms of culture and civilisation, in the broadest sense. Today, they seek to teach but also research. This means that the values debate in turn has become evermore complex.

It is important in all this is to both have a conceptual overview and also to place the values debate in the context of the practice of higher education. And when this happens then surprises might occur. Perhaps the historic values of higher education are not as clear as we thought? Perhaps the recent changes in higher education have brought in a new set of values around the concepts of accountability and transparency? Perhaps higher education has many purposes and with those many different values, not all of which rest easily together?

To articulate and test such values, this book brings together many different perspectives, based on the premise that no single discipline or perspective can claim to understand this issue or solely own any of the values in question. Hence, the book brings together representatives of many different disciplines and professions including: an engineer, a physicist, a mathematician, a theologian, a philosopher, a counsellor, sociologists, a chaplain, an administrator, a poet, teachers, and researchers.[2]

In the first part of this book, the different perspectives are subjected to critical scrutiny, and it soon becomes apparent that there are further questions about the foundation of any values. Peter Scott examines the rise of the civic university and the way in which the university and the city are in constant dialogue. The underlying values are not fixed but shaped by this continuing discourse.

Rowan Williams takes us into the learning enterprise, through reflection on human nature. The basis of values in higher education is humankind's capacity to reflect and ultimately to be aware of his own learning. This 'learning about learning' is at the heart of personal and social development, enabling the person to keep value questions alive in practice. Some of the invariant values that Bauman points are precisely necessary for that purpose, the values of commitment to, and of faith *in* the university, in particular. It is such a faith that enables reflection and dialogue.

Zygmunt Bauman suggests something more of a culture clash between the 'invariant values' of education and the values of the liquid-modern age. Education embodies commitment to people and projects, patience, durability, and resilience, all of which he argues are lacking in an age of instant gratification and constant movement, an age of 'thin ice' where the most valued skills facilitate swift skating. In the light of such a clash, there is the danger that education will move towards such values, perhaps with a concern to be 'value neutral'. In this light education becomes a commodity rather than development mediated by dialogue.

Dialogue is central to Thomas Bender's work. His focus, however, is the academic disciplines. From an American perspective, he contrasts 'strong disciplines' (with clearly defined boundaries) and 'weak disciplines' (with more open boundaries). Each has its own problems and limitations. Above all, none can claim an objective summary of the truth. Objectivity, so far as this is possible, he argues, needs the 'countercheck produced by a plurality of partial views'. Hence, Bender argues for interdisciplinary dialogue and democracy as critical to any search for truth. This is not simply a cosy respect or tolerance for each discipline, but a strong model of collaboration and creativity.

The theme of discourse continues in Alan Wilson's chapter, with Habermas at the centre of values that are constantly evolving. Alongside teaching and research, he notes the importance of the 'third arm', the university's work with industry and community. Working with the third arm is partly a matter of value dialogue, but also a matter of integrity. The pressures to commercialise can be resisted so long as the university remains true to its core values, especially its focus on students. Hence, universities are increasingly seeing the 'best student experience' as a key part of any long-term planning.

Bob Fryer then looks at core social values of citizenship and equality. Widening access to higher education can itself enable improved life chances for many more. But the very enterprise of higher education is also an equalizing enterprise. R.H. Tawney saw this as the kingdom of ideas in which inequalities of class faded before the shared search for truth, and a shared concern for the common good. Higher education can also enable reflection which helps the student to focus on responsibility and thus citizenship.

In chapter seven, Miriam David looks at the contribution of feminist perspectives to higher education and to pedagogic developments in particular. The broader qualities of care, empathy and holistic thinking are seen to have a proper place in a higher education that need lose nothing in terms of rigour, and gain much more in terms of reflective practice. How the virtues are developed and the kind of learning community that enables that development is then examined by Chris Megone. Megone's chapter underscores the underlying values of the practice and practices of learning which have to be embodied in the community and which are thus shared with the members of that community.

'Chapter' nine is a little different. Sue Vickerman wrote this poem for the University of Leeds Centenary Service, held in April 2004 at Leeds Parish Church. This is widening participation from the inside, an invitation to look again at what this means to identity, self understanding and community.

The second part of the book focuses on practice. Tom McLeish offers a perspective on research from the coal-face, which reflects on some of the tensions there. To extend the metaphor, though, he digs deeper to look at the values beneath the values, and to the relationship between the researcher and her data, not least the physical world. He suggests a powerful image of the researcher in therapeutic relationship with that world, not simply disinterested and standing back, but actively helping to heal. This resonates with theological concepts such as *shalom* (justice and peace). He also looks at the arrangements for research which prevent such engagement.

Hilde Nafstad continues this reflective process, inviting us to examine the values which underlie disciplines per se. She focuses on her researches in psychology. Her work reminds us of the old Tawney dictum there is no social organisation that does not have core values underlying it. The key to understanding these and to the development of institutional integrity is the articulation of these values in relation to practice. Nafstad examines the assumptions about human nature and value which underlie much of modern psychology.

John Cowan focuses on the values which are central to the teaching and learning relationship. He argues that learning cannot be value-free. From a student-centred perspective emerges the value of collegiality, which is central to any learning community. The learning relationship outlined by Cowan cherishes autonomy and mutuality, offering major challenges to task-centred models of learning in higher education and beyond. Cowan's insights come from long practice of enabling learner-centred learning.

Nigel Humphrys then looks at the way in which student support as a central service has grown over the years and the underlying values. It is striking that whilst *in loco parentis* care has gone, this has been replaced by a duty of care and a resultant massive increase in student support services. Has this very conscious response to student need been generated by a more systematic understanding of personal and educational needs? Or has it arisen through the ever-present value field of customer care? How does customer care relate to a broader, more holistic care? This in turn asks basic questions of higher education as an industry.

Clement Katulushi then invites us to view the university as a global community. The local university is itself global with the increase in international students. This heightens the view of the university as a polyvocal community, asking how any inter-cultural dialogue can best be achieved and what challenges the diversity of values make to all stakeholders, from the local student to the university institution. The university also reaches out, with 'local' branches and recruitment centres throughout the world, bringing further potential value conflicts and tensions as well as opportunities for learning.

Gwen Collins shares ongoing research into the underlying values and motivations of university teachers and how they relate to major global issues. It becomes clear that what motivates is often not articulated and worked through, and that connections to wider issues are therefore fragmentary. Collins suggests ways in which such connections can be made as part of the teaching enterprise.

Character, community, and personal and moral development were all at the heart of Cardinal Newman's vision of the university, one often claimed by the Christian religion which was very much the key to the founding of the university in the first place. Simon Robinson charts the power struggles behind any such vision, leading to the Anglican Church being forced to let go of its domination of university life in England and Wales. With universities 'liberated' from religion, it is interesting that through diverse influences, from consumer care to human rights, religion and spirituality are gradually returning to the campus. No longer coming from a privileged position, they now take part in the reflective dialogue on values, and support of students.

Finally, the editors try to bring this wide-ranging debate to a conclusion, focusing on the concept of integrity in the university. We suggest that this involves handling very different value areas, in the academic profession, learning, society and management. This is a long term dialogic process, central to any learning organization. It recognizes that any claim to what higher education is about must be tested through the participation of various stakeholders.

The debate about values in higher education will go on, and this is perhaps the point. If it stops then the purpose of the university as a reflective, learning organization is lost. What follows is an offering to that debate from the University of Leeds as we enter the second century, we trust with the same confidence and clarity about values as shown by Arthur Smithells, PVC at Leeds in 1906, whose thoughts will draw this work to its close.

We dedicate this book to Alan Wilson, who helped shape the last decade for the University of Leeds, and especially to the memory of all the staff and students who contributed to the first century of the University of Leeds.

Leeds 2004

PART ONE

THE VALUES

1

The university and civic values

Peter Scott

Introduction

The university was, is and probably always will be a civic institution. This is true culturally – the idea of a university is inextricably bound up with the growth of urban civilisation; spatially – the university is an important element in many cityscapes; politically – many universities were founded either by or with the support of civic élites; socially – universities shape the social structures of cities, and influence their political and cultural agendas; and economically – universities play a key role in urban and regional economies. It is in recognition of these powerful links between the university and the city that a key group of universities in Britain is labelled 'civic universities'. Indeed it can be argued that this group of universities, established in the second half of the nineteenth and earlier years of the twentieth centuries in the industrial heartlands of Victorian Britain, still represents the bedrock of the modern British university system.

Of course, this articulation between the university and the city takes many, complex and contradictory, forms. There are universities which visually and spatially dominate their cities yet intellectually and scientifically appear to be distanced from their urban environments. The most obvious examples are Oxford and Cambridge. But in both cases the histories of city and university are deeply entwined – whether in the form of the architecture of north Oxford with its dignified streets of donnish houses; or of modern

Cambridge's penumbra of science and technology parks. It is misleading to conclude that these universities and their cities were remote from each other simply because in Oxford Cowley with its car works seemed to have little connection with the University (a misleading assumption, contradicted by the foundation of Nuffield College), or the University of Cambridge seemed a world apart from the lives of the East Anglian country people who shopped in the city. There are other universities which are visually inconspicuous, embedded in the routines of urban life like the bus station or the department store. Most of the 'new' universities, the former polytechnics, still scattered across cityscapes on former college-of-technology or art-college campuses, fall into this second category. 'Campus', a word resonant of Sylvian aloofness, is a misleading description. 'Precinct', spatially distinctive but penetrated by public spaces and other uses, is the most that such universities can hope to achieve.

There is a third group of universities which, literally, created their cities. The University of California was built on farmland but is now the centre of a city (in turn embedded in the sprawling San Francisco Bay conurbation). Much the same happened at Ann Arbor with the University of Michigan – or Madison with the University of Wisconsin. Indeed the universities of the New World were among the most active instigators of urbanism, which continues to be reflected in the intensity of the engagement between communities and their colleges in the United States. In Britain provincial towns have been revitalised by the foundation of universities. Lancaster and York come to mind. Also Brighton, its decaying Regency splendour and post-war loucheness transformed by the foundation of the University of Sussex in the 1960s (Graham Greene's 'Brighton Rock' succeeded by Malcolm Bradbury's 'History Man' perhaps); or Coventry, transformed from the drab 'Middlemarch' memorialised by George Eliot into the quintessential modern Middle-England city with the active help of the University of Warwick.[3]

There is a fourth group of universities which grew up with their host cities, perhaps the most important group of all. In these cases the foundation of a university became the hallmark of the development of the city – in both a traditional sense, in terms of status and esteem; and a modern sense, to satisfy the voracious demands of the new industrial society for expert skills and scientific knowledge but also to reduce dependence on imported élites (whether from surrounding shires or metropolitan centres). The best examples are the great cities, and universities, of Victorian Britain – Leeds and Sheffield, Manchester and Liverpool, Cardiff and Belfast.

The University and the City, it could even be argued, are different manifestations of the same force – the civilising urge or, more recently, the drive towards modernity. In the Ancient World the city was conceived of as the most advanced form of social organisation. Relics of this conception still litter our everyday language – 'pagans', literally country people excluded from the benefits of urban civilisation; or the semantic proximity of the 'civic' and the 'civil'. The city in this idealised form, which was taken up again during the Renaissance, intensified during the industrial revolution and reached its apogee (even apotheosis) in the world-cities of today which reach deep in rural worlds, was seen as transcending the particular and the traditional and espousing instead the universal and the modern. The university, which first appeared during the revival of cities in the high Middle Ages, was seen as discharging a similar role – but in a different sphere. The city enlarged the physical potentialities of human civilisation, while the university enlarged its intellectual (and, for half a millennium, its spiritual) potentialities.

The city and the university were also twinned as creative agents in state-building. And the centralised nation state remains the dominant form of social organisation, despite the onslaughts of globalization. The establishment of the University of Berlin in 1810, which became the archetype of the modern university (outside the English-speaking world), was part of a much larger project, the modernisation of the Prussian state after the shock of defeat by Napoleon. Even in England the emergence of the University of London, and especially the foundation of University College London in a radical and utilitarian spirit, owed much to a similar impulse.[4] To the ideas of city and university was added an even more powerful idea – the idea of a rationally ordered state, as the embodiment of an increasingly expert and professionalised society. It was the state that gave the impetus to the growth of great cities, and it was the state that founded (or permitted the foundation of) modern university systems.

But the city and the university also offered routes for emancipation. Cities, especially the new metropolitan cities, became the cockpit of revolution (whether Paris in 1789 or Petrograd in 1917), where conventional ties of deference were at their weakest. During the course of the nineteenth and twentieth centuries the university became the agent of individual improvement and enlightenment (although *ancien régime* universities had played a rather limited role in the Enlightenment as such). To an extent the ideas of modernity and democracy became fused, powerfully so in educational systems. First, Mechanics Institutes, ancestors of many of today's universities in Britain (notably the technological universities and the former polytechnics), were established to promote popular education. Next Oxford and Cambridge were de-clericalised – and opened up to new social groups, if only to intensify the education of new social and governing élites.[5] The 'civic', and 'red-brick', universities offered new ladders of opportunities, celebrated and imagined in the lives and work of people like D.H. Lawrence or Richard Hoggart.

The histories of both the city and of the university, therefore, demonstrate remarkable affinities – which over time intensified (and continue to intensify). Academic life in all its manifestations – from the street life of students, through donnish society and the influence of universities on cityscapes, to their impact on the formation of expert professions and the generation of scientific and technical knowledge – was a major contributor to the emergence of broader urban cultures. The normative structures of city and university were, and are, also remarkably similar. Both encouraged the emergence of individualism and secularism, scepticism and rationality which became the key values of modernity.[6] This dynamic engagement between the city and the university continues in the interaction between post-industrial and consumerist urban structures and post-modern intellectual cultures.

Universities as urban institutions

It is possible to describe three historical phases in the interaction between universities and their host cities. The first occupied the second half of the nineteenth century and the early years of the twentieth century. Two facts stand out. The first is that nearly all universities were founded as a result of civic endeavour and agitation, even if the subsequent grant of Royal Charters depended on the exercise of national patronage. In city after city – Liverpool, Leeds, Newcastle – the great men of the City came together to demand a university (and, more than demand, to mobilise the necessary resources). There was, after all, no other way to establish a university.[7] The national structures of policy-making and programme-implementation, which are now taken for granted as the stuff of politics and the substance of the state, only existed in embryonic forms. Universities were local institutions because no national model of a university yet existed. Instead an influential model was provided by the Scottish universities which continued to be under civic control until late in the nineteenth century, the break between the University and the Corporation of Edinburgh only coming finally in the 1880s (and even then the motive was to reform not to 'nationalise').

The second fact is that, during this first phase the university was one among several civic institutions – the grammar school, the public library and (almost certainly) the town hall – which collectively defined the urban culture of industrial Britain. It did not yet possess the commanding position it has come to occupy at the beginning of the twenty-first century. It is important to locate the early development of universities (Oxford and Cambridge excepted – and also, to a lesser degree, London) within the context of these vigorous, self-confident civic cultures. The industrial Manchester that amazed (and dismayed) the world, the radical Manchester of the Anti-Corn Law league, even the revolutionary Manchester of Friedrich Engels were also the Manchester that created the Victoria University, the John Rylands Library and other temples of self-improvement. But the most notable, and last, of these civic cultures flowered in Birmingham in the 1880s and 1890s and was associated with a great urban dynasty, the Chamberlain family (and the involvement of this same dynasty with the great dream of Empire demonstrates the synergies between civic and imperial ambition). Joseph Chamberlain was sponsor equally of Birmingham as 'the factory of the world' and of a British Empire on which the sun never set, and of Birmingham's civic institutions and its newly founded university which were both crucial elements in that sponsorship.

The second phase lasted for much of the twentieth century. It is tempting to align its start and end points with the life-cycle of the University Grants Committee (UGC), which was established in 1919 (although there had been earlier ad hoc committees to channel state funding to universities) and was abolished in 1988.[8] The temptation is strong because a key feature of this second phase was that universities gradually withdraw from their civic connections and became increasingly 'national' institutions, and the UGC was the most potent totem of this change. But it was a long withdrawal. Still in the 1950s universities retained much of their old civic flavour. Students were predominantly local, commuting on trams and trolley buses to red-brick buildings only now being cleaned of decades of sooty grime; and universities were still modest in scale, higher grammar schools in their ethos, as Philip Larkin recalled his early days at post-war Leicester.[9]

The move to 'national' universities was not complete until the 1960s when three things happened. First, the idea of a higher education system was articulated with increasing power and frequency between 1956, when the colleges of advanced technology (now the technological universities) were designated, and 1965, when the polytechnics were first announced in Anthony Crosland's Woolwich speech (the so-called binary policy). The Robbins report two years before had been the most decisive stage on this road from a collection of 'local' universities and assorted colleges of technology, art and education to a coordinated system of higher education, a system that had to be 'national'. Second, the introduction of universal student grants broke the connections between students and localities; they became free to roam. Third, brand-new green-fields universities were founded – not bottom-up, as had been the pattern throughout the nineteenth and in the first half of the twentieth centuries, but top-down on national initiative. Even so, cities and counties competed to host these new universities.[10]

This loosening of the links between city and university reflected wider phenomena – the nationalisation of politics which had been under way for more than a century but only now radically undermined strong civic cultures; the strengthening of the bureaucratic state with its increasing concentration on national institutions, which culminated in the creation of the post-war welfare state; and the triumph of professional society in which professional expertise and scientific knowledge held unchallenged sway. Universities were implicated in all three changes. The nationalisation of politics freed them from the control of the civic and commercial élites which had been so prominent in their initial foundation; the new 'national' political class had little direct interest in the fortunes of individual universities, although it displayed a generic piety to universities collectively (and especially, of course, to Oxford and Cambridge as the predominant *alma maters* of this class). The waning of civic culture also deprived universities of creative partnerships; inevitably they sought new – metropolitan – connections. Change could no longer be engineered in local civic contexts. The strengthening of the bureaucratic state not only greatly stimulated the demand for university graduates (who were no longer destined to enter the liberal professions or become school teachers) but also enabled (required?) universities to establish national structures through which they could respond to this, and other, demands. Finally, the growing respect felt for professional expertise and scientific knowledge created the conditions for a far-reaching extension of the autonomy enjoyed by universities as a class of institutions distinct from the rest of the educational system, and also by the academic profession as a privileged social group.

Of course, it would be misleading to suggest that vigorous interactions between city and university declined during this second phase. But they took on a different – and, perhaps, more quietist – character. The mid-to-late twentieth century was the period when universities became key players in the cultural life of their communities – through museums, galleries, concerts, plays and other activities. To borrow Bagehot's celebrated terminology, the 'efficient' links between city and university were succeeded by more 'dignified' engagements.[11] Even that may be unfair. Extra-mural departments promoted popular, even radical, perspectives on liberal adult education. This, after all, was the age of Richard Hoggart, E.P. Thompson and Raymond Williams. But such efforts were increasingly pushed to the margins of both civic and academic life (or, in the latter case, absorbed in – or smothered by – a more open intellectual culture that had grown beyond its instinctive donnishness); they acquired some of the characteristics of principled (but impotent?) opposition. The new wave of post-war social science did contribute to the urban redevelopment and community regeneration projects of the 1960s and 1970s. During the brief flourishing of the New Left, it even seemed that student radicalism might engage with much broader quasi-revolutionary resistances to bourgeois democracy. But events quickly demonstrate how peripheral such activities were in the modern university and how feeble a challenge they were to a robust social order. There was never any real prospect that the radical university would re-engineer a radical city.

The third phase has occupied the past two decades. Two major changes can be observed. The first is the revival of the city – but as a focus for free-market enterprise and consumerism (whether described as post-modern or late-capitalist) rather than as a strong local polity. The dismantling of key parts of the bureaucratic state during the period when Margaret Thatcher was Prime Minister (and not reversed after the Labour Party's landslide victories in 1997 and 2001) arguably has loosened the reins of national policy – although this has not led to a revival of local democracy. The impact of globalization has had a similar effect, as cities relate more strongly to global networks rather than conforming to the old pattern of metropolitan-provincial relations.

The second change is the decline in the autonomy of the university over the past two decades.[12] This has many, contradictory, causes. One is the reversal in the fortunes of all professional experts – civil servants and lawyers, doctors and engineers as well as professors. The university has always been ambivalently poised between its attachment to elitism (and dependence on habits of deference) on the one hand and its sponsorship of critical inquiry and social mobility on the other. But the erosion of expertise has inevitably compromised the prestige of the university, the source and repository of so much expertise. Or, perhaps more accurately, the proliferation of competing experts has tended to politicise expertise, creating zones of controversy from which the lay public cannot be excluded. Another cause is the ever-widening distribution of expertise. As mass higher education has produced mass graduate populations, the demarcation between lay audiences and expert constituencies has become much more difficult to define. A third cause is the crucial importance of scientific knowledge and the technological processes produced by this knowledge in what has become a 'knowledge society'. Universities can no longer be left unmolested in their 'ivory towers'.

In this third, and contemporary, phase in the engagement between the city and the university their roles may be in the course of being reversed. A century ago the city was the dominant partner, the university being only one of several civic institutions. Local democracy flourished. Indeed civic prestige and power had never been greater (before or since). The bureaucratic – and early welfare – state was very much a local manifestation. Local, and regional, industry and commerce were not simply 'branch' economies of a larger national – or, later still, world – economy. Although integrated, they were not subordinated. Today the position is very different. Local government has been gutted, its role reduced to implementing (or, in the language of New Labour, 'delivering') a modernisation process decided elsewhere. The post-welfare state is an overwhelmingly national formation.[13] Local economies are clearly 'branch' economies, for all the emphasis placed on the contribution of small and medium-sized enterprises. Their dominant motif is the out-of-town shopping centre, an awesome aggregation of consumerist power.

The university, in contrast, has become the dominant civic institution. It is typically the largest single employer, and makes a decisive contribution to the economy of the city and its region (in ways that will be discussed in greater detail later in this chapter). The university is also often an important locus for civic culture – as the provider of theatres, galleries and museums in its own right; as a corporate patron of the city's own cultural institutions; and as a sponsor, or source, of the audiences that sustain cultural activities and events. The university is also an intermediary, or more active mediator, between national (and now global) markets and cultures on the one hand and local contexts and civic environments on the other. Indeed the university, although it plays an increasingly central role in market exchanges, is the only important non-market intermediary or mediator. Yet the university, although re-embedded in society to a degree deplored by advocates of autonomy, has preserved significant freedom of action – because without that freedom of action it loses its inherent utility. As a result, in the centuries-old dynamic between the city and the university, the university has potentially become the most powerful agent, the standard-bearer, for local identities and civic values. Only potentially – because universities are still stumbling towards a realisation of their new position (and power) as the inheritor, and now guardian, of the civic tradition.

Ancient and modern engagements

As a result of this shift, from the university being just one element within the city, to the university being, arguably, the leading element, an equally important shift has taken place in the quality of this civic engagement. In the past it was predominantly instrumental, in the sense that the university serviced the needs of other groups and organisations in the city (which themselves were often defined in largely utilitarian terms). Today this engagement has a much stronger normative element, because the university has become responsible for defining 'civicness' in a moral sense (at any rate outside the market arena, although universities of course make an increasing important and direct contribution to economic development in the city and its region). To illustrate the significance of this shift from the instrumental to the normative it is possible to distinguish between traditional and contemporary forms of civic engagement.

The first, the traditional and (I would argue) predominantly instrumental form of engagement between the university and the city, had three main elements. The first of these was the contribution that the foundation of a university made to civic prestige; indeed it became, during the course of the nineteenth century, one of the defining characteristics of a city which distinguished it from a town, more influential than legal incorporation. This element undeniably had a normative dimension, in the sense that it embodied a more explicit association between science and education on the one hand and other constituent parts of the life of the city on the other. But this association was not, in itself, new. Early modern cities had been proud to establish grammar schools. But in this earlier period the impulse was derived from a long tradition of philanthropy; the only difference may have been that this long established communal tradition gradually ceased to be the responsibility of the church and became instead the responsibility of the city. In contrast, during the later nineteenth and early twentieth centuries, the first great age of university foundations (we live in the second, which began in the 1960s and still continues), the impulse was one of modernisation. Universities were established to bring together, and to systematise, the scattered and fragmentary provision for higher education, technical training, scientific enlightenment, scholarly pursuit that already existed. The process of modernisation, of course, was far from being value-free, embodying as it did secular and rationalist values (which explains why the churches, having played a key role in the foundation of schools, played a much more limited part in the foundation of universities). Nevertheless it was expressed largely in instrumental terms.

The second element was the need to train sufficient doctors, lawyers and teachers – and, as state and corporate bureaucracies burgeoned, other experts – to satisfy the needs of the city and its region. To some extent this reflected the professionalisation of traditional roles that already existed. The medical and legal professions took on approximately their present structures during this period. In turn this created a need for more systematic education and training, which universities were well placed to provide. At the same time the increasing importance of science and technology in the industrial economy stimulated the development of new technical roles, which also created a need for more systematic education and training. This was partly satisfied by universities and partly by technical colleges (which later became universities). Finally the development of the bureaucratic state, and also of corporate bureaucracies in the private sector, created new expert roles which in turn stimulated the demand for more systematic high-level education.

The third element was the sponsorship of research and, to a lesser extent, scholarship. But research in universities was either strongly related to local industrial needs until well into the twentieth century (steel in Sheffield, mining in Newcastle, textiles in Leeds), or a continuation of an older tradition of the gentleman-scientist (of which there had been so many famous examples during the Victorian period). Britain lagged behind the United States and Germany in the professionalization of research, and the systematisation of research careers, which are now taken as axiomatic of university research. The Ph.D. was not introduced until after the First World War. The pattern of university scholarship was similar, either closely linked to teaching or difficult to disentangle from the 'amateur' scholarship undertaken by men-of-letters. The relationship between the urban intellectual and the academic scholar remained contested.[14] For example, the historian G.M. Trevelyan was as much a man of letters, and scion of a famous Whig family, as he was a professional historian. Arguably it took even longer to develop a fully modern approach to scholarship in the humanities (and the still embryonic social sciences) than to scientific research. The latter process was largely complete by the 1930s; the former not until the 1960s. But the key linkages with the city were through industrially relevant research and scholarly teaching.

These developments, of course, were not without normative significance. The rise of professional society in the last quarter of the nineteenth and first half of the twentieth centuries represented not simply a revolution in definitions of expertise and the emergence of new 'expert' roles. It also represented a social revolution; older ideas of social hierarchy as being determined by birth leavened by political advancement or economic success were replaced by new ideas of social differentiation which were at once more fluid (birth counted for less) and more determined (because the credentialisation of 'expert' roles became more important).[15] Universities, of course, were deeply implicated in both aspects of this social revolution. But the rise of professional society also represented a revolution in values. Traditional and customary values were swept aside by a new secular (utilitarian) rationality in which respect, and enthusiasm, for science played an increasingly important role. In this respect the city and the university were at one.

The modern, or contemporary, form of engagement between the university and the city feels – and is – very different. For a start the roles seem to have been reversed. As civic pride, and civic power, have waned, the modern university has gathered force, a mass institution in scale and range and also a scientific, or 'knowledge', institution. Once again there are three major aspects of this engagement. The first is that the university has become a much more powerful institution which overshadows, as has just been said, other civic institutions (certainly in the public sphere, but also arguably in the private, as communities have been eroded and notions of civil society have weakened, and as locally-based industry has lost its critical mass). As a result the university is now typically the largest local employer. In many cities it is also the largest single component of economic activity through its own purchasing of goods and services and procurement of new buildings and equipment and the spending power of its students and staff. The economic impact of an average-sized university is worth close to half a billion pounds. As has been argued earlier, the university is also a major cultural focus in the modern city directly by providing galleries, museums and theatres and indirectly by stimulating demand and creating audiences. Finally the university has become a major social presence. Patterns of society as well as patterns of consumption are shaped by the existence of large and influential university communities.

The second element is that the university now plays a key role in promoting not simply social mobility (as élite universities did in the past, however imperfectly) but also social inclusion (which is the particular responsibility of mass higher education systems). Its mission is no longer to train a civic élite of professional and technical experts, but to address much wider community needs for post-compulsory education. As a result specialist courses leading to professional (or quasi-professional) qualifications have been complemented (and maybe superseded) by much broader academic programmes that seek to inculcate generic 'graduate' qualities. Higher education is now close to being a universal entitlement for young adults from middle-class backgrounds. This is of particular relevance to the engagement between the university and the city because the modern middle class is very much an urban formation (as is indicated in the alternative description – bourgeoisie). Higher education has also become an important instrument for the integration and/or empowerment of ethnic minority and immigrant populations. This, again, is especially relevant to civic engagement because these populations are concentrated in cities. With regard to less privileged social groups, emphasis has switched from philanthropically inclined 'out-reach' (derived ultimately from university 'missions' in the poor quarters of Victorian and Edwardian cities) to politically mandated 'widening participation'. Instead of new student populations accommodating, and being helped to accommodate, themselves to the university it is now the other way round – the university must accommodate itself to these new student populations.

The third element is the crucial importance of the university within the knowledge society.[16] Universities have become powerful instruments of so-called 'glocalisation', the dynamic relationship between global 'knowledge' (whether in terms of research findings or, more diffusely, world concepts, images and brands) and local (or civic) environments. Not only do they act as a channel whereby global 'knowledge' is communicated, they also provide a feed-back loop through which the city – and, in particular, its diverse communities and its small and medium-sized enterprises – can 'talk back', and engage the forces of globalization. Universities are, quite literally, the sponsors of new enterprises through science and technology parks, atelier workshops and so on. More practically, universities make a decisive contribution to enhancing the skills bases of cities, not simply in terms of traditional expertise but also by educating key workers (such as nurses) and raising the general educational level of the population at large. They provide the intellectual (and cultural) capital on which successful and dynamic cities depend.

As a result the engagement between the university and the city has been transformed. Arguably the university now plays a more decisive role in shaping civic values. It shapes the 'culture' of the modern city – in terms of its employment and its consequent social structures, its access to science and (more broadly) knowledge, its capacity for innovation, its openness to new ideas. But the university may play a more baleful role – in two different senses. First, it is bound up (and implicated) in the inequalities of modern urban life, despite the drive to wider participation in higher education. In a knowledge society material inequalities are now more directly related than ever before to differential rates of access of education and skills. The new gulf in the modern city is between the knowledge-rich and the knowledge-poor. As a result, despite its best inclinations and best instincts, the university can be regarded as an active generator of inequality, rather than a passive accomplice. Second, as a result of our ability to reconfigure almost at will time and space (a direct result of the revolution in information and communication technologies and an indirect result of the emergence of global communities in sport or popular music as well as science), the modern city has become a fragmented space. The spatially contiguous may no longer be the socially, still less culturally, contiguous. Again the university may be implicated in this de-construction of the city – by developing the basic science and powerful technologies that enable us to un-bundle and re-bundle space and time; by allowing disruptive global influences to invade orderly urban space; and by educating mobile élites and rootless graduate populations.

Conclusion

There are two possible accounts of the contemporary engagement between the city and the university. The first emphasises the affinities between post-modern thought, and other relativistic and reductionist ideas, which originate largely within the modern university (with a lot of help from the mass media), and the normative and material structure of the modern city, both hyper-individualistic and super-consumerist. One of the favourite metaphors used to describe post-modernism is the shopping mall (or, in British terms, the shopping centre – especially, perhaps, the out-of-town shopping centre). Although the mall or centre does have a basic structure (of car parks, delivery bays and services infrastructure), it is generally out of sight. What is visible is a riotous medley of shops, cafés and restaurants all with their own themes and brands. The contrast is with the department store based on the orderly arrangement of different departments within an overall theme – which, consequently, can be taken as a metaphor of modernism, a rational system guided by general principles and with a clear sense of hierarchy and progression.[17]

It is a beguiling metaphor because the department store was one of the most distinctive developments of the late Victorian and twentieth-century city, which replaced the more chaotic arrangement of street markets and (a little later) arcades characteristic of earlier cities. The physical and mental worlds represented by Parisian arcades crowded with *flaneurs* and suffused with a restless romanticism is beautifully described by Walter Benjamin in his magisterial work *The Arcades*, the episodic and fragmentary nature of which mirrors the qualities of its subject.[18] The shopping mall or centre, arguably, represents a return to this older expression of culture, commerce and the city. Of course, there are difficulties with this interpretation because the principles of organisation that underpin the apparent chaos and playfulness of contemporary consumerism are far more rigid, far more over-determined, than in this earlier period.

Nevertheless, it is tempting to play with the idea that the city and the university have followed similar trajectories. The twentieth-century university, like the twentieth-century city, provided an orderly and progressive environment. This was true both organisationally, in the so-called public life of universities as new integrated campuses were built and coordinated national systems of higher education were articulated, and intellectually, as disciplines now arranged in logical taxonomies developed robust esteem and career structures. The university has much in common with the department store. The twenty-first-century university, like the twenty-first-century city, offers a different prospect – of increasing organisational and intellectual complexity, and of highly differentiated responses to that complexity. It has become a transactional rather than normative space. In this respect the university now has much in common with the shopping mall/centre.

But there is a second account of the contemporary engagement between the city and the university. The city has always been, and always will be, undeniably a communal organisation. Its historical origins were not exclusively economic, certainly not in a narrow commercial sense. Cities were centres of political power, social innovation and cultural experimentation. They remain so, to an ever greater degree. As a result cities have always represented arenas both for the expression of individualism (as has been argued earlier, the idea of the city was inextricably linked to the assertion of its 'liberties', later reduced to the singular) and for the fostering of collectivism. The early city was composed of guilds and 'nations' governed by a corporation. The modern city, too, is structured in terms of associations and communities, and its life is regulated by collective actions (whether on economic development, public transport or cultural policy); it cannot simply be regarded as a random space in which anomic individuals consume the delights of late capitalism (or huddle in its shadows).

The university also cannot easily be reduced to a simple aggregation of a large number of quasi-economic transactions – between students and their teachers, or between researchers and the 'users' of their research. First, the university is itself a community in which communitarian values jostle with individualistic values in the same way as in the modern city. Second, it continues to represent an ideal which transcends the immediate interests of its members. There is room for many different interpretations of that ideal – but it cannot simply be regarded, as some would argue, to a kind of 'brand'. Third, the transactions that take place within the university are highly complex, ranging from the unapologetically instrumental to the stubbornly altruistic. Fourth, the university is undeniably a 'public' institution, not necessarily in the sense that it must be publicly funded (although this is highly desirable) but in the wider sense that it is concerned to promote public goods (which include, but are not confined, to wealth creation). There is a tendency to argue that, because in a knowledge society the university has become a primary producer, these public goods can be assimilated into markets and, therefore, no longer need to be separately identified. But such an argument depends on a naïve account of how knowledge is produced; more subtle accounts emphasise the difficulty of distinguishing between 'producers' and 'users' and between market and non-market domains.[19]

At the start of the twenty-first century, the city and the university remain bound together by shared opportunities and common dilemmas, just as they were two centuries ago when modern cities and modern universities first emerged. In many ways their embrace is tighter than ever, with the university taking on many of the responsibilities which were once discharged by more traditional civic institutions. Both the city and the universities have been, and are being, reshaped by the more vigorous of the market. But both, in turn, are reshaping what is meant by the market – and in ways perhaps that incorporate older values, civic and academic. To emphasise the emergence of the 'market' city (as Philip Bobbitt has emphasised the development of the 'market' state), animated almost exclusively by the values of consumerism and individualism, and of the 'entrepreneurial' university, focused almost exclusively on its role as a wealth-producer in a knowledge society, is only half the story.[20] The other half – of the communal city and the liberal university – is equally important. The future of both city and university is being shaped by the continuing dialogue (dialectic even) between these two stories (or discourses).

2

*Faith in the university**

Rowan Williams

Introduction

Working in universities these days is not comfortable. Academics are being told, in effect, that they have never really understood the nature of efficiency or accountability, and are consequently being forced to put their house in order – that is, in the 'order' prescribed by governmental paymasters. There is pressure to justify oneself in terms of the quantity of our production – whether that is seen in terms of publications, contracts for research, or graduates suitably equipped to join the productive economic life of our society. And there is, simultaneously, pressure to reduce and rationalise staffing, to streamline teaching methods and so forth. National initiatives have been developed to bring more people into higher education; and at the same time fees are to be raised even further, putting extra pressure on students to find lucrative employment as rapidly as possible, and casting a fair-sized cloud over the chances of older students – housewives, workers, the retired – in the new world of higher education.

In short, it isn't clear what the university's paymasters think the university is there for; they only know that they want it to give value for money. Since there is no sense of why a university might be valuable, the only kind of value for money that makes sense is producing people who generate wealth; and the

---

* This chapter was revised from a paper given at Loughborough University Anglican Chaplaincy in 1989.

result is a vague but powerful notion that a university which doesn't produce wealth-generators is not pulling its weight. And if the student finance system means that people will naturally look for wealth-generating jobs, the circle is neatly completed.

In this chapter, I will explore two things (the ambiguity of my title is deliberate, of course): first, what it's like to live 'faithfully' in the context of the modern university, to live in a way characterised by faith or trust, and second, what kind of trust we ought to have in the university institution and its future – what we want to depend on, and so to defend and celebrate. And because living faithfully isn't something wholly abstract, divorced from how we learn about trust in the whole context of our experience, the latter point, about what is worth trusting and defending in the institution, will have much to contribute to the former concern. I write as an archbishop of the Christian church, and no doubt what I say about faith will be coloured by that fact; but I hope there may be resonances not restricted to the Christian frame of reference.

I begin then by offering a few thoughts on the general question of 'living faithfully'. Central to what I understand by these words is the recognition that I am not obliged to create or to justify myself. To live in faith is to be conscious at some level, perhaps only a quite deeply buried one, that your being there and your being who you are, are not under threat; your existence and your identity have roots and solidity. There are many ways of learning this, most obviously by knowing yourself to be the object of love or friendship; and for the religious person, it is most importantly anchored in the conviction of being created (i.e. God wants you to be). This sort of faith is the opposite of that attitude which suspects that you have no right to be there, and that other people are consequently out to remove you from the scene: faith*less* living assumes that we maintain who we are only at the price of keeping the threat of the other at bay. At its root is the fear that I can only maintain myself at your expense, and you at mine. Faithlessness is the absence of trust in my own reality and consequently the inability to trust anyone else.

Competition

Now a university environment looks, in many ways, as if it were deliberately designed to intensify faithlessness. You get to university, in the first place, by a process of competition in which it's more or less true that success is bound to be at the expense of others. Increasingly, within the university structure from top to bottom, competitive modes prevail; and in a shrinking job market its pressures will intensify. The relatively brief periods of residential study mean that there is not much time to succeed, to make an impression, create a *persona*. And the more you succeed, the more desperate the competition; you may even end up as a university teacher or administrator, devoting what feels like most of your working hours to explaining what you're doing and listing your scanty achievements for the benefit of the government, with something of the same feeling Scheherazade must have had in relating the Thousand and One Nights (if you stop, you get decapitated).

This also means that the university environment can produce what I'd call faithless varieties of faith. If you feel yourself under threat in one way or another, the temptation is strong to bind yourself to a scheme or system that tells you firmly what sort of being you are and what you should be doing. If your worth and significance is tied to something outside your own achievement, it will be – in some ways – a lot less vulnerable. But the problem then becomes one of making sure this system 'competes' successfully – that is, defending the system against all possible attack. Once again, the university is a place almost designed to make this maximally difficult. It puts a high premium on the asking of awkward questions, and positively encourages what can be maddening– and, at worst, destructive – habit of challenging conclusions. So you have the not unfamiliar combination of manic scepticism on the one hand and inflexible dogmatism on the other– the situation in which a good many people conclude that commitment, religious or otherwise, is somehow a disreputable and irregular element in the life of an intellectual community.

So it looks very much as if 'faith in the university' in my first sense is going to be extremely difficult. The environment encourages us not to trust ourselves or each other and colludes very readily with the temptation to take refuge in authoritarian systems in which I no longer have to take any risks, however much these help to isolate us as *persons* from the context we're in. There, in fact, is a rather substantial problem: if I can only survive as a person by a strategy of defensive withdrawal from questioning, that implies that the questioning I do as a student will not actually be relevant to me as a person. My intellectual questioning becomes no more than a series of skills that I learn so as to satisfy my teachers or my colleagues. Is it possible at all to imagine a kind of commitment that is nourished by the context I live in and doesn't need to be protected from it?

Answering that in fact suggests that we move over into thinking about the other meaning of 'faith in the university', before coming back to suggesting what sort of commitment is viable here. What is it about universities that is trustworthy, worthwhile, and important? What *is* a university? It's an institution which brings together a variety of intellectual activities in the conviction that, despite everything, they have something in common. At its heart is this recognition: that the situation of human beings in the world is neither clear nor static. It is characteristic of human beings not to take their environment completely for granted but to ask about it and modify it. We begin talking about humanity in the evolutionary story when see signs of animals modifying their environment and communicating about this modification; animals that are becoming capable of representing themselves to themselves, treating their own bodies as raw material for transformation. Where you have signs of the dead being buried, sometimes with pigment on their bones, sometimes with little artefacts buried alongside them, where you have shapes being made, in stone or pigment, crude statues, colours in a cave-wall, you have the record of an animal whose own body is not something taken for granted, a self-protecting, self-nourishing organism, but is becoming an object, even a stranger. It has become necessary to 'meet' yourself, to see your own organic life as if it were a 'thing' outside; and so it has also become possible to imagine something different from what is simply *given* in your biological needs.

Humanity appears when 'culture' appears – culture in the widest possible sense, the whole activity of seeing the familiar world from a distance and asking what might be different, the activity of imagining, making and planning. But culture contains a sort of contradiction as well: the body is no longer taken for granted, but it is not something that can be forgotten or ignored. Body and environment are not the last word, but they still impose limits. So, as human language develops, it brings to light the interlocking realities of a world not controlled, not at the disposal of human consciousness, and a world that also invites the consciousness to see it in constantly new and shifting ways and so to change it. Language itself, with its formal structures and its endless historical changes (you may say the same words twice, but you never say the same thing twice), shows us the kind of beings we are: innovative and reflective and limited, always looking for where the boundaries are and never sure they will stay in the same place.

Intellectual activity

What we call intellectual activity is simply the various ways in which we look at all this – at this reality which is in fact there in every word we speak, perhaps in our very ability to say 'I' and 'you'. It's a disciplined projection of ordinary human culture; and it's a *necessary* projection, because the history of human culture shows that we have a very persistent tendency to forget what it means to *be* 'cultural' and to assume that the way things are is natural. When you have a lot of people happy to assume that the way things are is natural (people who have forgotten that there is a process of history that gets you to the point you're at), then the intellectual life will look *un*natural and won't be very welcome. A society like that is a society that is in danger of forgetting what it is to be human: it will think that it's *obvious* what people want and how they should get it, and so its people will never learn to be strangers to themselves, to see their bodies from a distance, to meet and know themselves. They will be told what they are. Thus an institution which is about not taking your body and your environment for granted is an institution trying to keep in mind what's involved in being human.

One of the ways in which the university concretely does this is precisely by recognising that there are different sorts of intellectual activity. If you have to spend your time alongside someone who is perpetually asking different questions about the world from yours, you may be less inclined to assume that the questions you're asking are the natural or the only ones. This in turn means that you're less likely to think that your answers are the natural or the only ones; and it is this sort of perception which keeps alive the strong awareness that being human and being 'cultural' is essentially unfinished business. There will always be fresh questions about what can and can't be taken for granted. The co-existence in one institution of these different sorts of activity is, of course, only the bare minimum of what a university might be: properly planned and integrated interdisciplinary study at undergraduate level and some kind of boundary-crossing and sharing of experience and projects among teachers have always been part of what theorists have believed ideal in university life. Present reality – necessary specialisation plus constant erosion of time – makes this harder to achieve; but it remains true that no-one at any level in a university can be unaware of how differently the task of 'culture' may be understood – in biophysics, metallurgy, mediaeval history, theoretical linguistics, and so on. There are things I choose not to question, but I know others do; and their questioning ought to enhance my own awareness of living in a world that *systematically* invites human beings to new perceptions.

This relates somewhat to another aspect of intellectual life. I recognise that my questions and answers are one strand in a vastly complex tapestry; and that may well suggest that I can't know what questions will be right or interesting to ask as my activity progresses. Problems I am tackling now will generate others, if I have the honesty and energy to follow them through. Intellectual life carries on because it retains some capacity to be surprised; and intellectual training at any level must focus on this fact. To be *intellectually* competent is to know how to react appropriately and adequately to an agenda that I haven't set – just as to be competent in a language is to know how to reply to sentences I haven't heard before. So, if a university doesn't have scope for innovative work, it won't be training people very satisfactorily in intellectual activity. In plain English, a university without research is more or less useless. It will not convey anything of the sense that every discipline is 'unfinished', incapable of predicting what it will itself generate. Specialised research is bound to be a vocation of limited appeal; but I'm not sure any significant learning is ever without an awareness of what fuels the enterprise– the impulse to look for a proper response to the questions I haven't simply planned or invented, to look for a synthesis in and through what appears as discontinuity.

> The intellect in its present state, with exceptions which need not here be specified, does not discern truth intuitively, or as a whole. We know, not by a direct and simple vision, not at a glance, but, as it were, by piecemeal and accumulation, by a mental process, by going around an object, by the comparison, the combination, the mutual correction, the continual adaptation of many partial notions... Such a union and concert of the intellectual powers, such an enlargement and development, such a comprehensiveness are necessarily matters of training. And again, such a training is a matter of rule; it is not mere application, however exemplary, which introduces the mind to truth, nor the reading many books, nor the getting up many subjects, nor the witnessing many experiments, nor the attending many lectures. All this is short of enough; a man may have done it all, yet be lingering in the vestibule of knowledge; he may not realize what his mouth utters; he may not see with his mental eye what confronts him; he may have no grasp of things as they are; or at least he may have no power at all of advancing one step forward of himself, in consequence

of what he has already acquired, no power of discriminating between truth and falsehood, of sifting out the grains of truth from the mass, of arranging things according to their real value, and, if I may use the phrase, of building up ideas. Such a power is the result of a scientific formation of mind...

This process of training by which the intellect, instead of being formed or sacrificed to some particular or accidental purpose, some specific trade or profession, or study or science, is disciplined for its own sake, for the perception of its own proper object, and for its own highest culture, is called liberal education.[21]

Like most people trying to reflect on the life of the university, I've found it hard to improve on Cardinal Newman's account. And in case anyone should take fright at that term 'liberal education', believing it means a rather dilettantish formation in the arts, we should keep in mind the context of the expression here. Newman is talking about how critical and constructive habits of mind are formed by a process we might call 'learning about learning'. Learning itself is 'short of enough', says Newman, because it does not look at its own workings; and if it does not do this, it simply gives you access to a limited range of information. But if you understand the kind of thing you're doing when learning, you have acquired what people nowadays call a transferable skill; you are able to review your own starting-point, to question your questions, to learn not just about some object or activity but about your own capacities as a questioner – as an 'unfinished' being, capable of surprising and being surprised. This seems to be what lies at the heart of Newman's vision of 'liberal education', and of what he therefore believed to be essential for the university. It means that the university can never be either a simple training school or a pure research institute. A training school would do no more than provide certain limited skills: be no part of its essential job to reflect on what it *is* to learn. You can go to language school and emerge with a good grasp of Russian or Spanish or whatever, but none the wiser about what it's like to be a human subject in the world. No criticism is implied; the language school quite properly has limited goals, and sets out to attain them efficiently. And in a way the same is true of a pure research institute: quite properly, it seeks to extend a particular area of skill and knowledge, and only accidentally deepens the sense of what's involved in learning itself. Most philosophers of science are found outside specific scientific research programmes (and scientific researchers tend to think of them as rather a nuisance!) but the research programmes wouldn't last long if the researchers hadn't had a formation which introduced them to the notion of wondering whether they were asking the right questions.

That's the formation a university is meant to give. Professor Anthony O'Hear of Bradford wrote that:

> Education…requires both a deep understanding of at least one area of human knowledge as well as some idea of where and how that area fits into the whole of which it is a part. The former is necessary not only for the knowledge thereby acquired, but also because it is through engaging with a form of knowledge at an advanced level that one comes to understand what it is to submit oneself to the demands of reasoned enquiry… One of the main distinctions between a university education and career-directed forms of higher education ought to be the stress placed in the former on a sense of the interrelationships between the various studies and disciplines… [A] university cannot subordinate its educational function to its service role and continue to do that for which it is particularly suited and which provides the reason for grouping all the major intellectual disciplines in one institution.[22]

Learning alongside people involved in different kinds of learning is, in short, one of the most obvious and resourceful methods of learning about the nature of learning, steering you away from that taking for granted of your own agenda which is ultimately so dehumanising. And this means, as Professor O'Hear makes plain, that any attempt to redefine the university's role in terms of what 'society' believes it needs (i.e. what a particular bureaucracy decides a state needs) is an assault on the essence of the university institution. It implies that someone *does* know, fairly exhaustively, what questions are good or natural ones, and forecloses the opportunity of asking questions about questions. When this happens, it is a sign that politics has abandoned culture: which is normally the herald of politics abandoning humanity, abandoning the sense of a constant negotiation with a strange and challenging environment, in which we run up against both strength and resourcefulness and our powerlessness and finitude; the politics of environmental indifference, obsessional security-consciousness, the search for 'ultimate' military threats and military defences.

Believing in the university

Faith in the university, trust in its methods, structures and values, is a commitment to humanity and culture, in the sense I've been trying to define. It means believing, in spite of all discouragements that the university has something irreplaceable to offer to human society: by its deliberate pursuing, entertaining and criticizing of questions of widely differing kinds, by not allowing that variety to be limited by considerations of short-term profit and results, it reminds a society of the fundamental relation between human beings and their environment. A society that allows itself be reminded of this will be one in which it is still possible to talk of provisionality, hopefulness, even repentance, a society prepared to resist the anti-culture of totalitarianism.

Even in the short term, we have learned just a little of the folly of thinking that our practical needs– industrial, commercial and so on– are best served by restructuring university education towards those needs. Economics and technology are by no means fixed quantities, 'technical' skills that can be mastered once and for all. Now more than ever they involve the imagination; they require an ability to ask questions about the questions being asked. In other words, they require what a university education gives. Anecdotal evidence still suggests that employers in industry and business are often more interested in proven intellectual attainment than in training for specific tasks: in other words, they recognise that they cannot flourish without the creativity and critical sharpness of intellects that have found out how to think about learning.

What then does all this suggest about the faith people might be able to live by within the structures of the university? Intellectual inquiry of itself doesn't produce religious or other kinds of commitment; but it's fair to say that faith itself would not be imaginable if human beings were not the kind of beings who go in for the life of understanding, 'intellect' in its widest sense. If being human were not a matter of being unfinished, exploratory, not taking things for granted, committed to learning, then presumably they would never raise the questions or experience the responses that shape faith. Faith, however, is not confined by this basic ground. In effect, faith says: given that humanity is like this, the struggle for 'culture', the negotiation between our creativity and the inflexible facts of an environment, given that we are both finite and creative, we need to take a further step of imagination. We need to ask whether there is a way of fusing our creativity with limitations so that our life remains in harmony with our total environment. But to ask this question at all is to imply that there is an overall context for ourselves (mind and body) and the perceptible world, a context which makes sense of the idea that our reality is somehow an ordered whole. Religious practice, even at its most rudimentary, witnesses to some awareness of interconnectedness and balance, some sense of unified world held in its unity by a reality which the sum total of facts about the world doesn't exhaust.

Faith, then, is a commitment to the belief that our life is more than a struggle between a creative ego, individual or collective, and a lot of raw material; it trusts that there is a possible reconciliation ('atonement') between human selves and their world. Without necessarily entailing that the characteristic restlessness of being in the world is done away with, it sees that restlessness as pressing towards some kind of homecoming, an affirmation and acceptance of the reality we are in, instead of fear, hostility, naked conflict. Different kinds of faith envisage this hope in different terms: Christian faith, with its particular concern with human history, its recognition that we are bound to time, that learning entails giving time, sees our hope as linked with the story of certain human communities in which the perception of a total context of all things, a creator, had become inseparable from the conviction that this context had a personal, purposive character, that it was possible to relate to it not only in trust, but in love. The story presupposes that the creator not only creates but so makes him/ herself present in the world's history that people are set free from their fear of their environment and their defensive reliance on will and ego. In this freedom, they are able to trust themselves and each other, and so to become a human community without artificial limit. But it also presupposes that the presence of God in history is something which will profoundly unsettle what we are comfortable in assuming about ourselves. If, as Christians believe, God is somehow decisively present in the life and death of Jesus, God can be unrecognisable to those who want a fixed order in religion and politics. Jesus can appear as the most disturbing 'intellectual' question of all, the figure who most makes us strangers to ourselves, even as he promises the deepest homecoming, the acknowledgement of God as a loving parent.

Faith is not an alternative to the life of the intellect. On the contrary, it presupposes it, it presupposes our creativity, our life in questioning and culture. What it adds is the trust that all of this is an entry into a reality which affirms and holds together all our explorations, not an endlessly fragmenting series of independent enterprises. The very fact of a university's existence, with its unspoken confidence that different essays in understanding may learn from each other is a tentative step of faith, trust in some kind of possible human wholeness. One of the tasks of faith in the context of university life is surely to keep alive this tentative hopefulness about the human world by witnessing to more explicit accounts of the wholeness of things, especially in the fragmenting, trivial and anti-humanist context of our present pseudo-culture.

Human creativity

But to do this, faith has a responsibility to itself. What I earlier called faithless kinds of faith, authoritarian schemes which solve the problems of anxious or dependent personalities by a short cut, are not fulfilling their responsibility (their mission, if you like) to their own environment. Faith needs to keep reflecting on the two dimensions of human existence that it presupposes: the restless creativity of persons, their urge to remake the world, and the limitedness, the physical, historical boundaries, in which our lives are lived. 'Faith' which seeks to quench the creative, to treat all significant questions as answered already, simply colludes with our present political barbarism. But there is also a 'faith' which is so obsessed with the ideal of a boundless human creativity, that it cannot face the reality of the consequences of betrayal, failure, violence (sin, in short), the reality of *tragic* frustration. It lives by what the German radical sociologist and philosopher, Theodor Adorno, contemptuously called the 'jargon of authenticity', by the intense cultivation of private utopian fantasies and a refusal to call the ego and the will into question.

   If faith in the university can remain critical of its two great temptations, authoritarianism and utopianism, it will not only preserve its own integrity but proclaim what it ought to proclaim in its setting: a confidence in the human future, based not on any glib optimism about how nice or how clever human beings are, but on the generosity which it believes to underlie all things, on the possibility of human beings finding a way of being at home in the world because they have found that world (and themselves in it) to be the objects of love, pity and purposeful engagement. This leads on to a final reflection: faith in the university needs to be self-critical, perhaps even iconoclastic; but this does not mean that it has any business to be without confidence. By confidence I don't mean an arrogant sense of rightness, and exclusive and dismissive attitude to other visions; simply the trust that, however inadequately, the language of faith is genuinely about reality; that it connects with truth.

Only if faith looks to something beyond the state of my – or anybody's – consciousness, only if it shows itself to be answerable to, criticisable by, what it does not have under its control, can it claim any integrity; only so can it claim also to have anything to say that would prompt change or renewal in those who hear. For faith to be any more than a utopian fancy or psychological crutch, it must believe, passionately and argumentatively, that it is capable of opening to human beings a new possibility of unillusioned, unafraid living. It must see itself as a gift and as judgement. And this, far from making the language of faith more easy or smooth, can make it more uneven, more agonised: if we really *are* answerable to something beyond our scope of control, we can't get away with repetition, with jargon or platitude. The language of faith becomes an art – like the poet's or the physicist's – seeking for the least trivial and inadequate way of giving voice to a reality that is outrunning us. And, in the university, faith has the opportunity of constantly varying and challenging conversation with the styles of human learning, so that its language has every opportunity of being tested and refreshed.

The university as an institution is to be trusted and defended because it speaks from and for our distinctive human identity as cultural, learning animals, bound to, yet not trapped by, our environment. It brings to light and nurtures what faith builds upon. Faith separated from the life of intellect is no longer a human activity, but belongs in the bleak 'post-human' world of totalitarian captivity. Faith, in short, needs the witness of the university. But, like all the institutions of culture, the university also needs to be related to the sphere of human commitment and hope – otherwise it will equally dehumanise itself by isolating intellect from engagement, by nursing the image of itself as a realm of secure and disinterested work. It cannot of itself, of course, insist upon or teach commitment: its value is in its distance, its different perspective. But it can and must be prepared to reflect on the human project it represents, and how that relates to wider stories, political and artistic as well as religious, about this project. It needs the presence of commitment within it, in case it should think it has an alibi when questions of human import are raised. We cannot afford to sit light to the task before us, the task of preserving the human-ness of education itself.

3

The liquid-modern
challenges to education

Zygmunt Bauman

In the 2 January 2001 issue of the *Washington Post* Caroline Mayer reported a new range of fast-food products, time-and-effort saving and ready for instant and trouble-free consumption, which flooded American supermarkets in the year that just ended.

It is true that the Americans (and not just them) came long ago to identify progress with shortcuts: with rising opportunity to *buy* things which before they had to *make*. It is also true (and true to the point of triviality) that once such an understanding of 'improvement' is in place, it tends to spiral out, recasting ever more previously performed activities into the category of avoidable and resented chores. Things that used to be done daily, mostly without complaint and often with pleasure, come to be seen and felt as off-putting, abhorring and detestable waste of time and energy. This tendency is by no means novel, but the speed with which the 'new and improved', time-saving foods have landed recently on supermarket shelves only to be promptly swept into the trolleys of enthusiastic customers would astonish a most acute observer of fast-food markets and its addicts' habits.

We learn from Caroline Mayer that ever more American children, and ever more often, find the effort involved in eating an apple oppressive: too much hard work for jaws and teeth, and altogether an investment of time too big for the amount of resulting pleasure. They also resent having to peel an orange and prefer drinking ready-made juice. Is not the new custom of drinking beer straight from the bottle, a habit that swept over American bars and later over English pubs with the speed of a forest fire, related to a growing resentment of the drudgery of pouring beer from the bottle into a glass before quenching the thirst?

Smucker, a fast-food factory, has introduced a widely acclaimed novelty: the crust is cut out from the bread slices on which peanut butter and fruit jelly are spread in American children's favourite sandwiches. It seems that the innovation answered an urgent need, as it was an instant commercial success. Apparently, children came to consider the task of biting their way through the slice's hard edge as too tough a challenge for their jaws.

Their parents, though, do not seem to lag far behind. Iced tea is one of the Americans' favourite drinks. Alas, to prepare it the orthodox way one needs to boil water first, fill the teapot, brew the tea, and then wait for the brew to cool down. A lot of labour, and a lot of time – would the thirst and the desire to quench it survive that long? Fortunately, another food industry potentate, Lipton, spotted the vexation of iced-tea lovers and offered the distressed iced-tea addicts teabags with contents soluble in cold (even already iced) water. Satisfaction can be now instantaneous, just as in the case of newly marketed instant-tuna powder, which puts paid to the fingers-wrenching and time-wasting drudgery of tin opening. Gratification no longer needs to be delayed. The *waiting*, as the commercials enticing prospective customers to use the freshly introduced credit cards once announced, has been indeed taken out of tuna and iced-tea *wanting*.

Impatience syndrome

Caroline Mayer quotes Professor David Shi of the South Carolina Furman University: 'Waiting has become an intolerable circumstance'. That new mood of American public Shi dubbed 'the acceleration syndrome'. Myself, I would rather speak of the *impatience* syndrome. Delay, picked up by Max Weber as the paramount virtue of the pioneers of modern capitalism and the prime source of their astounding success, tends now to be experienced as a waste of time. Time has become one resource (perhaps the last one) whose waste is unanimously resented as abominable, unjustifiable and intolerable; indeed, a snub and a slap to human dignity, an offence against human rights.

Nowadays, all delay, procrastination, waiting, turn into a stigma of inferiority. The drama of power hierarchy is daily re-staged (with the secretaries cast in the role of stage-directors) in innumerable waiting rooms, where some (inferior) people are asked 'to take a seat' and kept waiting until some others (superior people) are 'free to see them now'. The badge of privilege (arguably, one of the most potent stratifying factors) is the access to shortcuts, to the means to make the gratification instantaneous. Position in the hierarchy is measured by the ability (or ineptitude) to reduce or cut out completely the time-span separating want from its fulfilment. Rise in social hierarchy is measured by the rising ability to have what one wants (whatever one may want) *now* – without delay.

As in the case of other widely coveted goods, the market is quick to supply consolation prizes styled in the idiom of the new era: iced-tea bags or tuna powder sachets, the mass-production replicas of the *haute-couture* 'real thing', reserved for the enjoyment of the selected few. Interviewed by Oliver Burkman of the *Guardian*,[23] an 18-year-old English girl declared: 'I don't want to look back on my life and see that I went into a job because it was safe and stayed there forever'. Dads who stuck to their jobs for life (if there are such dads left, that is) are viewed as a warning and a deterrent: this is the kind of life we must do whatever we can to avoid. While a New York baker complained to Richard Sennett[24] about the dads' side of the quandary: 'You can't imagine how stupid I feel when I talk to my kids about commitment. It's an abstract virtue to them, they don't see it anywhere'. Little evidence of commitment in their dads' lives, to be sure. They might have tried to commit themselves to something more solid and durable than themselves – a vocation, a cause, a workplace – only to found that there are few if any solid and durable targets willing to accept their commitment offer.

Benjamin Franklin's discovery that 'time is money' was an accolade of time: time is a value, time is important, something to be cherished and cared for, just like your capital and your investments are. The 'impatience syndrome' conveys an opposite message: time is a bore and a chore, a pain, a snub to human freedom and a challenge to human rights, neither of which must or needs to be suffered gladly. Time is a thief. Agree to wait, to delay the rewards due for your patience – and you'll be robbed of the chances of joys and pleasures that are in the habit of coming once and disappearing forever. Passage of time is to be recorded on the debit side of human life-projects; it brings losses, not gains. Passage of time portends the waste of opportunities that ought to have been grasped and consumed as they came.

Having compared the pedagogical ideas and educational settings of thirteen different civilisations, Edward D. Myers[25] noted (in a book published in 1960) 'the increasing tendency to view education as a product rather than a process'.

When it is regarded as a product it is conceived as something that can be 'got', complete and finished, or relatively so; for example, it is not uncommon now to hear one person ask of another, 'Where did you get your education?', expecting the answer, 'At such-and-such college'. The implication is that the graduate has learned all he needs to know of the techniques and skills of language and mathematics and of all the accumulated knowledge about man's relations to other men, his debt to the past, the natural order and his relation to it, and about the realm of aspirations and values – all he needs to know, that is, of what is required for his particular job.

Myers did not like what he found; he would rather have education treated as a continuous, whole-life endeavour, since he resented the tendency to cut the knowledge cake into thin slices, one for every trade or profession. Not to be satisfied with one's own 'professional slice' – this was in Myer's view the duty of a 'cultured person', and to perform the duty the years spent in a college cannot suffice. The objectively accumulated and potentially available knowledge was enormous and still expanding, and the effort to assimilate it should not stop on the graduation day; 'the appetite for knowledge' should be boosted throughout life, for the man 'to continue to live and grow' and so to be altogether a better kind of person. But the idea that knowledge could be appropriated and made into a durable property of the person, Myers took for granted and did not contest. Like other property in the then 'solid' stage of modernity, big was beautiful and *more* equalled the *better*. What Myers found wrong in the current educational thought was but the view that one should 'get education' in *one* go, as a *one-off* purchase, rather than being on a continuous look-out for ever more and richer possessions to *add* to the already acquired ones.

Knowledge

The image of knowledge reflected that commitment, and the vision of education replicated the tasks that commitment put on the modern agenda.

Knowledge was of value since it was hoped to last, and *education was of value in as far as it offered knowledge of lasting value.* Education, whether seen as a one-off episode or a life-long endeavour, was to be an activity aimed at the delivery of a product which like all other possessions could, and would, be desired to be held forever.

Here we come across the first of the many challenges contemporary education needs to face and withstand. In our 'liquid-modern' times, durable possessions, products meant to be appropriated once for all and never replaced, let alone not meant for one-off consumption, have lost their past attraction. Once seen as assets, they are now more likely to be viewed as liabilities. Once the objects of desire, they have turned into objects of resentment. Why? Because the 'life world' of contemporary youth patched together of their life experiences no more resembles the orderly, steady, 'learnable' corridors of laboratory maze which were used half century ago to explore the mysteries of successful adaptation through learning. Harvard Business School professor, John Kotter,[26] advises his readers to avoid being entangled in long-term employment of the 'tenure track' sort; indeed, developing institutional loyalty and to become too tightly engrossed in any given job for a long time to come is ill advised. No wonder that baker Rico complained to Sennett of the difficulty in explaining what a commitment could mean.[27]

The history of education has been full of critical periods in which it became evident that the tested and seemingly reliable premises and strategies were losing their grip on reality and called for repair or reform. It seems, though, that the present crisis is unlike the crises of the past. The present-day challenges deliver heavy blows to the very essence of the idea of education, as it had been formed at the threshold of the long history of civilisation: they put in question the *invariants* of the idea, the constitutive features of education that thus far withstood all the past challenges and emerged unscathed from the past crises – the assumptions never before questioned, let alone suspected of having run their course and being in need of an overhaul and replacement.

In the liquid-modern world solidity of things, much as the solidity of human bonds, is resented as a threat. Any oath of allegiance, any long-term (let alone timeless) commitment, augurs a future burdened with obligations that would (inevitably) constrain freedom of movement and reduce the ability to take up new, as yet unknown, chances as they (inevitably) come by. The prospect of being saddled with one thing for the duration of life is downright repulsive and frightening.

The most coveted things are known these days to age fast, to lose their lustre in no time and to turn abruptly and with little or no warning from a badge of honour into stigma of shame. The editors of glossy magazines feel the pulse of time well: alongside the information about the new 'you must do's' and new 'you must haves' they regularly supply their readers with advice on 'what is out' and needs to be dumped. Even the habits meant to stay for a bit longer are not meant to stay *still*. A recent commercial of a mobile telephones outlet appeals to the telephone seasoned users: Come to us, since with the mobile you have you can no more show yourself in public... Our world is ever more reminiscent of Italo Calvino's 'invisible city' of Leonia, where 'it is not so much by the things that each day are manufactured, sold, bought that you can measure opulence; ...but rather by the things that each day are thrown out to make room for the new'.[28] The joy of 'getting rid of', discarding and dumping, is our world's true passion.

The ability to last long and serve the owner to no end no more speaks in things' favour. Things and bonds are expected to serve for a 'fixed term' only and be shredded or otherwise disposed of once they outlive their usefulness – which they must sooner rather than later. And so possessions, and particularly the long-lasting possession one cannot get rid of easily, are to be shunned. Today's consumerism is not about *accumulation* of things, but their one-off *enjoyment*. So why should the 'knowledge package' obtained during the stay in the school or college be exempted from that universal rule? In the whirlwind of change, knowledge fit for instant use and meant for one-off use, knowledge ready-for-instant-use-and instant-disposal knowledge of the kind promised by software programmes coming in and out of shop-shelves in an ever accelerating succession, looks much more attractive.

All this shrinking of the life-span of knowledge by the sheer 'contagion' – by the impact of demoting the value of durability from its once venerable position on the values' list – is further exacerbated by the commodification of knowledge and access to knowledge.

Knowledge is today a commodity; at least it has been cast in the mould of commodity and prompted to shape itself after the pattern of commodity. Bits of knowledge may be patented and so barred from replication, while those that do not fall under the patent laws are closely guarded secrets when still in the process of development (like a new car model before being put on display in the next year salon) – in the well-grounded belief that, as in the case of all other commodities, commercial value reflects the differential rather than the quality of the product as a whole of the product. Differentials are as a rule short-lived, the impact of novelty wears off quickly, and so the fate of commodity is to lose market value fast and be replaced by the 'new and improved' ones, claiming new differentials, as transient as the ones just dumped as having passed their power-of-seduction age. Focusing value on the differential obliquely devalues the rest of the body – the rest unaffected by change, the rest that 'stays the same'.

And so the thought that education may be a 'product' that is meant to be appropriated and kept, treasured and protected, is off-putting and most certainly no more speaks in the institutionalised education's favour. To convince their children of the use of learning, the fathers and mothers of yore used to tell them that 'what you've learned, no one will ever take away'. Such advice might have been an encouraging promise to *their* children taught to build their lives like houses – from foundations to the roof, and accumulate furniture in the process – but the odds are that it would look a horrifying prospect to the *contemporary young*. Commitments tend to be resented unless they come with an 'until further notice' clause. In a growing number of American cities, building permits are taken only together with demolition permits…

Contemporary change

The second challenge to the basic premises of education comes from the erratic and *essentially unpredictable nature of contemporary change* and adds power to the first challenge.

At all times knowledge was valued for its faithful re-presentation of the world; but what if the world changes in a way that continuously defies the truth of the extant knowledge, constantly taking even the 'best informed' people by surprise? Werner Jaeger, the author of the classic exploration of the ancient roots of the Western concept of pedagogy and learning,[29] believed that the idea of education (*Bildung*, formation) was born of the twin assumptions: that underneath the friable layer of variety, of varied and shifting human experience, lies the hard ground of the immutable order of the world, and that similarly hard and solid are the laws that underlie and govern human nature. The first assumption justified the necessity and the benefits of knowledge-transmission from teachers to pupils. The second imbued the teachers with self-confidence needed to carve on the pupils' personalities, like sculptors do in marble, the shape presumed to be, at all time, right, beautiful, and good – and for those reasons virtuous and noble. If Jaeger's findings are correct (and they have not been refuted), then 'education as we know it' is in trouble – since it would take nowadays quite an effort to uphold any one of the two assumptions and even more effort to perceive them as self-evident.

Unlike the behaviourists' maze, the world as lived-through these days, feels more like a contraption for forgetting than as a setting for learning. Partitions may be, as in that laboratory maze, opaque and impenetrable – but they are on castors and on constant move, carrying the tested, previously explored passages with them. Woe to people with sticky memory, when yesterday's trusty tracks are found a short time later to end up in blank walls or quicksands and as the habitualised, once foolproof behavioural patterns begin to curry disasters instead of securing success. In such a world, learning is bound to endlessly chase the forever elusive objects that in addition have the nasty and infuriating habit of melting or losing lustre the moment they are grasped. And since the rewards for proper action tend to be moved daily to different locations, reinforcements may mislead as much as they reassure: they are traps to beware and be avoided, since they may instil habits and impulses that in no time will prove to be useless, if not harmful.

Nigel Thrift, the insightful analyst of contemporary business people, has noticed the remarkable change of vocabulary and the cognitive frame that mark the new global élite of industry, trade and finances – and the most successful among them, such as 'call the tune', set the pattern of conduct for the lesser or still aspiring members to emulate.[30]

To grasp the rules of their strategies and the logic of their actions, contemporary business leaders use the tropes of 'dancing' and 'surfing'. They no longer speak of 'engineering', as their grandfathers and still their fathers did, but of 'cultures' and 'networks', 'teams' and 'coalitions' – and of 'influences' rather than of control, leadership, or for that matter management. In opposition to the now abandoned or shunned concepts, all such new terms convey the message of volatility, fluidity, flexibility, short life-span. People who deploy such terms are after loosely-knit organisations that could

43

be put together, dismantled and reassembled as the shifting circumstances require – at short notice or without notice. It is such a fluid form of assembly that best fits their perception of surrounding world as 'multiple, complex, and fast moving, and therefore 'ambiguous', 'fuzzy', and 'plastic', uncertain, paradoxical, even chaotic'. Today's business organisations tend to have a considerable element of disorganisation deliberately built into it; the less solid and more readily alterable they are, the better. And like everything else in such a liquid world, all wisdom and know-how cannot but age quickly and quickly use up the advantage it once offered and so it is the 'refusal to accept established knowledge', unwillingness to go by precedents and suspicion against accumulated experience that are now seen as the precepts of effectiveness and productivity. You are as good as your successes; but you are only as good as your *last* successful project.

It has been pointed out already in the pioneering years of cybernetics that there is no such thing as 'perfect organisation'. There is no way to say with any degree of certainty which of the alternative organisations is 'better', unless account has been taken of the environment in which that organisation is destined to function. Complex, multi-functional organisms of higher mammals may be seen as the prize achievements of the species' evolution only because the planet Earth they inhabit is protected from the outer space full of maverick meteorites by a thick layer of atmosphere. Were this not the case, a blob of a fluid, shapeless plasma would be a much more 'perfect' form of life. We may say that the global frontier-land we all inhabit these days seems to favour plasma and dis-privilege the complex, tightly integrated, monotonously self-reproducing organisms.

And as Ralph Waldo Emerson observed long time ago, when skating on thin ice your salvation is in speed. Salvation-seekers would be well advised to move quickly enough not to risk overstaying any spot's endurance. In a volatile world of liquid modernity, in which hardly any form keeps its shape long enough to warrant trust and gel into a long-term reliability (at any rate, there is no telling when and whether it will gel and little likelihood that it ever will), walking is better than sitting, running is better than walking and surfing is better yet than running. Surfing benefits from the lightness and sprightliness of the surfer; it helps surfing as well if the surfer is not choosy about the tides coming his way and always ready to cast aside his received wisdom, together with the customary preferences it warrants.

Memory

All that goes against the grain of everything that learning, and education, stood for in most of their history. After all, learning and education were made to the measure of a world that was *durable*, hoped to *stay durable* and intended to be *made yet more durable* than it had been to date. In such a world, memory was an asset, and the further back it reached and the longer it lasted the richer asset it was. Today, such a solidly-entrenched memory seems potentially incapacitating in many cases, misleading in many more, useless in most. One wonders to what extent the rapid and spectacular career of the servers and the electronic networks was due to the waste-storage, waste-disposal and waste-recycling worries that servers promised to mitigate. With the work of memorising resulting in more waste than usable products and without a reliable way to decide in advance which is which (which one of the apparently useful products will soon fall out of fashion and which one of the apparently useless will enjoy a sudden upsurge of demand), the chance of storing all information in containers kept at a safe distance from brains (where the stored information could, surreptitiously, take over control over behaviour) was a timely, tempting proposition.

In our volatile world of instant and erratic change the settled habits, solid cognitive frames and stable value preferences, those ultimate objectives of the orthodox education, become handicaps. At least they have been cast as such by the knowledge market, for which (like for all markets of all commodities) all loyalty, unbreakable bonds and long-term commitments are anathema – so many hindrances to be forced out of the way. We have moved from the immutable maze modelled in the behaviourist laboratories and the monotonous routine modelled by Pavlov's collaborators into the open marketplace where anything may happen at any time yet nothing can be done and fixed once for all, and where successful steps are matters of luck and in no way guarantee another success if repeated. And the point to remember and to be appreciated together with all its consequences is that in our times the market and the *compleat mappa mundi et vitae* overlap. As Dany-Robert Dufour recently observed – 'capitalism dreams not only of pushing…the territory in which every object is a commodity (water rights, genome rights, living species, babies, human organs…) to the limits of the globe, but also to expand it in depth to cover previously private affairs, once left to the individual charge (subjectivity, sexuality…) but now included in the merchandise'.[31]

In the present day 'liquid' stage of modernity, demand is fast drying up for the orthodox 'disciplining and surveilling' managerial functions. And it is easy to understand why: domination can be gained and assured with much less expenditure of effort, time and money – through the threat of *dis-engagement* or better still from the *a priori refusal to engage*, rather than by obtrusive and continuous, day in day out, control and surveillance. The threat of disengagement or refusal of committed engagement shifts the *onus probandi* onto the other, the dominated side. It is now up to the subordinates to behave (and daily) in a way likely to find favour in the bosses eyes and entice them to 'buy' their services and their individually designed 'products' – just like the other producers and traders seduce the prospective customers to desire the commodities put on sale. 'Following the routine' would not suffice to achieve that purpose. As Luc Boltanski and Eve Chiapello found out,[32] who wants to succeed in the arrangement that has replaced the 'rat maze' kind of employment settings, needs to demonstrate conviviality and communicative skills, openness and curiosity – offering for sale one's own person, the whole person, as a unique and irreplaceable value that would enhance the quality of the team. It is now up to the current or would-be employee to 'monitor oneself' in order to make sure that the performance is convincing and likely to be approved – and will stay being approved in case the taste of the viewers change. It is no more the task of their bosses to smother the idiosyncrasies of their employees, homogenise their conduct and lock their actions within stiff frames of the routine.

The recipe for success is 'to be oneself', not 'like all the rest'. It is the *difference*, not *sameness* that sells best. Having knowledge and skills 'ascribed to the job' and already shown by the others who did the work before or are applying for it now, would not suffice; most likely, it would be considered as a disadvantage. One needs instead unusual ideas, exceptional projects no one before suggested, and above all the cat-like inclination to walk one's own solitary ways. Such virtues are unlikely to be gleaned and learned from textbooks (except for ever more numerous handbooks that teach, or promise to teach, how to defy and kick out of the way the received knowledge and wisdom and how to muster the courage needed to go it alone). By definition, such virtues ought to be developed 'from inside', by letting free and expanding the 'inner forces' presumably dormant in the obscure innards of personality and waiting to be awakened and set to work.

This is the kind of knowledge (*inspiration* rather) that men and women of liquid-modern times covet. They want counsellors who show how to walk, rather than teachers who make sure that the one and only road, already crowded, is taken. The counsellors they want, and for whose services they are ready to pay as much as it takes, should (and would) help them to dig in into the depth of their character and personality, where the rich deposits of precious ore are presumed to lie clamouring for excavation. The counsellors would probably reproach the clients with sloth or negligence, rather than ignorance; they would proffer the 'how to' kind of knowledge, *savoir être* or *vivre* rather than 'savoir' in the sense of wisdom that the orthodox educators wished to impart and were good at transmitting to their pupils. The current cult of 'life-long education' is focused partly on the need to update the 'state of art' professional information – but in an equal, perhaps even greater part it owes its popularity to the conviction that the mine of personality is never exhausted and that spiritual masters, who know how to reach the yet unexploited deposits the other guides could not reach or overlooked, are yet to be found – and will be found with due effort and enough money to afford paying the price of their services.

The triumphant march of knowledge through the world inhabited (lived) by modern men and women proceeded on two fronts. On the first, new yet unexplored territories of the world were invaded, captured, domesticated, mapped, colonised and converted to cultivation. The empire built, thanks to the first front's advances, was that of information meant to represent the world: at the moment of representation, the represented part of the world has been assumed conquered and claimed for the humans. The second front was that of education: it progressed by expanding the canon of 'educated man' and stretching the perceptive and retentive capacities of the educated. On both fronts, the 'finishing line' of the long and tortuous effort – the end of war – was clearly visualised from the start: all blank spots will be eventually filled, a *compleat mappa mundi* drawn, and all the information necessary to move freely through the mapped world will be laid available to the members of human species through the provision of the needed number of educational transmission channels.

The further the war progressed and as the chronicle of victorious battles grew longer, the 'finishing line' seemed however to recede. By now it is prudent to assume that the war was, continues to be and will remain un-winnable, and un-winnable on both fronts.

To start with, mapping of each freshly conquered territory seems to increase rather than diminish the size and number of blank spots, and so the moment of drawing a *compleat mappa mundi* seems no more imminent. Besides, the world 'out there', once hoped to be grasped and held fast, incarcerated and immobilised, in the act of representation, seems now to seep away from every recorded shape; it looks more as a player (and a crafty and cunning player to be sure) in the game of truth, rather than the stake and the prize that human players hoped to share. In Paul Virilio's vivid description, 'Today's world no longer has any kind of stability; it is shifting, straddling, gliding away all the time'.[33]

Even more seminal news come however from the second, the distribution-of-knowledge, educational front. To quote Virilio, 'The unknown has shifted position: from the world, which was far too vast, mysterious and savage' but into 'the nebular galaxy of the image'.[34] The explorers who are willing to examine that galaxy in its entirety are few and far between, and those able to do so are even fewer. 'Scientists, artists, philosophers...we find ourselves in a kind of 'new alliance' for the exploration' of that galaxy – a kind of alliance which ordinary people could as well abandon all hope of ever joining. The galaxy is, purely and simply, un-assimilable. Even more – much more – than the world of which the information narrates, the *information itself has become the prime site of the 'unknown'*. It is the information that feels like 'far too vast, mysterious and savage'. It is the gigantic volumes of information vying for attention that ordinary men and women feel nowadays considerably more threatening than the few remaining 'mysteries of the universe', of interest solely for a small bunch of science addicts and even smaller one of Nobel Prize contenders.

All things unknown tend to feel threatening, but different kinds of the 'unknown' prompt different reactions. The blank spots on the map of the universe arouse curiosity, spur into action and add determination, courage and confidence to the adventurous. They promise an interesting life of discovery; they augur a better future freed one by one of the life-poisoning nuisances. It is different, though, in the case of the impenetrable mass of 'objectively available' information: it is all here, available now and within reach, yet tauntingly, infuriatingly distant, obstinately alien, beyond hope of ever being grasped. Future is no more a time to look for. It will only magnify the present trouble, adding exponentially to the already stultifying and stifling mass of knowledge, barring the salvation it seductively offers. The sheer mass of knowledge on offer is the main obstacle to taking the offer up. It is also the main threat to human confidence: surely there must be somewhere, in that awesome mass of information, an answer to any of the haunting problems, and so if the solutions fail to be found, self-deprecation and self-derision immediately and matter-of-factly follow.

It is the mass of accumulated knowledge that has become the contemporary epitome of disorder and chaos. In that mass all orthodox ordering devices – topics of relevance, assignment of importance, usefulness-determining needs and value-determining authorities – have been progressively sunk and dissolved. The mass makes its contents look uniformly colourless. In that mass, one may say, all bits of information flow with the same specific gravity – and for people who are denied the right to claim expertise for their own judgments but are buffeted by cross-currents of contradictory expert claims there is no way to sift the grain from chaff.

In the mass, the parcel of knowledge cut out for consumption and personal use can be evaluated by its quantity only; there is no chance of comparing its quality with the rest of the mass. One bit of information equals another. TV quizzes faithfully reflect that new dull and confusing formlessness of human knowledge: for every right answer the same number of points is awarded to the contestant, regardless of the topic of the questions. The gravity of questions and the consequentiality of answers does not count. If it did, how would one go about comparing and measuring it?

Conclusion

Assigning importance to various bits of information, and even more assigning to some more importance than to others, is perhaps the most perplexing task and the most difficult decision to take. The sole rule of thumb one can be guided by is the *momentary* topical relevance – but then the relevance *shifts* from one moment to another and the assimilated bits lose their significance as soon as they have been acquired and often well before they have been put to a good use. Like other commodities in the market, they are for instant, on-the-spot and one-off consumption.

Education took in the past many forms and proved able to adjust itself to changing circumstances, setting itself new goals and designing new strategies. But let me repeat – the present change is not like the past changes. At no turning points of human history did educators face a challenge strictly comparable to the one the contemporary watershed presents. Simply, we have not been in such a situation ever before. The art of living in a world over-saturated with information is still to be learned. And so is the even more difficult art of grooming humans to such a living.

4

From academic knowledge to democratic knowledge

Thomas Bender

A strong case can be made to the effect that the academic disciplines, at least in the humanities, have collapsed.[35] Still, I think that such a proposition overstates the case. We are, however, in the midst of a major transformation in the character of the academic disciplines in the human sciences, and I would describe this as the emergence of 'weak' disciplines. I do not think this development is necessarily bad news. These changes carry important democratic possibilities, but like Alexis de Toqueville, we must seek to guide forces and processes we do not wholly control.

Much of the current concern with the state of the disciplines derives from worry about four issues (often telescoped together in a way that suggests a tighter linkage than in fact exists[36]). One is the challenge of recent intellectual currents to inherited disciplinary notions of verification and objectivity; another is the arrival and supposed impact of new populations in academe, as faculty and students. The emergence of interdisciplinary studies programs worries some, especially those programs that seem to reflect the interests of the new university populations or political agendas (gender studies, ethnic studies, African-American studies, and Sabaltern studies). Finally, traditional disciplines seem threatened by what Clifford Geertz called the 'blurring of genres' and the loss of a consensus on proper objects of disciplinary inquiry, a situation that seems to be fuelling an explosion of metadisciplinary scholarship.[37]

While it is true that there has been a certain nesting of these phenomena, they are not interdependent. Neither are they inherently threatening to academic disciplines. In fact, I want to argue that each of these problems can be recoded as an asset, one that carries the promise of intellectual revitalization – a stronger and still disciplined pursuit of truth. The issue ought not be the preservation of disciplinary boundaries as we found them but rather the sustenance of disciplined scholarship that expands understanding of the world we inhabit.[38]

Both traditionalists and avant-garde academics fail to recognise how historically specific is the disciplinary formation that they wish to defend or dismantle. It is a model realized only briefly, if at all, in the middle of this century.[39] This parochial but typically universalized characterization of the disciplines has four elements. They are (1) autonomous, safe from contamination from other disciplines or worse, ordinary public discourse; (2) founded upon disinterested and rigorous analysis on the supposed model of science; (3) internally generative, thus impervious to external influence in the establishment of intellectual problems and in judging the significance of scholarly work; and (4) above all, elitist and authoritative, their certified knowledge giving to scholars and scholarship standing in the public realm.

I want to acknowledge the considerable analytic power gained in that formulation and formation of the disciplines, but I want also to emphasize the consequent narrowing of focus that has produced as much blindness as insight. For me, two sociological aspects of this ideal are most worrisome: autonomy and elitism.

There is a big question to be asked at this point. How much distance do disciplines need between themselves and our democratic life? I would not assimilate the one to the other, but neither do I want the pretence of a wall of separation. Academics profess democratic sympathies, but rarely are they prepared to live them at work. At heart, we are more often than not unacknowledged Platonists. Like Hannah Arendt, whatever our praise of the democratic public, we deeply believe that our specialized, disciplinary knowledge is superior to the intelligence of democracy. In an elegant essay on 'Truth and Politics', Arendt neatly distinguished between academic and political truth.[40] With characteristic intelligence, she noted the tension between the academy and the polity. For her, and for many of us, the former is the custodian of truth that would pass the Kantian test, while the latter is the generator of vitally important but lesser order truths. Following John Dewey, I want to argue against, or at least significantly weaken, this conventional hierarchy and distinction between academic truth and political knowledge. If we understand politics and academic inquiry, as Dewey did, as convergent, both committed to a collective and continuing search for better and better truths, we open the way for a democratic academy.

The academic culture thus defined will not be hostile to disciplines. Surely, it will not be post-disciplinary, whatever that is supposed to mean. But neither will its disciplines be so tightly bounded, autonomous, disinterested, or authoritative. Dewey described the relation of disciplines to democracy and the larger society that I have in mind here. While he had the greatest respect for specialized, technical scholarship, the model scholar he sketched in *Experience and Nature* began his or her inquiry not within the disciplines but rather with the ordinary life experience he or she shared with others. Dewey's scholar then brought those issues into the world of disciplinary knowledge, always, however, with the expectation of returning to quotidian life for further common dialogue. The special contribution of scholarship to this public conversation is its access to esoteric knowledge and to a refined and severe method of thought. The value of academic knowledge was not to be found within anything like an autonomous discipline but in the larger world. When special knowledge is 'referred back to ordinary life experiences, does it,' Dewey asked, 'render them more significant, more luminous to us, and make our dealings with them more fruitful? Or does it terminate in rendering the things of ordinary life more opaque?'[41]

The first graduate schools, we shall recall, were founded in a civic context. They were established to train political leaders, journalists, and social reformers. And they did a pretty good job: the first Ph.D. in history at Harvard was awarded to Henry Cabot Lodge, and W.E.B. Dubois earned his history Ph.D. there about the time Lodge entered the Senate. One of the first Ph.D.s in history and politics at Johns Hopkins went to Woodrow Wilson. A good number of social reformers – from Albert Shaw to Frederick C. Howe – came out of Herbert Baxter Adam's 'History Seminary' at Hopkins. Theodore Roosevelt was one of the first students to enrol in the graduate program in Public Law that preceded the formal creation of the Graduate

Faculty of Political Science at Columbia. Women like Edith Abbott and Mary Kingsbury Simkovich, who sought advanced degrees, were particularly prominent as reformers.[42]

The American Economics Association was founded in 1885 by Richard Ely and E.R.A. Seligman with the explicit intension of undercutting the laissez-faire economics of the Gilded Age. Knowing that an ideological attack on laissez-faire would only generate conflict, the new economists adopted a particular methodology from their German counterparts: historical or institutional economics. They made no global claims for government intervention in the economy, but they did successfully establish methodological principles that pointed to the same result. They insisted that close examination of particular conditions would indicate whether specific interventions were appropriate for that time and place. Methodology in this instance was political strategy, and out of it emerged the regulatory state. It was only later, in the waning years of the 1890s that Seligman and his colleagues at Columbia realized that the students who earned Ph.D.'s were entering the academy, not public life. The unanticipated reason for the development was the rapid growth of colleges and universities between 1870 and 1914. That growth, combined with the decay and dismantling of the classical curriculum, produced a shortage of professors in the modern subjects: natural science, social science, modern history, and the modern western European languages.[43]

My point so far is this: the modern disciplines, the ones within which we work, were established in the context of public life. They were not so inward looking as many disciplines have since become. Second, they did not shy away from open engagement with large political issues, though – as the academic freedom cases of the 1890s reveal – there were limits both from within and outside the disciplines. Still, academics openly and enthusiastically took their research and teaching problems from the general cultural and political discourse of their time. This is true even of someone like John Bates Clark, who in the 1890s developed the theory of marginal economics upon which the modern discipline of economics is substantially built. For all abstraction of his contribution, his interest was political, not disciplinary development. He was seeking to address the widely debated issues of labour, capital, and monopoly.

The disciplinary models at the centre of so much current debate bear too little relation to practice, past or present. A moment's reflection reveals how variable disciplinary categories and practices can be. For example, they are formed differently in different countries, even limiting the universe to those nations, like the U.S., that based their academic systems on the nineteenth-century German model. The intellectual ecology of different national academic terrains is divided up differently; law and the social sciences are nearer neighbours in France and Germany; sociology until very recently had almost no presence in Britain. To the colonial or semi-colonial scholar in India, Congo, or Brazil, the distinction drawn in the U.S. between anthropology and sociology makes no sense, and in Mexico anthropology and history have a relationship that contrasts starkly (and revealingly) with the case in the U.S.

Within the U.S., there are interesting variations. Stanford's anthropology department recently divided into two departments, and at Berkeley there were for a period five biology departments. Robert Kohler's illuminating study of science patronage shows how some very local office politics in the Rockefeller Foundation enabled, almost urged, Warren Weaver to support certain scientific ideas that led to the creation of the new discipline of biochemistry.[44] One could go on with these comparisons.

Two points need to be made here. First, we must always keep in mind the historical character of the disciplines we 'grew up with.' Second, disciplines are more like holding companies than singular entities. Compare the number of scholarly journals and associations with the number of arts and science departments. The former are nearly innumerable, while the latter have changed little since 1950, and not much more since the 1920s. We ignore this internal differentiation when we refer to the singular or unified *discipline* of History or Sociology or Psychology.

We can press this line of inquiry in yet more radical directions. My colleague Mary Poovey, in the English department, has recently shown that the *fact* as we know it, what she calls the 'modern fact,' a unit of social datum without context or relevant associations, is an invention with a long history that begins with Renaissance double-entry bookkeeping.[45] Such historical deconstruction of a conventional 'given' does not discredit it or render it useless, but it should make us at once more confident and more modest in our navigation through the currently troubled waters of academe. Five centuries of usefulness should be taken seriously; still, it differs importantly from timeless Platonic forms or natural phenomena.

Disciplines are not reflections of the world; they are semi-institutionalized protocols and research strategies for the incremental and interminable work of understanding the natural and social worlds. For this work, they can take many forms. And the forms can change. Form, in fact, *should* be affected by changing objects of inquiry. With all the permutations of academic disciplines, past and present, there is a core work that they do: they sustain conventional truths and supply the research protocols that enable knowledge to be cumulative. They also provide a social and intellectual space for critical debate over those conventional truths. That participants who enter this terrain carry agendas – or interests – from outside of the academy enriches the possibilities of deeper and wider truths.[46]

Let me turn again to American academic history, to the moment of a second founding. Between 1940 and the mid-1950s, the social science and humanities disciplines committed themselves to what Carl Schorske, describing this re-founding, has characterized as a 'new rigorism'.[47] These recast disciplines were positivist in method and they were premised on modernist assumptions of autonomy. Consider for a moment the parallel and well-documented movement in art identified with the critic Clement Greenberg, who in the 1940s claimed for art the related ideals of autonomy, abstraction, and self-referentiality. Each art, each discipline, had its own work to do, its own qualities and capacities to explore and realize. For painting, it meant the rejection of subject matter outside of itself. No more murals about workers. The work of painting was to express its own two-dimensionality. That implied abstraction. One cannot make a realistic picture, whether of a worker or anything else, without some sense of the canvas as a window. But for Greenberg that was a corruption of the autonomy of painting. It allowed external subject matter into the painting. The subject of painting, then, was properly itself; according to Greenberg, that was the ever more radical revelation of its flatness. Other arts and disciplines would fasten upon other essential tasks. Economics, for example, would explore and develop the equilibrium model that Keynes had constructed for them in the interwar years.[48]

How do we explain this massive cultural shift? Part of the explanation is very short-term. Certainly Greenberg – and many academics, most notably Lionel Trilling – wanted to escape the ideological politics of the 1930s. Senator McCarthy and his ilk offered further motive for claiming autonomy. There was in the modernism of the 1940s a deep contempt for the 'masses' and the culture of Kitsch.[49] Turning inward provided sanctuary, which is how Richard Hofstadter described the value of the university in his important book on academic freedom, published in 1955, his book on anti-intellectualism in 1963, and his eloquent commencement address in 1968.[50] But were the refounding of the arts and human science disciplines based solely on such negations of the cultural surround, neither the arts nor the disciplines would have been so vital and creative in the 1950s. There was a positive aspiration as well. In the academy it was a grand and optimistic commitment to rigorous and objective knowledge.

A new Cartesianism drove the refounding in the academy. Here I follow the philosopher Stephen Toulmin, whose book, *Cosmopolis: The hidden dimension of modernity* (1990) opens up the interpretive terrain I am now crossing. He points out that the Enlightenment legacy involved at least two modernities. He associates one with the 'sceptical Enlightenment' of Montaigne, while the other is the quest for certainty identified with Descartes. For the former, absolutist thought was the danger, while for the latter the danger was uncertain or incorrect thought. It was the latter modernity that was embraced at mid-century.

Recall that Descartes wrote in the midst of the devastating Thirty Years War. For mid-century intellectuals, having come through the first half of the twentieth century, marked as it was by ideological conflict and war that brought humanity to the brink of annihilation, the promise of truths so certain as to definitively displace ideology and resolve conflict had enormous appeal. Such, I think, was the underlying attraction of the quest for certainty that drove the mid-century construction of strong disciplines. If the strong disciplines looked to Locke and Descartes, I propose that we now recall Montaigne, Montesquieu, and Dewey (among others) as we respond to the emergence of weak disciplines over the past quarter century.

All disciplines went through the mid-century refounding; indeed, there is a remarkable parallelism across academic culture. Political science may be the most revealing, however. Dreaming of a behavioural science of politics that would bring forth a rational politics and better political management, foundations poured money, more than a hundred million dollars in the 1950s, into that discipline. The Centre for Advanced Studies in Behavioural Sciences in Palo Alto was founded upon the same premise, though its agenda was quickly broadened.

For a moment, I want to focus more closely on English and Philosophy.[51] Both were refounded on a scientific, rigorous model, but they ended up in very different places by the 1990s. In the 1940s, the New Criticism displaced philology and biography in academic literary studies. There were good reasons to displace those approaches. Neither got very close to the literary qualities of the text itself. For criticism, one had to turn from the academics to the amateurs, like Edmund Wilson. But the New Criticism changed that. It promised a professional but distinctly literary criticism.

By leaving history, biography, and external reference out of literary readings, by focusing upon the literary language of the text, literary studies gained an impressive and arguably scientific method of reading. Clever young academics found this method both powerful and exciting, and they quickly transformed the field. It was a method that could sustain expansive professional ambitions. By establishing a theory and technique, like a science, literary scholars could make a claim of professional expertise. And there was an added virtue: the New Criticism offered a method for teaching relatively uneducated college students how to effectively read literary texts without the wide range of historical and literary reference Edmund Wilson deployed.

Philosophy was also transformed. As late as the 1930s, the discipline was still significantly shaped by the tradition of John Dewey and the Golden Age of the Harvard Department of Philosophy – with Royce, James, and Santayana. But the introduction of logical positivism moved the discipline in an analytical direction. By the 1950s, Dewey was regarded as a kindly old man, but not one who had a grasp of real philosophy. Hans Reichenbach, who in fact had some sympathy with Dewey's commitment to science, spoke for the logical positivists when he declared that Dewey's career was irrelevant; the future belonged to specialized and technical philosophy. Dewey's larger ethical, social and political concerns were abandoned for narrower, more rigorous and professional puzzles of symbolic logic and language analysis.[52]

In the 1960s, a group associated with Thomas Nagel and, especially, John Rawls sought with the new journal, *Philosophy and Public Affairs*, to re-engage the world. Yet in the journal – and in Rawls' great book, *A Theory of Justice* – the effort is more to test the discipline than it is to test society. It demonstrated both the power of analytical philosophy in public and established the capacity of the method to engage and argue substantive social justice issues. The discipline of philosophy policed its borders rather vigorously and rigorously; it has no place for explorers or for the old quest for wisdom. The fate of Richard Rorty perhaps makes the point. When he published *Philosophy and the Mirror of Nature* (1979), a book that is far more formally rigorous than his later more literary work, it was enough to cause philosophers to disown him, a compliment he gladly returned. For that discipline, a particular definition of rigor has become more important than the broadly public issues of politics and society earlier addressed by Dewey *as a philosopher.*

Philosophy and Literature – and one could similarly pair economics and history – followed different courses through the 1960s and 1970s. Philosophy and Economics became ever more formal and rigorous disciplines, but they did so partly by shedding questions that could not be addressed by their new disciplinary methods. While English and History were being profoundly affected by various public concerns, particularly those associated with race and gender, philosophy and economics seemed not at all to be distracted from their formal agendas.

Economists reified their discipline, substituting it for the experience they sought to explain. Put yet more strongly, they confused means with ends. In good Greenbergian fashion, they researched and taught Economics *as a discipline* as opposed to using the discipline to understand the general experience of realizing human material needs.

English and History were more open, absorbing new ideas and movements in a spirit of inclusion, becoming weaker disciplines along the way. Of these two, History was the more fortunate, having the ordinance of time, which insured focus amidst diversity. Literature seemed to lose its object of study – work classified as literature. But recent commentators, like John Guillory and Mary Poovey, have suggested that functionally its object was and can still be writing, made clearer by being more inclusive of disciplinary practices that tend to be administratively separated, from composition through criticism to creative writing.[53]

The firming up of disciplinary walls by the strong disciplines (economics and philosophy) and the opening up of weak ones (literature and history) are both plausible responses to the challenge the sixties posed to the aspirations of the mid-century refounding. But I want to argue that it is the weak disciplines that now offer the greater opportunity for vital, objective, and democratic knowledge.

The weaker disciplines have moved beyond or around the formalist ideals of stronger disciplines. They have turned instead to a re-historicization of knowledge, a movement that has been called, with slight differences of meaning, 'the hermeneutic' or interpretive turn, the 'cultural turn,' or the 'historical turn'. Whatever terminology we choose, the weak disciplines emphasize the constructed character of knowledge, including their own. While strong disciplines have quite firm egos that may all too easily become arrogance, the historical and cultural disciplines (or interpretive disciplines), with weaker egos, should be more humble but also, as a result, more capable of participating in and learning from what Dewey might have called (and the Political Scientist Charles Lindblom does call) the method of democracy.[54]

The danger of strong disciplines is that they will sacrifice relevance and significance for rigor, while the danger of the more open weak disciplines is that they may be vulnerable to the corruption specified by the literary critic David Bromwich in his claim that scholarship, especially in the humanities, has been reduced to a form of 'group think' that amounts to 'politics by other means'.[55] An allied but distinct worry is that we in the weak disciplines today too often treat our interpretations as facts.[56] The solution to this danger, which is real, is more democracy, not less, more inclusion, not less, the proliferation of interests and points of view in good Madisonian fashion.

It is conventional, especially in the ideology of disciplinary professionalism, to link disinterestedness and objectivity. The special claim of the academic disciplines, we are told, is their disinterestedness. But if we mean by disinterestedness something like neutrality, we should be careful. Objectivity is not neutrality, a point effectively made by Thomas Haskell.[57] A discipline based upon neutrality is unlikely to achieve objectivity, though it may deliver banality.

I want to focus on a wider definition of interest, one that can be phrased as 'positionality' in contemporary parlance, but which I would rather call, following Karl Mannheim, 'partiality' based upon 'social location'. My argument is that any ideal of objectivity depends upon recognition and incorporation of this sort of interestedness into the social act of making knowledges.[58] Objectivity, in so far a it can be achieved, depends upon the sort of countercheck produced by plurality of partial views.

The consequence of the absence of a lively plurality frequently finds manifestation; here I want to mention one instance in my own discipline.

I refer to the fate of W.E.B. Dubois' great book, *Black Reconstruction*, published in 1935. Dubois was committed to a universal or cosmopolitan culture, but, like Dewey, he recognized the fundamental importance of one's social circumstances and consequent interests. In 1898, for example, he told graduates of Fisk University that in our education, we 'must start on the earth where we sit.'[59] For him and the students he addressed that meant a focus on African American life and culture. That point of view informed his history of reconstruction, something he pointed out in a 'Note to the Reader', where he explained his particular interest. 'In fine', he wrote, 'I am going to tell this story as though Negroes were ordinary human beings, realizing that this attitude will from the first seriously curtail my audience.' Indeed, it did, and one of those audiences who refused the book were his fellow historians. The *American Historical Review* never reviewed the book. A discipline that pretended to objectivity failed, largely because it was far too homogeneous in its membership and too narrow in its sense of discipline.

We are today intensely aware of the distortions that derive from the assertions of difference. The discomfort that results from our difficulty with difference, a discomfort which is clearly political, threatens our capacity for critical debate, and that threatens to undermine the essential contribution of weak disciplines. If academe is going to address that matter, strong feelings will have to be accommodated.

Less emphasis on achieving consensus, which is usually a form of triumph, but rather on developing a working system of what I will call 'non-consensual reciprocity' will help us find the real value of higher education as described by William James almost a century ago. When we learn 'how diverse the types of excellence may be, how various the tests, how flexible the adaptations, we gain a rich sense of what the terms 'better' and 'worse' may signify in general. Our critical sensibilities grow both more acute and less fanatical.'[60]

Academic disciplines do not erase origins or interests; they need not, nor ought they. We must acknowledge the particular illumination that interest contributes, and, equally important, we must be catholic in our appreciation of the kinds of interests a diverse social life produces. Only the widest possible participation in the making of knowledge will protect us from our own partialities and consequent blindness. We too often treat partiality as simple falsehood, when it is in fact the beginning of ethical inquiry. And it may be, even if false, the path of access to a sphere of knowledge or ethical insight otherwise closed.[61]

While I am anxious to rehabilitate interest and positive value of difference, which is admittedly an invitation to politics in academe, I want to challenge any *a priori* or formulaic understanding of interest. Our present sense of the menu of difference or interest is much too confident and much too limited. Serious scholarship must listen for the unexpected interest, for the quiet whisper that may hold an important new perspective. A wide range of social, intellectual, and emotional experiences, individual and collective, form interests. All of that difference represents a remarkable human resource that is partially lost with the rather pervasive tendency toward the reduction of difference to re-essentialized, or, more generously, strategically essentialized notions of race and gender.

The impulse to escape complexity, to purify, to police deviation, undermines the actual use value of the disciplines. It is a logic that forgets Thorsten Veblen's insight that every trained capacity is also a trained incapacity. If academic socialization is a good thing and in fact the work we rightly do, particularly at graduate level, we must recognize that it soon enough reaches a point of diminishing returns. What good is the seminar if everyone has the same social and intellectual formation and thus shares all the same premises and perspectives? How likely are new and unexpected data to be introduced, silences and blindness be discovered, novel argumentation offered?

Difference and diversity talk is omnipresent. But as it spreads through academe (and elsewhere) it is being thinned and rendered painless.[62] It elides power and conflict. That trap must be avoided. Our work is worthwhile because it deals with issues that are important, issues for which students and colleagues will fight. Such conflict may have no permanent solutions; we have no choice, then, but to proceed with our thinking and acting.

Power and ideology will always play a role in those resolutions, but the real work of the disciplines is to provide a place where evidence and logic are expected and honored, whatever one's motive for deploying them. Enabling multiple perspectives to bear upon a given claim to truth is what justifies the disciplines and the academic community. A century ago, when the disciplines were founded, authority was as important as epistemology, more so for some intellectuals. American intellectuals sought, in the words of Thomas Haskell, institutional authority for 'sound opinions'.[63] More recent debates have been understood to be about epistemology, but I think we err if we overlook the historical concern for intellectual authority. In fact, much that we today see as dissolution of the disciplines or the ideal of objectivity is little more than a pluralization of interests in the discussion, something uncomfortable but positive rather than otherwise. Democracy carries that kind of discomfort, because some differences are not easily accommodated.

I have been emphasizing historical change in the disciplines. In conclusion, let me now emphasize continuity. I want to reach back a century to suggest that we still live in the world that John Dewey confronted. I further suggest that his solution can be ours. Like us, he found the stable world of knowledge he knew in graduate school challenged by Darwin and Nietzsche, who together undermined any notion of fixed truths. Thus spake modernity.

Dewey's response, like that of William James and Charles Peirce, was pragmatism. In a very brief definition, his pragmatism fused theory and practice, substituted history for epistemology, and placed the responsibility for the fixing of truths in communities of inquirers. Pragmatists judged the worth of knowledge by its consequences for future 'action' in the work of living. For Dewey, the communities of inquirers had borders rather than boundaries; science and democracy inquiry virtually merged. Truths were historicist, and they were constructed *by active and interested participants*.

Dewey's metaphysics sought to establish that the world we live in is one that would allow a faith in democracy. Any philosophy that apprehended it in terms of rational law and scientific certitude was to him a 'metaphysics of feudalism'. He offered a 'philosophical anthropology' that assumed a world in which 'there is real uncertainty and contingency, a world which is not all in, and never will be, a world which in some respect is incomplete and in the making, and which in these respects may be made this way or that according as men judge, prize, love, and labour.' He deeply believed that for a democrat, 'any notion of a perfect or complete reality, finished, existing always the same without regard to the vicissitudes of time, will be abhorrent.'[64]

Many today have accepted his (and Peirce's) notion of communities of inquirers as the means of achieving a reasonable level of objectivity. But few of them worry enough about who is included in that community. Two analysts who have been enormously influential in my discipline – Thomas Haskell and James Kloppenberg – find a community of inquirers a sufficient foundation for validating knowledge. There are differences between them. Haskell hews more closely to Peirce's conception of truth, which unlike

Dewey's anticipates, at least in principle, completion.[65] Kloppenberg is more Deweyan. He is open to an endless train of inquiry, with one contingent truth following another. At the institutional level, however, they share an inattentiveness, Haskell more than Kloppenberg, to the constitution of these communities.[66]

That is a mistake. If we take Dewey seriously, as I think we should, his democratic commitments and his understanding of the verification of knowledge brings to the fore the question of the *distribution of access to the community*. If we follow Dewey and privilege interested participation, it is incumbent upon us to inquire about any socially structured constraints affecting participation in the critical discussion that establishes the status of conventional truths and proposed truths.[67]

Dewey's words on this point, though they sound a bit antique, are telling:

> The ultimate contradiction in classic and genteel tradition is that while it made thought universal and necessary and the culminating good of nature, it was content to leave its distribution among men a thing of accident, dependent upon birth, economic, and civil status. Consistent as well as humane thought will be aware of the hateful irony of a philosophy which is indifferent to the conditions that determine the occurrence of reason while it asserts the ultimacy and universality of reason.[68]

That is the justice argument, but its demand for access has additional implications that point toward the work of disciplines, the testing of conventional truths and fashioning of new, better, but never complete truths. Without access we will be farther from both justice and truth. With access, with interested challenges to the conventional, and with more appreciation of uncertainty, our weak disciplines will flourish and so will democracy.

5

Values in higher education: a social and evolutionary perspective [69]

Alan Wilson

Introduction

The argument of this chapter is pursued in three stages: first by asking what the purposes of universities are; secondly then to relate value questions to these purposes; and thirdly, to explore the consequences of change over time. The structure of the argument is rooted in concepts in the works of Andersson and Habermas. The former provides a framework in relation to 'purposes' (Section 2) through his 'conditions for successful regions' – which are then applied in the context of universities. The latter identifies different types of knowledge in a constructive way and through this, offers answers to the question of how the values represented by universities are determined – in effect in an evolutionary process of social interaction, and hence the chapter title (Section 3). The next three sections then explore value issues associated with learning and teaching, research and engagement respectively. Some concluding comments on change in universities are then offered.

Starting points: purposes and value questions

I begin by seeking to describe the purposes of the university. Paramount is a concern with knowledge. [70] A useful framework for this is provided indirectly by Ake Andersson, a Swedish economist, who argued [71] that the conditions for a region to be successful in the knowledge economy involved appropriate development of cognitive, creative and communications capacities. Because of the centrality of knowledge in the higher education mission, the argument can be applied to universities. Andersson's conditions can be identified with *teaching and learning* (cognitive), *research* (creative) and *engagement* – often through partnerships and alliances (communications). These three dimensions can be identified with key purposes.

We can also bear in mind an alternative perspective on higher education purposes by adding to what are, or could be seen as, essentially instrumental roles within the knowledge economy. Universities also have social obligations – 'civilising' and opportunity-creating roles – making knowledge universally available. This begs a lot of value-related questions about what is 'civilising', 'good', 'honourable' – and in this sense universities are partly like any other organisation, but are partly special, as we will see. Some of these questions are answered in part by the values that the University of Leeds, for example, formally commits itself to:[72] critical independence and academic freedom; lifelong learning; inclusion; responsiveness; and openness and transparency.

Of course, from the students' point of view, the economic and social dimensions combine. Work provides income and job satisfaction; social development provides the basis of responsible action and 'life satisfaction'. Economists might try to measure both kinds of satisfaction in terms of some utility function: but we are still begging questions here! Halsey[73] attributes much of the rationale for higher education to Alfred Marshall's 1872 paper[74] 'The future of the working classes': 'Marshall's faith in education to bring rising wealth, cultural progress, and narrowing income differentials has since provided the orthodoxy of educational reform for more than a century'. He judges the theory to have been 'falsified' – presumably in its failure to reduce income *differentials*, albeit while increasing income – and he notes that 'Robbins rewrote it and more'.

Knowledge and values in a social context

The next step in the argument is to explore types of knowledge and in this case we turn to a German philosopher, Jurgen Habermas, for a framework.[75] He writes of three kinds of knowledge: technical (concerned with work, the empirical and analytical sciences); practical (social interaction, intersubjective communication); emancipatory (ideology, power). These ideas were summarised by Habermas (as quoted by Bernstein)[76] as follows:

> The systematic sciences of social action, that is economics, sociology and political science, have the goal, as do the empirical-analytic sciences, of producing nomological knowledge. A critical social science, however, will not remain satisfied with this. It is concerned with going beyond this goal to determine when theoretical statements grasp invariant regularities of social action as such and when they express ideologically frozen relations of dependence that can in principle be transformed.

These ideas link the 'purposes' of my first section through the concept of *communicative understanding*. The *Times Literary Supplement*[77] in a review of Habermas' work asked whether he represented *realistic utopianism* or *utopian realism*. As we proceed, we open up more questions. Habermas' framework implies that we need *depth, breadth* and *engagement* – the first two echoing Isaiah Berlin's 'the hedgehog and the fox'.[78] It can now be argued that this framework helps us to tackle the question: how are values determined?

Habermas, in effect, articulates the issue as the task of finding a set of common values. In the higher education context, there may be tensions between what students want and what staff want – for example, between the vocational and professional on the one hand, or something more 'academic' or 'rounded' (with all the questions that begs)[79]. But we have to make a start. The values we might expect to find supporting HE might include: understanding, mutual tolerance, democracy. In this last context, we have to worry about how to protect minorities – that is, how to deal with the problems of a selfish majority. This again raises questions about what is civilising and civilised.

We can link Habermas' argument to Kant's categorical imperative: colloquially, 'do unto others as you would be done by'. More formally, everything you do should be justifiable as though it was a manifestation of a universal law. The *Times Literary Supplement* article[80] argues that Habermas has fallen back on to Kant but has sought to make the imperative more active: the Kantian argument is argued to be based on *hypothetical* consent – presumably you think it through yourself and make a judgement. Habermas wants to this to be *actual* consent – through his emphasis on communication. Thus, in the Habermas model, values are determined through an evolutionary process of social interaction.

Higher education values will, through the processes of communicative action, to an extent reflect society's values; but can also have a major impact on them;[81] so we need to decide what they mean for higher education. It re-emphasises the concept of engagement – presented earlier – as a key purpose. We can again use knowledge as the core concept for further exploration. We have to recognise that knowledge is *socially produced*. The Habermas argument is that we all have a *critical responsibility* to dig deep. We also have to recognise that the key value question associated with knowledge is: what is true? This connects directly then to another Habermas idea – *that truth is derived by consensus*. This will seem odd at first sight, but a little thought shows its plausibility. That is how science works, for example. We know what is true in physics because we (or at least physicists) can agree about it; it is tested in an open society, and universities play a key role in this process. It is perhaps more interesting to look at areas of knowledge where we cannot agree: the arts, the social sciences, politics. We are then involved in critical explorations. Perhaps it is this kind of understanding of the nature of truth – and that in many areas we will have to argue things out – that provides the basis of *tolerance* as a key value in universities. And in this respect, they can be models for the rest of society. 'Thinking things through' also means 'arguing things through in a spirit of tolerance'. Note that in this context, tolerance is not simply about letting people do what they want, it is about critical and constructive social engagement.

So perhaps what is most important is the role of universities in these critical social processes – research, and teaching in an atmosphere of research, and constant critical inquiry; not simply teaching from received texts; certainly being deeply suspicious of the idea of *facts*. It is this continuing critical assessment that gives universities such important broader roles in society – key nodes in networks of communicative action – and therefore key roles in the evolutionary processes through which values are determined.

How do we make progress? How do we decide what to do in a university in the context of a developing knowledge of underlying values? What we are about? We can explore through the headings introduced in the second section.

Learning and teaching: cognitive capacity

Universities contain much of the world's knowledge base – its cognitive capacity. This mainly resides in people – the staff and the students, and the external community with which it communicates. It is expressed through curricula and core skills. To an extent it is contained in 'libraries' – the quotation marks indicating that the concept now extends to IT databases. Information systems are increasingly complex and powerful – expressed through concepts like the Leeds Virtual Knowledge Park.[82] We work through interactive people-machine systems in which the power comes from combining human and computer-driven intelligences.

This raises deep questions about what any individual 'ought' to know – the 'ought' implying value questions for any of us, whether as student, teacher, researcher, or citizen. As implied by the earlier analysis, it can be argued that we need both breadth and depth. The breadth is needed because that is the only way in which judgements can be made about where to search. Depth is needed as a demonstration of how to confront real difficulty and to solve hard problems. These arguments underpin the debates on 16–19 education: a broad 'pick and mix' curriculum, or the 'gold standard' of specialised A-levels. The adjectives show how loaded the debate can be. We are arguing very strongly that both are needed at all levels.[83]

A critical value in education, whether in breadth or depth, is *understanding* – as distinct from 'training'. Understanding involves the capacity to reflect on and apply reasoning ability to new problems; modify skills to deal with similar but significantly different problems; and an awareness of why this modification is appropriate.

Research: creative capabilities

The key question for the researcher is to identify the knowledge frontier. This is a value question and involves some subjectivity. Two questions have to be asked. What is interesting? What is important?[84] And there is a related question: how to be ambitious? Most academic work is organised through disciplines, and what we have to remember is that, to an extent, disciplines are social constructs. Certainly much of their present power is based on the power of the coalition that constitutes the discipline. In so far as disciplines have a rationale, this can be argued in terms of the prime systems: physical systems (physics, chemistry), living systems (biology), environmental systems (geology, ecology), social systems, (sociology) and so on. Many research problems, however, are interdisciplinary. If the systems' definitions are different – consider 'cities' for example – then many of the traditional disciplines contribute.

There are other shifts to consider. Biology, for example, has been dominated by the molecular scale. The 'systems' levels have been neglected – a judgement, again by socially-determined and constructed coalitions – that have led some commentators, erroneously it can be argued, to say that we have reached the 'end of science'[85]. In practice, there is likely to be a shift from reductionist to systemic perspectives. Indeed, it can be argued that there is a big shift to come – a concern with increasingly complex systems. And this involves stitching together our micro knowledge. It can be argued that in this territory, there is nothing like enough work being done. If we use this kind of thinking to help determine the research agenda, then this also will have longer run implications for what is on offer in terms of the teaching curriculum.

Value questions in research are in part questions of what resources ought to be spent on. And this exposes the research version of the Newman argument: knowledge for its own sake, or for utilitarian purposes? This is brought sharply into focus by the magnitude of problems facing governments of all kinds – and at all scales – today. Consider for example: poverty, education, health, an ageing population, crime, city and regional planning, housing, environment, transport.[86] These are interdisciplinary problems – and at the same time, 'basic science' problems for the social sciences![87]

There is a complex web of value questions associated with the choice agenda related to research. There is a high-dimensional combinatorial space of possible problems. The way these choices are made – for example with a focus on 'blue skies' research, economic instrumentalism or social development – involves an engagement with value questions.

Engagement: partnerships and alliances – communications capabilities

Universities do engage beyond their own networks on an increasing scale, but this is what they are least good at. Hence the argument for the so-called *third arm* – or third leg, or third mission – that takes universities beyond teaching and research. Universities should be able to *serve* their communities with this engagement; and they should be able to *learn* what is important outside the academic community. This would force universities to *engage* with the value questions which emerge from these explorations – and this links to the core of the Habermas argument.

In practical terms, what does engagement mean? Essentially, the extension of research and teaching to new constituencies. The research is therefore likely to be applied research – 'interesting and important', and hence 'useful' to those organisations that can apply it. Such research can be carried out in the university. An extension of this argument is technology transfer or, more broadly, knowledge transfer. This is in part accomplished by graduates and postgraduates migrating into the economy. But it can also be the result of direct engagement: through licensing and setting up university (part-) owned companies. The broader constituencies for teaching commit universities to supporting lifelong learning – a necessity in a time of rapid change. And this can be taken beyond its traditional role through electronic networks and 'distance delivery'. There are now many examples of such activities in universities. In Leeds, it represents about ten per cent of the total, and this figure can be expected to grow.

All of this is part of a broader argument that universities should have a more direct engagement with the economy – with commercial interests – and indeed they clearly do. The argument can be extended not just to relationships with the industrial components of the economy but with society through government and social agencies. Bok puts this very directly in an argument for Harvard setting up its School of Government.[88] And this obviously connects to the 'national problems' agenda of the previous section.

Much of the funding for applied research comes from industry for projects that are commercially driven; as we have observed, universities license the products of their own research or set up companies to exploit their research findings – in current jargon, they exploit their intellectual property. What does this imply for values in HE? Does this kind of commercialism threaten independence? Kennedy argues that this is not inherently a problem, 'the relationship between the academy and society has always been changeable', but he goes on to argue that the test of success in managing this relationship is whether universities can continue to put students 'at the centre'.[89]

This takes us to the nub of the value questions associated with the third arm. The relationships with wider constituencies can work provided that universities can be true to their own core values. This is essentially what Bok is arguing.

Concluding comments

Given this analysis, what should we be doing differently? What does the future hold? It is important to recognise the threefold focus: on knowledge capacity and creation (teaching and research); and, above all, engagement. Working through partnerships as part of that critical engagement.

Universities have proved remarkably stable entities. To quote Clark Kerr:

> About 85 institutions in the Western World established by 1520 still exist in recognisable forms, with similar functions and with unbroken histories, including the Catholic Church, the Parliaments of the Isle of Man, of Iceland and of Great Britain, several Swiss cantons, and 70 universities. Kings that rule, feudal lords with vassals, and guilds with monopolies are all gone. These 70 universities, however, are still in the same locations with some of the same buildings, with professors and students doing much the same things, and with governance carried on in much the same way. [90] [91]

'Much the same things' implies a continuity of purpose and value. The debates about 'knowledge for its own sake' – and an associated 'training of the mind' – versus something more utilitarian are of long standing. And the answer has always been something of each. However, the knowledge base changes – and hence the research map – along with new opportunities for the delivery of learning and teaching. And above all, new opportunities for engagement. The Andersson argument applied to universities implies that success – and in that sense the maintenance of the best purposes and value base for universities – involves effective progress on all fronts. The Habermas argument implies that appropriate value systems can *only* be worked out through constructive engagement. When Bok argues that universities can only maintain their values if they 'put students at the centre', then unpicking this must lead us back to something like the categorical imperative and its working out in a Habermasian manner.

What will be different in one or two decades time?[92] We can expect to maintain an academic core of disciplines like mathematics,[93] but increasingly, schools and faculties will be organised on an interdisciplinary agenda – because it is that agenda that will be judged to be 'interesting' and 'important'. Fundamental research in universities will continue to expand, but it will be increasingly complemented by an expansion of partnership-based applied research; and there will be a symbiotic link between the two sectors. The major expansion will relate to the 'engagement' heading. For example, there will be a growth in university-managed corporate universities and other institutions and companies which link university resources directly to the learning needs of organisations. There will be a serious commitment to lifelong learning both to professional organisations and to individuals. A consequence of these arguments, is that there will be more students linked to a university who are off campus than on campus – connected by high-bandwidth networks and powerful interactive workstations.

All of this can be compatible with the development of universities in ways that are consonant with 'old values' – rooted in being the knowledge core of society and an associated concern with truth and how to find and recognise it.

6

Universities and citizenship: the forgotten dimension?

R.H. Fryer

Dearing's four purposes

When Ron Dearing's National Committee of Inquiry into Higher Education reported in 1997, it commended four main 'aims and purposes' for universities in carrying out their key role in sustaining a learning society.[94] They were, first, 'to inspire and enable individuals to develop their capabilities to the highest potential levels throughout life, so that they grow intellectually, are well equipped for work, can contribute effectively to society and achieve personal fulfilment'. Second, said Dearing, universities should 'increase knowledge and understanding for their own sake and to foster their application to the benefit of the economy and society'. Third, they should 'serve the needs of an adaptable, sustainable, knowledge-based economy at local, regional and national levels' and, finally, universities should 'play a major role in shaping a democratic, civilised, inclusive society'.[95] It is that fourth purpose which is the focus of this chapter.

Of the four purposes identified by Dearing, this fourth, concerning democracy, civilisation and inclusion, is the one I suggest that has been given least attention in both subsequent policy debate and in its practical implementation. This is especially so in respect of the specific mobilisation of funding, resources and strategic initiatives, at both national and institutional levels, to secure achievement of the Dearing vision. If this is indeed true, it needs to be asked why this has occurred. It cannot be because this fourth purpose is obviously and evidently less important than the other three, centred, as it is, on such major and wide-ranging issues. And these are ones that are, after all, of concern to all members of the community and not just those people already routinely involved with universities.

Perhaps that is the real problem. Because the matters in question are simply so broad, 'philosophical' and daunting, even, it has been hard to bring them down to specific actions or to measure their achievement through particular and agreed metrics. Or perhaps this fourth purpose is seen by the universities, and by those who fund and lead them, as normal or likely by-products of the successful pursuit of the other three, and therefore not requiring any specific consideration or measures to secure their accomplishment. Or, maybe, it's just another sign of the times. Perhaps such an apparently ideal and altruistic purpose has found little resonance with the dominant and more cynical discourses of an era seemingly pre-occupied with a more individualistic, instrumental, market-oriented and economistic conception of the prime role of higher education. Finally, for those of a post-modernist bent, any purpose that is predicated on such 'grand narratives' as democracy, civilisation or inclusion is bound to be regarded as meaningless under conditions of infinite relativity and diversity.[96]

Whichever of these, or other, explanations offers some insight (and none is entirely convincing), the relative neglect of this aspect of universities' functions and, it should be said, of what really should be their *responsibilities* towards the rest of society, is still surprising. After all, it can be argued with little difficulty that this fourth purpose, or rather cluster of purposes, could be depicted as universities' most noble, challenging, fundamental and even transcendental activity. Indeed, this fourth of Dearing's purposes for universities might with justice be termed their core 'public' or 'civic' mission and underscores the role of universities in helping both to define and to uphold core values in a democratic society. And it can be argued that such a mission and a commitment to such values are even more important in a period of rapid social change. As the Dearing committee itself argued, 'higher education contributes to the health of society by helping it to understand itself, its history, culture and institutions'.

Enlarging on the vision, Dearing argued that it is through their engagement in universities that students are afforded an important chance 'to consider the values needed in a democratic society'. In their studies, university students can develop their capacity 'to debate issues rationally and openly' in the context of a 'commitment to a pluralistic society, the rule of law and the protection of individual liberties'.[97] In reporting and advancing these views, and as a 'fitting conclusion to this section of our report', Dearing also drew on submissions it had received during its inquiries, including one from Professor Stewart Sutherland. The latter's argument set out universities' central contribution to what he termed 'civic virtue', the inter-relationship between the role of education and what he termed the 'pillars of democracy'.[98] What witnesses to Dearing looked for in universities was that they should be 'even more *engaged* with the wider society and, indeed, the world'.[99] As Dearing powerfully summarised the submissions that adopted this same point of view, where universities can make a major contribution to the wider society, 'higher education can legitimately, it is suggested, become a vehicle for social justice'.[100]

According to this view, universities should play a pivotal role in the education and development of citizens and enlarging social inclusion, especially in the lives of those who might be expected to provide leadership of all kinds in civil society, if this doesn't sound altogether too grand. Universities' work in pursuit of this fourth of Dearing purposes would include action in all matters of contemporary concern such as the meaning and implications of globalization, living with risk and the challenges of sustainable development. As the Association of University Teachers' Northern Ireland Advisory Committee put it in their own evidence to Dearing, 'it is a clear duty upon higher education institutions to exert leadership in providing an arena in which diversity is recognised, variety flourishes, and members of all communities feel at home'.[101] The Further Education Development Association argued that 'students must be prepared for their responsibilities as citizens, including the responsibility to use resources sustainably' and St Mary's University College expected university graduates to be able to 'probe the human implications of scientific and technological progress' of the contemporary world.[102]

Some antecedents of Dearing

In many respects, the core purposes of higher education identified by Dearing echoed those set out in the celebrated Robbins report over thirty years earlier.

For Robbins, the main aims of universities had been first the 'instruction in skills suitable to play a part in the general division of labour'. Second, said Robbins was the promotion of 'the general powers of the mind' not to produce mere specialisation, but rather 'cultivated men and women'. Third, he called for the advancement of learning and partaking in the nature of discovery; and fourth he termed 'the transmission of a common culture and common standards of citizenship'.[103]

At the time of writing his report, Robbins himself was only the most recent in a distinguished line of authors to underline the responsibilities of universities in defining, upholding and transmitting culture and values. For example, in his landmark book on universities, first written in the aftermath of the First World War and re-published after the second as Germany struggled to reintegrate itself into the world family of democracies, Karl Jaspers succinctly summarised the four principal functions of universities. For Jaspers they were research, teaching, professional education and, here again, the transmission of culture.[104] Naturally, the latter purpose was of particular importance in considering universities' contribution to the re-making of Germany in the aftermath of the assault not only on them as institutions, but also after the sustained and violent degradation by fascism of wider civilised values, democracy and citizenship. Thus, universities had a key role to play in the reconstruction of German citizenship and in the regeneration of civil society in the post-war world. For Earnest Boyer, there were four key inter-related aspects of scholarship – those of discovery, integration, application and teaching – and each might be more prevalent at any one time or in any one sphere or domain.[105] These four 'faces' of scholarship may each be expected to bear upon the issue of universities and citizenship.

In similar vein to Robbins and Dearing, the most recent UK Government White Paper on higher education envisages a 'higher education sector which meets the needs of the economy in terms of trained people, research and technology transfer'. At the same time, says the White Paper, 'higher education needs to enable all suitably qualified individuals to develop their potential intellectually and personally, and to provide the necessary storehouse of expertise in science and technology, and the arts and humanities which defines our civilisation and culture.'[106] In detail, this vision comprises eleven elements including:

• Recognising and valuing universities 'as creators of knowledge and understanding and as engines for applying that knowledge for the benefit of all';

• Recognising 'their role in educating their students to live life to the full, through the acquisition of skills and through fostering imagination, creativity and contribution to society';

• Acknowledging and celebrating 'the differences between institutions as each defines its own mission';

• Building 'strong and purposeful collaborations';

• Meeting 'the developing needs of students for new modes of study and delivery of courses as well as pastoral and learning support';

• Offering 'the opportunity of higher education to all those who have the potential to benefit'; and

• Having 'the freedom to be innovative and entrepreneurial'.[107]

The main difference between Dearing and Robbins centred on their respective fourth purpose. The Dearing committee explicitly felt unable to repeat exactly what Robbins had proposed in respect of the transmission of a 'common culture'. This was because 'since the time of the Robbins report, the UK has increasingly become a society which includes many cultures and one in which there is active debate about any system of values'. Hence, in such a society 'those in higher education may not see themselves as custodians of a culture and a system of values which they are entitled to advocate and transmit on behalf of society'.[108] Indeed, many witnesses who submitted evidence to Dearing, in generally endorsing the Robbins principles, suggested that Robbins' aims for higher education should be reinterpreted, reformulated and extended, to deal with the more 'complex' cultural mix of contemporary society.

According to Dearing's summary of the national consultation undertaken at the time, the revised aims for universities should meet the growing need for more personal flexibility and development, widen life chances and social inclusion and enhance the quality of life. They should also contribute to the development of a learning society with 'enhanced capacity for society-wide reflection and critical nous'.[109] At its best, higher education 'can impart tolerance, openness, and the capacity to inject positive forms of social interaction'.[110] So, despite the undoubted shift to a more diversified and culturally mixed society, there remained, argued the committee, a core group of shared values and standards that should continue to characterise universities and, more generally, a civilised community. These were the pursuit of truth, sharing knowledge, freedom of thought and expression, rigorous analysis based on evidence and reason, listening to alternative views to be judged on their own merits and concern with the ethics of different findings or practices.[111]

Continued adherence by universities to such values in a more culturally diverse and pluralistic world harks back to the noble and challenging aims for them first set out in full by Cardinal Newman over a century-and-a-half earlier.[112] This emphasis also draws attention to the key role of universities in still sharing responsibility for what one witness to the Dearing inquiry termed acting as the 'conscience of the nation' or what others, more radically still, have termed 'speaking truth to power'.[113] What is more, Dearing's completely understandable grounds for modifying the Robbins' committee's fourth purpose in this way, by reference to increased cultural diversity and social change, are all the more reason for exploring how universities can best fulfil and strengthen their responsibilities in the context of contemporary democracy.

This is precisely why this chapter is concerned to review the implications of this for their role in upholding and advancing citizenship in the late modern world. For democracy and citizenship are but two sides of the same coin in any serious consideration of the development of civil society. It is exactly in these circumstances of a greater diversity and plurality of lifestyles and identities that the issue of what constitutes a valid, inclusive, tolerant and legitimate notion of citizenship requires critical investigation, clarification and dissemination. Such considerations centre on the questions of how we are to live together in such a diverse society and according to what standards and norms we are to conduct our contemporary lives, both public and private. All of this should constitute most fertile and apposite grounds in universities not just for investigation and analysis but also for promulgation and application.

Democracy, citizenship and inclusion
In making a connection between democracy, civilisation and citizenship, the Dearing Committee's thinking was the most recent contribution to

a long line of distinguished, and often quite contentious, philosophical debates and political practices. These date right back to the city state *polis* of Ancient Greece and, specifically, to the writings of Aristotle. For Aristotle, citizenship was not only the principal *means* to being free; most importantly, it was itself the *very way* of being free. According to Held, 'from classical antiquity to the seventeenth century, democracy, when it was considered at all, was largely associated with the gathering of citizens in assemblies and public meeting places'.[114] Links between democracy and citizenship, between active involvement in decision-making and the consequent legitimacy of authority are central to both the theory and the practice of democracy. In this world of the *polis*, citizenship expresses the democratic ideal where each citizen is both ruler and ruled: citizens join each other in making decisions where each decider respects the authority of the others and all join in obeying the decisions…they have made'.[115] Thus, for Rousseau, sovereign authority rested with the deliberative involvement of citizens in the determination of the 'general will'.

The linked domains of democracy and citizenship are rich in controversy and dispute. For those favouring the theory of *participative* democracy in the tradition of Aristotle and Rousseau there is in their approach an emphasis on the active participation of the citizenry in political discussion and decision-making. Being a full citizen confers both *status* and social position. By contrast, and in part in pragmatic response to the challenges of scale and numbers involved and in part refusing to trust in the rule of governments, those who advocate *representative* democracy often couple this with an associated bundle of *rights and obligations* for citizens. For liberals of this latter persuasion, the role of government is to secure for all individual citizens the best circumstances for them to pursue their own legitimate personal interests and ends. States and authorities should secure for citizens the greatest possible degree of individual liberty consonant with the liberty of their fellow citizens. Both approaches have in common a concern with the issues of equity and equality where the citizenry is concerned, especially where formal rights or status are at issue.

Communitarian critics of late modern society, such as Amitai Etzioni, mourn what they see as the loss of community and social solidarity between citizens. For them, the lifeblood of democracy is found less in the formal institutions of democracy, such as the franchise or equality before the law, important though these are, but in citizens' everyday engagement in, and self-government of, the complex and cross-cutting web of social relations and voluntary organisations in society. This is the realm of 'trust' relations and so-called 'social capital' that universities and other educational institutions can do much to support and promote.[116] As Robert Putnam, one of the most influential authors in this field puts it; 'social capital here refers to features of social organisation, such as trust, norms and networks, that can improve the efficiency of society by facilitating coordinated actions'.[117] According to Putnam, voluntary associations are 'places where social and civic skills are learned – "schools for democracy". Members learn how to run meetings, speak in public, write letters, organize projects and debate public issues with civility.' Voluntary and community groups serve as 'forums for thoughtful deliberation' over vital public issues, as 'occasions for learning civic virtues, such as active participation in public life' and networks through which to develop trustworthiness and reciprocity. They are places where 'opposing sides in a democratic debate...agree on the ground rules for seeking mutual accommodation after sufficient discussion even (or especially) when they don't agree on what is to be done'.[118]

In this domain of largely self-organised 'intermediary' bodies, which stand between the potentially overwhelming might of the state and the insecurity and isolation of the individual, active, participative democracy and thriving engaged citizenship are vital and enrich society in a wide variety of ways. As Putnam succinctly puts it, 'citizenship is not a spectator sport'.[119] That is exactly why, on the basis of his extensive research into the latest trends of community participation in the United States of America, he has expressed such concern at an apparent current decline in active, face-to-face involvement of citizens in voluntary organisations, in public life and in social engagement. It is in these domains that universities in our late modern age can, and in my view should, make a major contribution in clarifying the vital and continuing social functions of positive social capital, not just for individuals and communities but for societies at large. In implementing the fourth dimension of Dearing's vision it is here that universities should deploy their influence, expertise and resources in advocating and supporting the creation of and access to social capital by a wide cross-section of citizens, associations, interests and social groups.

Not surprisingly, demands for and struggles to secure full citizen rights and status for different social groups have often been the occasion of major political and often violent confrontations. Even in recent years, they have provided the basis of mobilisation for notable social movements, especially where 'minorities' are involved. In his major revision of the theory of citizenship immediately after the second world war, T.H. Marshall signalled the expansion of the concept to take full account of historical developments in which it was possible to distinguish between citizens' *civil, political and social* rights.[120] *Civil rights* confer formal freedoms on citizens before the law and in the face of the power of the state. *Political rights* have to do with the extension of the franchise and parliamentary representation. *Social rights* are about securing for all citizens the opportunities to share in the economic and social benefits of society. For Marshall, one of the paradoxes of citizenship was that, at least until the late nineteenth-century achievement of collective bargaining by trades unions and the advent of the welfare state, it could co-exist with, or even legitimate, certain forms of social inequality and the overall system of class relations.

In this domain of the 'social', education plays a particularly significant role, including through its links to the occupational structure and hence in its relationship to citizens' life chances. Important to remember in this context is the fact that education can thus be the domain not only of the *expression* of different class interests and opportunities, but also of their *distribution* and, what is more, *legitimation* and perpetuation. And too often, education can emphasise passivity and receptivity rather than autonomous action. As the nineteenth-century sociologist Herbert Spencer once gloomily commented: 'the established systems of education, whatever their matter might be, are fundamentally vicious in their manner. They encourage *submissive receptivity* instead of *independent activity.*'[121] These issues should be of central concern to universities, desirous as many of them are of opening access to all the talents, regardless of social origin, but also of playing the key role assigned to them by Dearing in the realm of citizenship.

What Marshall's critique opened up, but was unable to resolve, was the large gap that was too often manifest between *formal* equalities for all citizens and the *substantive* reality which different individuals faced in the world where marked inequalities persisted, including in access to education and attainment. In response, increasingly, minority and 'special interest' groups have argued the case that their actual needs or circumstances deny them access to full citizenship and indeed 'exclude' them from the good life or key aspects of social experience. Whilst the question of who is and who is not to count as a 'citizen' has always been a core issue for democracies, an explicit focus on the matter of what is often now called 'social' inclusion is very much a product of contemporary European debate and policy. Its particular recent emphasis has been to identify and tackle all those aspects of civil society, including education, that result in the systematic social exclusion of certain groups from genuinely equal opportunities. These conditions range widely. They may include the circumstances of family life, housing, neighbourhood, schooling and learning more generally, labour market status, leisure, community engagement, ethnicity, sexual orientation or disability indeed a whole raft of domains in what is often called 'civil society'. Perhaps less tangibly but none-the-less with at least as serious consequences for inequality, by the very circumstances of their lives some social groups are systematically excluded from the benefits of the social capital of networks of trust, contact, influence, know-how and community involvement. Examples of these groups of people include those whose poor levels of standard literacy and numeracy (some millions in the UK) serve as barriers to their social inclusion and access to the good life generally. They also include some ethnic minorities and groups of refugees as well as poor, white unskilled (and often unemployed) working class groups housed on so-called 'sink' housing estates, and travellers' groups living their lives largely excluded from the wider society.

Hence, within a *general universality* of citizenship, and in an increasingly *pluralistic and diverse* society, authors such as Iris Marion Young argue that certain social groups continue to experience exclusion from full citizenship and deserve, even, special attention and support.[122] Here precisely are the contemporary issues of diversity and social complexity that the Dearing committee raised, but certainly not so that they could be avoided by universities because of their intricacies and difficulties, any more than by other responsible elements of a democratic society. They were raised by Dearing precisely so that universities could help them to be better understood and responded to fairly in all of their various nuances and subtleties. At the same time and in this same connection, Smith and Spurling issue a vital warning about the lures and dangers of what they term 'cultural hegemony'. In responding to such examples of social exclusion, the 'moral majority' should not see in education and lifelong learning an opportunity to devise, and maybe even impose, learning programmes 'in an instrumental fashion to show the marginal population the error of their ways through narrowly defined citizenship courses and the like.'[123]

More radically still, Ignatieff has warned against what he sees as the self-deluding 'moral narcissism' inherent in some contemporary and 'pious' social democratic critiques of market values and associated pleas for a more 'caring' approach. Ignatieff discerns in such essentially nostalgic critiques a misleading kind of sentimentality about a 'lost' notion of citizenship once underpinned by the welfare state and 'Butskellite' consensus of mid twentieth-century Britain. For many in Britain at least, he argues, the *practical experience* of such citizenship was not always beneficial and liberating but quite the reverse – in council housing, state enterprises and in their involvement with unresponsive public bureaucracies. What is now needed, according to this point of view, is a vigorous debate not about substituting a more 'caring' society for market capitalism but about what is meant by citizens' rights and entitlements. This is a world where markets can be expected to persist and, indeed, to perform some functions perfectly satisfactorily according to their own criteria. 'Any invocation of citizenship as an ideal that is not just heart-warming words has to make its peace with the indubitable efficiency of markets and then to define and implement its redistributive goals in such a way that they do not crush the liberty that equality of opportunity exists to enhance.'[124] This kind of tough intellectual territory ought to be precisely the arena which universities, with their commitment to independent and critical inquiry, ought to relish. Further, they should debate and share the product of their studies with the wider community of citizens to whose benefit such deliberations should, rightly, be oriented.

So, whilst there are clearly many points of difference in both the theory and practice of citizenship and democracy, broadly speaking, the principal distinctions centre on two main continua and the resulting tensions between them. These are the continua running from individualism to collectivism on the one hand and from homogeneity to diversity on the other. In simple terms, this gives us four 'modal' types of citizenship and democracy. For example, those who are committed to a communitarian perspective will tend towards that quadrant of the simple model where collectivism and homogeneity intersect while those centring on the interplay of diversity and individualism will emphasise citizens' individual liberty and their substantive equality in a more 'atomised' society. The role of universities is to review and clarify understanding of all of these dimensions and possibilities, to enquire into them critically, in theory and by empirical study, in teaching and research and to prepare citizens for active engagement with the issues facing modern democracies. As Carr and Hartnett have shown in a sustained and powerful analysis that focuses largely on school-level education, for more than a century models of democracy and society are often paralleled by theories of education and learning.[125]

In short, citizenship is, for universities, both a proper topic for systematic and critical enquiry and an appropriate focus or their various programmes of teaching, learning, research, community engagement and dissemination. Hence, it also quite appropriate for universities also to respond to these various conceptions and conditions of citizenship by opening up their resources, facilities, learning opportunities and ability to influence the development of society and to enable citizens at large to secure social change and improvement.

Teaching, learning and research

At one level, there is nothing especially new in the idea of universities making a major contribution to citizenship and, through this, contributing to the core values and central institutions of society. In the first instance, it can fairly be claimed that the direct and routine output of universities' research and teaching, in the forms of knowledge and alumni, constitute their principal contributions to the kinds of societies that obtain in the contemporary world. Universities' graduates and research output also may be seen to represent their main ways of shaping both the conceptions of citizenship that prevail at any time and, in part, the sorts of opportunities that people in general have of enjoying or benefiting from them. In that sense, the major 'outputs' of universities, by way of the people qualified by them and the knowledge contributed through universities research, may be deemed to be major contributions to and influences on definitions and practices of citizenship in any given era. This is not to be underestimated and it was, no doubt, in part what Dearing and his colleagues had in mind with their fourth purpose for universities in the late modern age.

In this connection, the demand that universities should play a fuller role in widening and deepening access to study in them and in diversifying participation in the opportunities to learn that they provide for all sections of the community is, of course, central. Indeed, any obstacles or intervening practices that artificially and maybe systematically limit access to learning by people whose intellectual capability is otherwise of the level required fruitfully to benefit from, and successfully to contribute to the work of universities, can rightly be seen as illegitimate and undesirable. All this constitutes an aspect of the 'fair access' debate that is rarely discussed.

In the UK, still only a little more than ten per cent of young people from the lowest socio-economic group go on to university by comparison with an average of more than 40 per cent from the age cohort overall, and of almost 80 per cent from the highest socio-economic group. This constitutes a palpable and serious failure to extend democracy, citizenship and inclusion in this way to the community at large. Of course, universities cannot be held solely responsible for the current pattern of unequal opportunities in higher education. Nor, acting alone, can they be expected to resolve the problem. But, to the extent that more of a society's citizens from different walks of life are enabled to join the ranks of the universities or to study in them, the more likely is the promise of Dearing's fourth and most challenging purpose for higher education to be achieved.

In similar fashion, in so far as the output of university research extends or enhances citizenship or secures greater social inclusion, then universities' contribution to what might be termed the 'common social good' ought, quite understandably, be expected to increase. Some university researchers, and all taken together, will necessarily contribute to contemporary notions of democracy and citizenship, albeit often indirectly or unintentionally. Some university researchers will directly address limited *aspects* of these dimensions of society in their inquiries and some (in truth, a small minority) will be centrally concerned with the very conditions and circumstances of democracy and citizenship, by virtue of their chosen intellectual focus. One positive way in which citizenship may be strengthened by university research is in the development and embedding of research skills, critical analysis and reflective practice amongst citizens at large and in the wider community. For example, especially in research undertaken in the field of development studies, it has increasingly been advocated that one aspect of social and educational research especially should be to foster and transfer some research skills into the people, groups and social relations being studied. In this way people can become active participants in and users of research and not merely its passive objects or, worse still, its victims, knowingly or otherwise. This has been a valuable and notable extension of citizenship through commitment to a more enlightened and empowering ethics of social enquiry.

However, it should be noted that not all of higher education's contributions to society can be *assumed* automatically to be benign: indeed, some may actually be thought to undermine citizenship, weaken civil society or represent a challenge to civilised values, mostly but not always, it should be said, inadvertently. In any case, these university 'outputs' are not always, or even mostly, first designed with their expected contribution to citizenship explicitly in mind. In fairness, it might be contended that this is not the chief purpose in universities of producing either knowledge or graduates, although any such consequence is always to be welcomed. The same may be said of universities' research activities and outputs.

But, even at their very best, contributions to upholding and advancing the cause of citizenship in these ways is largely about what universities can do either *to* or *for* the wider community rather than *with* it and the citizens that people it. Nor is the agenda of universities set *by* the wider community in any recognisable or tangible way, either directly by its citizens or by representatives of the community at large. Indeed, one of the key freedoms that universities rightly and greatly cherish is their independence of mind and governance in their pursuit of truth. In this sense, universities do not really welcome the direct setting of their agenda for teaching, learning and research by 'society', or more accurately by those who happen to wield power or pull the purse strings at any particular point in time. This point of view is understandable, noble indeed, if its main purpose is consciously to shield universities from the overbearing influence of particular (and potentially malevolent or distorting) social or political interests. But insistence on absolute university autonomy betrays either a certain naivety or some disingenuousness. For it is difficult to see how any institution so closely linked to the rest of the world through its people, money, contracts, the exercise of power and the web of social relationships can really stand 'above' or 'outside' it.

Community involvement

A second way in which universities' contribution to citizenship may be said to be manifest is in the various roles and responsibilities undertaken in the wider community by the graduates and staff of universities. They do this in their everyday work and in their participation in a wide variety of voluntary, community-based, political, religious and social settings. In this, people from the universities may be seen both to exemplify and to enrich citizenship by their active participation and may also provide leadership to others in so doing. Of late, some individual universities and the Higher Education Funding Council (HEFCE) have encouraged the extension of such community involvement to undergraduates through a variety of organised volunteering activities, and some higher education institutions also now enable students to gain credits through such activities. This work is supported by HEFCE's small but innovative Higher Education Active Community Fund.

Over the past five years or so in England, HEFCE has developed what is often referred to as 'third leg' or 'third stream' funding to support universities' outreach into and collaboration with local businesses and the local economy. The specific aim of this element of financial support to universities is to enhance universities' contribution to the community through knowledge transfer, joint business ventures with the private sector, in 'spin-out' companies and by wealth creation generally. In the first iteration of the higher education reach-out to Business and the Community Fund, launched in June 1999, up to £83 million was made available. In the first round of allocations a total of eighty-seven awards was made, ranging from just £25,000 to over one million pounds, and a further fifty in the second. This initiative is now being taken forward by the Higher Education Innovation Fund and both HEFCE and Government have signalled their intention to build such funding into the core allocations to all higher education institutions.

One of the most valuable consequences of these welcome initiatives is what HEFCE calls the subsequent 'embedding' of such third stream activities into universities' normal routines of learning, teaching, and research. This helps universities to strengthen their direct contribution to the economy and to local and regional communities and, in some limited ways and indirectly at least, to some aspects of citizenship. But, as HEFCE itself fairly remarks, this stream of financial support to universities is still only tiny by contrast with its main fields of funding for teaching and research and, according to some preliminary research findings from Slowey, is scarcely recognised as being of any significance by many academics.[126] Nor is a preoccupation with this sort of activity likely to lead to academic preferment or promotion.

Even so, this is all very much to be applauded, but mostly these engagements by the graduates, staff and undergraduates represent what might be called a range of largely indirect or implicit contributions to the upholding or advancement of citizenship. Much of the undoubtedly valuable participation by people from the universities in all sorts of community settings, from schools to old people's homes and from voluntary organisations to political parties, still only constitutes a contribution to citizenship through processes more accurately understood as diffusion rather than direct and mutual engagement. More critically, such contributions might sometimes even be seen as amounting to some kind of unwelcome 'missionary', interfering or domineering impositions by university people on their (presumed-to-be less fortunate or capable) fellow citizens or as a more or less deliberate attempt to shape or direct their thinking. In any case, this kind of involvement is mostly not undertaken on reciprocally agreed terms between the university-based individuals concerned and the wider society or with democratically accountable community representatives.

However valuable such contributions to citizenship might be, it is also fair to say that they rarely constitute the principal or core activities of contemporary UK universities. Nor is any staff and student involvement in them likely to bring very much institutional reward to the individuals or universities themselves, by way of promotion, achievement, recognition or social honour. What is more, very little of this useful activity demands the allocation of substantial university resources to support it and, truth to tell, most of these sorts of engagement in civil society are largely by-products or even accidental consequences of universities' mainstream activities. It would, as Dearing rightly argued, require the development of some sorts of new deal or 'compact' between universities and the community, or more likely their *local* communities. Such a new compact would make explicit that all kinds of participation in the wider society and in active citizenship and its promotion by university staff and students should be recognised by universities themselves as significant contributions to their missions.

Cultural resources and facilities

Another and important way in which universities can support and enhance citizenship and also constitute a civilised, civilising and valued resource for the wider community is by opening up their cultural activities to people at large. They do this by virtue of their ability, thanks to a concentration of effective demand, to devote resources to such facilities as libraries, theatres, cinemas, museums, art galleries, exhibitions, sports facilities and so on. On the whole, where this happens, it tends to be the local communities of a given university that benefit most. Where there is no local institution of higher education or where problems of geography or transport intervene, such opportunities may not arise or may be more theoretical than substantive. Moreover, some members of the public may not consider that such cultural facilities are 'for the likes of them', given their own identities, self-images and social origins. In those senses too, some groups of citizens may be 'excluded' from enjoying the benefits of making available universities' cultural resources for wider use.

Again, such opening up of universities' resources is much to be welcomed but, once more, some caveats need to be entered. First, the main objective in providing such facilities is not often, if at all, for securing public or community benefit and even less for their expected contribution to upholding or advancing contemporary citizenship. Second, even when such facilities are genuinely open to the wider public, they are rarely enjoyed by more than a minority of citizens, and even then the composition of such groups is usually highly selective in terms of class and race and, where sport is concerned, gender. These valuable and often high quality facilities are aimed principally at the members of the *university* community and, increasingly, are used as an additional attraction to would-be students or staff. In the worst circumstances, where little public participation is possible or welcomed, such cultural facilities may be regarded as the privileges or unfair advantages enjoyed by the university 'élite' and their friends.

Adult and community learning

The most direct and explicit way in which universities have contributed to citizenship, or at least to a particular version of it, is by opening up opportunities for learning to the wider and, most often, adult community. In this they have especially sought to extend their educational reach out to those social groups whose members have been traditionally under-represented in, or excluded from, university-level education, particularly to adults from the lower middle and working classes. In the UK universities have done this variously over the past century-and-a-quarter through a range of university 'extension' or 'extra-mural' provision and through the use of the university-level tutorial system, first pioneered by the universities of Cambridge and Oxford. This is part of what is often seen as the 'great tradition' of so-called 'liberal adult education' and what is often meant by those who advocate what they call a greater 'social' purpose for universities.

Different authors use the notion of 'social purpose' higher education in a variety of ways, not all of them consistent with one another. Some are more inclined to liberal notions of individual citizenship development, some leaning more to the idea of sustaining the common norms and standards of an integrated community of citizens and some are more committed to a radical critique and collectivist transformation of society. But, mostly they all have to do with establishing a firm relationship between learning, and especially the taking of a critical and challenging perspective on existing practices or knowledge, and movements for social change. One such approach explains that its purpose is to provide 'individuals with knowledge which they can use collectively to change society if they so wish'. Thus, social purpose higher education is aimed at equipping 'members of the working class with the intellectual tools to play a full role in democratic society or to challenge the inequalities or injustices of society in order to bring radical social change'.[127]

In a lecture given to celebrate the contributions of Albert Mansbridge and the Workers' Educational Association to the social purposes of adult learning, Lalage Bown drew explicit links between what she called the rich and radical 'inheritance' of adult education and the people's quest for liberty. In her lecture, Bown traced this tradition of the promise in citizens' learning back to the radical writings of John Milton in support of enlightenment and emancipation in the political, social and intellectual turbulence of the English revolution of the mid-seventeenth century.[128]

UK universities have made this kind of adult education and 'extension' provision sometimes alone and sometimes in joint work with voluntary bodies such as the Workers' Educational Association.[129] They have done so in part-time and evening programmes, in occasional lectures and seminars open to the public, in summer schools and in so-called 'open learning' activities.

Most remarkably, such extension activities have in some notable instances provided part of the original basis first for creating 'university colleges' and subsequently universities in their own right, such as in Liverpool, Sheffield and Keele.[130] Traditionally, the involvement of voluntary organisations in such learning have brought three distinctive characteristics to their educational activities: 'they are membership bodies, they have adult learning as a major or primary function; and they are held together by some sort of collective purpose'.[131]

Universities' entry into this field in this country largely followed, and often was deliberately intended by those in authority to counter, contain or re-direct, the perceived threat of a variety of independent working class education initiatives. These initiatives were frequently and deliberately aimed at promoting the economic and political emancipation of the working class and at securing progressive social change, sometimes including revolution. In the UK, the roots of these quests for independent learning reach deeply into the past of the making of modern class society and into origins of a variety of working class institutions and other social movements. Claims for the liberating promise of learning have been associated with what Edward Thompson memorably coined as the 'planting of the liberty tree' and were taken up in earnest in the late-eighteenth and early-nineteenth centuries.[132] They were reflected in the late eighteenth-century radical writings of Tom Paine, Mary Wolstonecraft and Godwin and were taken up by Corresponding Societies, by the advocates of Owenite co-operation and early socialism, and with the Chartists' slogan of 'bread, knowledge and freedom'.

A commitment to and conviction in the emancipatory promise of learning was carried forward variously in dissenting religion, in the enterprising ranks of working class autodidacts, through proletarian self-help organisations and in the practice of mutual support, in reading aloud to groups of fellow students and in independent educational work. It thrived too in scientific, literary and secular learned societies, in adult Sunday Schools, in nineteenth-century women's organisations and the early trade union and labour movements and Labour Colleges, and in independent working class libraries.[133] Opportunities such as these for engagement in learning and serious debate constituted the 'proletarian equivalent of an artistic café, literary magazine, or university common room'.[134] Frequently, the purposes here for embracing education were explicitly focused on its expected contribution to the democratisation of society, its challenge to autocracy and privilege and its anticipated help in bringing about emancipatory and radical social change. Here again can be discerned a clear and legitimate link to Dearing's democratic and inclusive agenda for universities. As Anthony Giddens has rightly noted, 'emancipatory politics makes primary the imperatives of *justice, equality and participation*'.[135]

Disputes

Where universities are concerned, this potential involvement of education with social change has, not surprisingly, often been the occasion for bitter differences, for accusation and counter-accusation and has frequently constituted fertile ground for expressing sharply different points of view on the legitimacy or real value of such educational enterprise. For some, linking up with wider democratic and social movements has been nothing less than the right and proper extension of universities' duty both to society at large and to the search for truth. Some, more bluntly, saw in the opening up of universities to more working class students a chance more effectively to hitch higher education to their own political quest for radical social change. By contrast, as I have already indicated, others looked to universities' extension and extra-mural classes, and to bodies such as the Workers' Educational Association, to counter the threatening zeal of revolutionary ideas and insurrection. This was especially the case where such subversive thoughts and arguments were perceived as being promoted or endorsed by allegedly 'ideological' approaches to teaching and learning, approximating more, it was felt, to the spread of propaganda and agitation than to 'responsible' and 'disinterested' inquiry. At Oxford University, in the first decade of the twentieth century, such was the rancour and depth of feeling in this dispute that it led to a strike of students at the newly established Ruskin College. This was followed by the dismissal of the Principal for siding with the more radical and dissenting views of the striking students, the establishment of the breakaway independent National Labour College and the founding of the celebrated Plebs League.[136]

There were many critical portrayals of the stance taken by the universities' chief partner in their adult extension and tutorial class work, the Workers' Educational Association, reflecting the hope of some in authority that its dispassionate approach to learning would quell the radical and revolutionary ardour of the working class. As an examination of the intentions or rhetoric of the authorities and some WEA leaders such criticisms were often well founded, even if such high hopes of moderating political commitment were frequently frustrated.[137] The students' own experiences often told of quite other journeys of intellectual enlightenment and invigoration. As Jonathan Rose demonstrates in a careful analysis of the impact of study through the WEA and Ruskin College, the outcome at grass-roots level was 'an articulate and obstreperous working-class intelligentsia'.[138] Those who went through these sorts of studies grew markedly in self confidence, were well able to hold their own in learned political debate, could analyse parliamentary reports, understand statistics and, above all, think for themselves.

It comes perhaps as no surprise that university adult education of this 'engaged' and socially purposive kind has often attracted individual scholars and academics who have been themselves been intellectually curious about, or committed to, the idea of promoting active citizenship and social change. They have often also been outstanding scholars in their chosen field of study, and have led both teaching and research in areas connected to various struggles for democracy, emancipation and equality. Thus, the provision of university-level adult education has been supported or even led in the UK by outstanding intellectuals and distinguished academics such as R.H. Tawney, T.H. Green, G.D.H. Cole, Raymond Williams, Ken Coates, E.P. Thompson, K. Alexander, Lalage Bown, Royden Harrison and Michael Barratt Brown.

By no means have such intellectuals always approached their university adult education work from the same political point of view. Nor have they always agreed precisely on the role and contribution of universities to debates about the great social issues of the day and, especially, to social movements of one kind or another. Frequently, such academics have been accused by some of their university peers of undermining universities' only 'true' and valid purpose in the quest for disinterested and even, on occasion it has been argued, value-free 'truth'. They have been accused of political or ideological bias and of abusing their positions of academic tutors to spread a particular point of view or interpretation of society. Some of these academics have even forfeited their careers, or at least their otherwise well-deserved promotion, by remaining committed to their conception of a socially purposive higher education.

On the other hand, outside of universities, some radical political activists have ridiculed what they see as university intellectuals' noble but vain attempts to reconcile the academic demands and conventions of higher education with an unswerving political drive for social and economic change. These particular critics' preoccupations have been to challenge and overturn the existing *status quo* in society, of which universities are perceived to be prime supporters and beneficiaries. In the tradition of Karl Marx they have argued that the priority should be to seek to *change* the world and not merely to study, understand or interpret it. For critics of this persuasion, in so far as university adult education has role at all it is only to afford those who will eventually usher in a new society some chance to refine their revolutionary ideas and proselytise amongst their fellow students and members of the university. Not for them a domain of rigorous inquiry, self-critical reflection and genuinely open debate. To the extent that university adult education successfully gets learners, and a wider public, to subscribe to these values, such critics maintain that it should be vigorously opposed.

The Russell report
In the major public review of adult education led by Sir Lionel Russell, in the early 1970s, attention was drawn to the key role played by universities in this field. Russell underlined the major contribution that such education already had made, and should continue to make, to democracy, citizenship, political education and to people's capacity to engage with social change, and areas of social life that are always bound to be controversial:

> The way of democracy is to submit areas of controversy to debate, in the belief that right judgements are built upon knowledge, critical enquiry and rational discussion. Those who lack the knowledge, or the tools of enquiry, *and who therefore feel excluded from a say in the decisions that govern their lives, are effectively disfranchised.* The need for education in social and political understanding, recognised from the early days of Chartist and Co-operative adult education and re-affirmed by the WEA, will continue to be one of the prime needs of the future.[139]

In like fashion, trades union and labour studies have long constituted a significant element of university adult education, and, since the 1970s especially, this has embraced extensive training of shop stewards, health and safety representatives and, more recently, new 'learning representatives'.[140] This work reached its zenith in the late 1970s and early 1980s, as union membership in the UK grew to thirteen millions and to 57 per cent of the employed workforce. In this growth, the WEA played a key role in the development of higher education trades union work in this country especially through its joint work with university extra-mural and continuing education departments. The trades unions have themselves long acted as training grounds for developing the skills of analysis, debate, argument, representation, leadership, accountability and the art of imaginative compromise through rigorous discussion. For many working class people it has been principally through access to and participation in union education programmes that they have come into contact with higher education. In some universities, joint programmes with unions, notably with miners and steelworkers, led to three-year day-release programmes for union workplace representatives. For some individuals, of course, this has also been the start of a learning journey that eventually took them into full-time study and sometimes academic employment in the universities, thus constituting one route to widening access.

University-level trades union education too has been an arena of adult higher education open to many different approaches, to conflict and, on occasion, to hostile criticism from both within and without. But, more generally, there have always been limitations on the scope and, particularly, on the prevalence of the more critical and socially oriented aspects of such provision, especially where state sponsorship, funding or inspection has been involved. John McIlroy has tracked what he sees as a loss of the more critical, independent, wide-ranging and liberal traditions in much trades union education a gradual narrowing towards a triumph of 'technical' education.[141] Even so, some practitioners have seen in university-level provision of learning for trades unionists as being a major way in which both *industrial citizenship* and citizenship more generally might be supported and enhanced.

Naturally, in any genuinely open society, citizens' and communities' interests may be expected not always to coincide with official perspectives and, often enough, these are arenas of debate, conflict and struggle and not always susceptible to easy incorporation or official domination. So, universities and their academic staff that venture on to this territory should do so with their eyes wide open as this is bound to be dangerous and contentious and, like as not, will be susceptible to criticism both from within the wider university community and from without.

Community activism
The tradition of deploying university-level education as one dimension of winning social change has been revived in some aspects of community education and regeneration. Learning in this field is organised principally for, and more often *with* community groups and community activists. Higher education learning of this kind has been part of the traditions of the work of some of the short and long-term adult residential colleges, such as Ruskin in Oxford, the Northern College in Yorkshire and Fircroft in Birmingham. They have developed their own close links with the labour movement and with community-based social movements and initiatives, and this has been reflected not only in the composition of their student bodies and curricula, but also, often, in their forms of ownership and governance. This tradition is evident, too, in the struggles for a distinctive 'voice' and perspective engaged by the contemporary women's movement and black and ethnic minority groups, and by environmental, gay and lesbian and disability campaigners.

Working with such groups, radical community academics connect their 'social purpose' approach to campaigns for popular education, to the teachings of Paulo Freire on the pedagogy of the oppressed and to avowedly critical perspectives. Thus, for Johnston, 'its key values can be identified as social justice, greater social and economic equality, the promotion of a critical democracy, a vision of a better, fairer world where education has a key role to play'.[142] In Johnston's challenging scheme, university-level 'social purpose' adult education should concern itself with four principal objectives in the field of citizenship: learning for inclusive citizenship; learning for pluralistic citizenship; learning for reflexive citizenship; and learning for active citizenship.

Lifelong learning and citizenship
More recently, the links between adult learning, citizenship and social engagement have been included explicitly with universities' engagement with lifelong learning. Of course, it easy enough, and sometimes quite right, to criticise the contemporary rhetoric of 'lifelong learning' for either its evident vacuity or its excessive concern with narrow matters of skills, the labour market and economy.[143] However, the notion that none of these issues really matters to individual citizens and communities but only to 'authorities' or governments who seek to manipulate them certainly does not follow from

this. These are also core concerns for citizens as much as for employers and governments. Moreover, people's lives are not defined entirely in terms of their involvement with jobs and the economy: they have 'life-wide', 'life-course' as well as lifelong learning needs of their own, and these are often reflected in universities' adult and continuing education provision.

In an early and sustained argument for universities' active engagement with lifelong learning for citizenship, Stewart Ranson predicated his case on what he perceived as the need for essentially public solutions for the problems confronting contemporary society in the face of what he called a dangerous 'vacuum' in the polity. 'The challenge for our time is to renew the purposes and institutions of democracy, which allows citizens to participate in the creation of a society that enables each to develop as a person but also to contribute to the good of the community.'[144] Drawing on Aristotle and other political theorists of democracy and citizenship, Ranson points out that the very notion of being a citizen ideally expresses a *duality* of being, on the one hand, an autonomous person and, on the other, a member of a wider whole. This duality links the world of individuals with the public domain and a higher education for citizenship should properly concern itself with both. It is, he argues, only through a full understanding of ourselves in relation to others that we can truly develop and flourish, including through the use of learning such as that provided by universities. 'Citizenship establishes the right to the conditions of self-development but also the responsibility that the emerging powers should serve the well-being of the common wealth.'[145]

Watson and Taylor, writing explicitly in response to, and in support of Dearing, again emphasise the importance of the variety of 'social purpose' traditions of adult, community and trades union education.[146] They note that a renewed commitment to engagement with their communities represents a welcome return to the roots and founding Charters of many universities and constitutes a natural feature of ex-polytechnics and 'new' universities in the UK, not least in their patterns of local student recruitment. However, the two authors comment that much of the emphasis on community links has centred on relationships with business and the economy. In contrast, Watson and Taylor set out a challenging 'post-Dearing' lifelong learning 'agenda' for contemporary universities to address. In this a defining characteristic has to be 'a concern with and commitment to the widest possible involvement of the adult population in post-compulsory education and training, in order to contribute to the development of a democratic, participative society and culture'.[147] Watson and Taylor note the concerns of this tradition as much with collective as personal interests, with social action, enlarging democracy and social change and with questions of what is now referred to as 'social inclusion' as much as with individual academic achievement and progression. Moreover, successful socially purposive university education needs to be based on genuine partnership. 'For community education to be successful it must arise from a genuine dialogue between the community and the university, and not be imposed by the university. It is not a question of the university offering its provision on a 'take-it-or-leave-it' basis, rather, the university must adapt and develop its provision to meet the needs of the community.'[148]

A distinctive pedagogy

It is important to recognise in this connection that the overlapping domains of lifelong and adult learning have generated their own *distinctive*, and *valuable traditions* of learning, pedagogy, and the recognition and valuing of experience active citizenship. Not infrequently, universities' contribution to citizenship in this aspect of their work has been in both the *form* and *content* of the learning programmes mounted. Thus, they have not only widened *access to* learning amongst some sections of the community but also provided opportunities to study and debate core aspects of society, what constitutes the 'good life' and what are key debates on the very *theme* of citizenship.

Similarly, it has been in the domain of adult learning that pedagogic recognition has been given to the value and authenticity of learners' own experiences as a contribution to their own learning and the learning of their fellow students and teachers. The role and skill of the university adult tutor is – through discussion, challenge, guided reading, reflection and writing – to bring those experiences into critical articulation with the experiences of others, and with concepts, theories and evidence. Adult educators also take as their legitimate starting point for teaching the given positions of the students themselves, make a virtue of the so-called 'negotiated curriculum' in which students themselves help in the process of determining the focus of their studies. In this tradition, too, especially in the approaches of the WEA and trades union programmes, there has often been an element of class or study group 'democracy', in contrast to the largely authoritarian, if often largely benign, approach to curriculum and learning programme development in the rest of university education.

Marginality, fragmentation and closure

Despite all of this, and despite university adult education's undoubted and valuable contribution to the theme of citizenship, once more some important reservations need to be entered. First, it should be noted that, even in the best university 'extra-mural' or 'extension' provision, this was never more than a tiny element of the universities' operations. Richard Hoggart, himself a celebrated champion of such work, tellingly characterised universities' attitudes to extra-mural activities: they were often 'left in a corner, a sort of sop to the community, higher education's red flannel.'[149] Extra-mural and adult education provision was often little more than a marginal activity of the university, carried forward on shoestring budgets and with poor resources. It was always susceptible to cuts and financial restriction and never likely to attract large-scale funding or high profile support (other than rhetorical) from the higher echelons of the universities. This has been not least because the field of adult learning always threatens to be 'dangerous' intellectual territory for those in authority. And an explicit concern with Dearing's fourth and demanding purpose has seldom been more than marginal concern, fragmented rather than being central to universities' plans, strategies and critical self-assessments and always threatened by a lack of commitment from the top or by the reduction of allocated resources.

Second, success in this sort of university-level adult learning has mostly depended upon the devoted enthusiasm and commitment of a few dedicated individuals. Not infrequently, these individuals witnessed their own academic careers and progression being limited by their involvement in adult education work, looked down upon even when 'admired' by their mainstream academic peers. Some of them have felt obliged to switch to more conventional university activity in order to win full academic recognition. Third, some sorts of university adult education, especially of the more sharply critical and 'engaged' kind, have routinely attracted criticism from university authorities and others for their alleged 'bias' or even 'political' or 'ideological' character. Fourth, especially in recent times, such programmes have suffered cuts or other restrictions, including the requirement to be 'mainstreamed' or certificated in order to retain public funding.

Finally, in many universities, traditional adult education and extra-mural departments have of late been closed down and their resources dispersed throughout the university or, occasionally, changed into 'lifelong learning' initiatives. Sometimes this has amounted to little more than a change of name merely to reflect contemporary thinking or academic fashion. Most often, these moves have been more concerned with generating additional income from providing programmes of continuing professional development and training to business than with the noble objectives of learning for citizenship of the radical kind envisaged by Watson and Taylor. This is not an argument against universities' engagement in such kinds of community-oriented learning as a perfectly legitimate function and extension of their routine educational operations. But, it is an insistence that such work should not be confused with the more challenging and explicitly 'political' educational enterprise implied in Dearing's vision and championed at the margins by a minority of university academics. The differences are to be seen in the very purposes of such education, in the social composition of the student populations involved, in the resources committed, in the curricula studied and the mode of their determination and in the forms of academic governance deemed to be appropriate.

An 'earnest minority'

Partly because of all of these reasons but mostly because of previous experiences of and attitudes to education in wider society, it is important always to remember that university adult education has never really engaged more than what Richard Hoggart has memorably referred to as an 'earnest minority'. In making this telling point, which is still accurate despite the marked expansion of student numbers in higher education since he wrote, Hoggart had no intention of decrying the admirable achievements or contributions to civil society of this minority. But his principal concern in making this point was with the implications for the majority. How was it possible that for most members of the community such involvement with universities and the opportunities they afford for learning and development continued to be rare and a highly unlikely future choice? Any concern with citizenship, democracy and social inclusion needs to adopt the same critical perspective, deriving more from Aristotle's conception of active participation for all citizens, as it were, than from Plato's very different reliance upon an élite to lead and govern the majority. And, so long as such people continue to be few in number they are always vulnerable, can be labelled as 'odd' and risk separation from their peers in the community. As Hoggart remarked of this devoted and engaged minority: 'the enquiring and serious working class student is easy game…; people who insist on getting knowledge against the odds, whether the odds are material or less tangible, can soon appear stodgy and over-earnest'.[150]

In any case, argued Hoggart, there were (and, truth to tell, still are) too few forms of cultural, intellectual, social and literary support for these notably valuable and often courageous members of the community. Without such support, they always risked suffering either a suffocating incorporation into, and subordination to, established ways of thinking and being or enduring isolation and alienation from their own roots, or a combination of both! The risks here, he rightly saw, were not simply to the individual pleasure and happiness of such devoted and often self-denying citizens, but also to the achievement of the visions and possibilities of social change and improvement that their singular engagement with education for citizenship and democracy promised. This is the most important difference between widening access to university-level education so as to open up welcome and valid *individual* progression and improved life chances by moving up the social 'ladder' and a quite different emphasis on education for citizenship to secure wider democratic and *collective* benefits for *citizens at large*.

Conclusion

First of all, there is a problem of shifting the kind of valuable experience of higher education in the realm of citizenship afforded through the best of university adult learning from a minority, and maybe somewhat 'deviant', activity to forms of *majority* engagement and wider social advantage. This, indeed, is a huge challenge to our universities. It will not be achieved by adding a few pious words to university 'mission statements' or by inserting a radical paragraph or two in universities' strategic plans. Nor will it suffice for Vice-Chancellors and University Councils simply to offer much needed protection and growth to the best kinds of university adult education, welcome though this would be as an indication of the beginnings of a reversal of recent and depressing trends of decline and demise. Again, even if the current target of securing fifty-per-cent participation in higher education by those under thirty years of age were to be achieved, there will still be the ugly and persistent imbalance of highly differential participation rates of different social groups to contend with. And what, in such circumstances, should universities have to say and do about the post-school learning of the 'other' half of the young adult population not expected to progress to university, let alone the millions of adults already beyond the arbitrary age limitation of thirty? The tradition of university adult and community learning is to make provision according to need, capability and interest, not to meet arbitrary and frankly ill-conceived age category targets.

However, no real shift in the exciting directions envisaged in Dearing's demanding vision and mapped out by authors such as Bown, Watson and Taylor or Johnston is likely without serious commitment from government, HEFCE, university Vice-Chancellors and governing bodies. It will require the allocation of real financial and learning resources, the diversification of forms and locales of engagement with the intellectual work of universities and new career pathways for those staff skilled in engaging with the wider community. To signal the kind and scale of the change I have in mind would be immediately to earmark no less than five per cent of the sector's total learning and teaching budget for work of this kind, rising to a minimum of ten per cent over the next five years. That would represent a real commitment to implement Dearing in this field.

Second, a start could also be made in higher education itself by recognising, at the highest levels, the value and legitimacy of the enterprise of university academic and administrative staff engaged in the difficult work of community outreach, partnership, curriculum negotiation and engagement in 'risky' areas of study and debate. This would be a singular act of principle by those charged with leading our institutions of higher education. But steps should also be taken by HEFCE, the DfES and other funding departments of government to recognise and reward those institutions that excel in the demonstrable promotion of active citizenship, possibly with a scheme that gives public support and additional resources to university centres of excellence in the field.

Third, universities should learn from and build upon the best traditions of democracy and self-organisation of the adult and voluntary education movements. There need be no threat in this to universities' rightly cherished insistence on autonomy of governance and academic freedom. But, whatever else they may legitimately claim to be, UK higher education institutions could advance no legitimate claim currently to be miniature democracies internally or to be genuinely representative of the diversity of community interests in their overall systems of governance and accountability. As Carr and Hartnett have convincingly argued this implies for universities, as for other educational institutions, a process of 'double democratisation' giving rise to a simultaneous process of democratisation for both education and society. '(W)ithout a democratic development of society a more democratic system of education cannot be promoted, and...without a more democratic system of education the democratic development of society is unlikely to occur.'[151]

Fourth, implicit in Dearing's challenge is the much more fundamental task of securing reform across the whole higher education curriculum, as well as in universities' research agenda, forms of governance, decision-making and determination of strategic priorities. The aim first would be for serious intellectual and practical engagement with matters connected to citizenship, democracy and inclusion to become the normal experience of all involved with this level of learning, as staff, students, leaders and governors. No doubt, something can be learned from the initiatives already advocated for schools by the National Commission on Education, authors such as Tom Bentley of Demos, recommended by the Crick committee on citizenship in the curriculum and already beginning to be implemented in schools as part of the revised National Curriculum. Of all the so-called 'core' and 'transferable skills' espoused by governments, employers and universities in recent years a genuine understanding of and commitment to the values and inclusive practices of dispassionate and tolerant enquiry and debate in a pluralistic and diverse society is surely amongst the most important.

Fifth, there is an urgent need for a wholesale shift in the profile and diversity of individuals and social groups *engaging* routinely and with self-confidence in the intellectual, research, cultural, leisure and learning activities and resources of universities. The current debate on *'fair access'* to universities is vital in this connection, but needs to go well beyond the artificially narrow targets of adults under the age of thirty. Not everyone will want, or have the capability, to enrol in formal courses of learning at undergraduate or post-graduate levels, but a greater diversity in the forms, locales and objectives of university-provided learning opportunities will do much to broaden and deepen participation, including through the use of e-learning. Some will gain the advantages of engagement through the support given to their employment or voluntary and community activities, including by their involvement in project work or action research. Some will benefit from a genuine and open welcome to join in public debates, lectures and conferences that are deliberately geared to involve the wider citizenry.

Sixth, university-level learning is not only different in respect of the *levels* of learning, inquiry, debate and reflection involved. It is also a matter of what might best be termed the overall intellectual orientation and responsibilities of universities and the characteristic 'turn of mind' of those involved in or benefiting from university learning. In a series of stimulating and influential publications, Ron Barnett has emphasised the role of both criticism and reflection as distinguishing features of higher education and as core characteristics of best university practice in relation to knowledge.[152] Sustaining a truly critical discourse in higher education requires action on three fronts: critical *reason,* critical *self-reflection* and critical *action.* Moreover, Barnett considers that this essentially liberal, 'human' and emancipatory conception of higher education can be fully reconciled with he requirements for university-level professional qualification.

Seventh, as the Delors Commission report for UNESCO on education for the twenty-first century emphasised, higher education cannot limit itself to bringing individuals together to pass on the common values shaped largely by the past. It must also help 'to answer the question as to *what for and why we live together* and give everyone, throughout life, the ability to play an active part in envisioning the future of society… As education for citizenship and democracy is *par excellence* an education that is not restricted to the space and time of formal education, it is also important for families and for other members of the community to be directly involved.'[153] This is part of what Delors termed 'living democracy' in which lifelong learning is used to build an active civil society.

Eighth, in calling for universities to be what Delors termed 'a place of culture and learning for all', it was made clear that this is not simply a matter of putting lifelong learning at the heart of their future provision. It would mean making every university an 'open' university but, challenging though all of this will be, this would not sufficiently encompass universities' responsibilities to the wider community, local, national and global. This is because, in the Delors Commission's view, universities also 'constitute the living repository of the human heritage'. So, the Delors vision, prefiguring Dearing, constituted also an 'affirmation of a major task of the university – even a moral obligation – to participate in the major debates concerning the direction and the future of society'.[154]

Finally, if higher education institutions embark on the pathways outlined here in a quest to implement the Dearing vision, such a course of action will necessarily impact positively upon each of the other purposes that the Dearing Committee set out for them in respect of individual attainment, the advancement of knowledge and supporting a sustainable knowledge-based economy. In other words, this is far from a focus on Dearing's fourth purpose threatening to become either a distraction or an obstacle in the path of universities' pursuit of their chief and vital objectives.

In reviewing the Dearing Committee's report and recommendations, Richard Pring suggested that the Dearing trajectory represented the first major revision in the idea of the university. In so doing, he argued, it probably 'captured a mood and policy aspiration' spelt out in the committee of inquiry's call for a new 'compact' between higher education and society Pring believed that this notion of a compact raised some major issues to be addressed. He summarised Dearing's new vision as one 'in which "relevance", "utility", "social inclusion", and "accountability to a wider public" seem to predominate'.[155] The burden of this chapter has been that it is precisely in pursuing this powerful idea of a new kind of relationship, a new compact between universities and society, that energy at all levels of higher education policy and management should now be deployed. In matters of funding, teaching, recruitment, research, reward, governance and strategic development there is now urgent need for universities' engagement with and enhancement of democracy, citizenship and inclusion.

7

Feminist values and feminist sociology as contributions to higher education pedagogies and practices

Miriam E. David

Introduction

Using feminist methodologies of personal and critical reflections, I reflect on the contributions that feminist sociology has made to the academy and consider how feminist values and perspectives have become embedded in the wider pedagogies and research practices of aspects of higher education, such as in learning and teaching at the turn of the twenty-first century. How have the notions of personal development and reflective practice been developed and how might they develop?

I want to argue that the key transformations in the landscape of higher education, over the last three decades, have been the contribution and critiques of women and feminists as both academics and as students.[156] The changing forms of social, economic and neo-liberalism have had major implications for changes in families, labour markets and the economy, in the context of changes in information technology and global transformations.[157] These have led to moves towards 'a knowledge economy', contested though these concepts are, and one in which feminist theories and 'knowledges' play a key part.[158]

I consider how these developments build upon the increasing

involvement of women as both students and academics within higher education, and sociology and/of education in particular. I situate these changes in the expansion of higher education and the changing balances between undergraduate and postgraduate education. Women are now a majority of undergraduate students and a substantial proportion of postgraduate, including doctoral students, across higher education in Britain.[159] In the social and health sciences and humanities, women make up a significant minority of academics, although they remain extremely rare in the top echelons and in management of British universities.[160] I will thus reflect upon how these involvements relate to, and reflect, more global, economic, familial and social transformations and the values on which they are based.

I will draw some conclusions about the contributions of feminist values, perspectives and methodologies for future directions in the practices of higher education. I want to argue that the future in higher education is likely to be based on such methodologies, pedagogies and research practices.

Theoretical and methodological background: feminist sociology?

The chapter draws on the themes and feminist methodology of my recent book *Personal and Political: Feminisms, sociology and family lives*.[161] The book was a personal reflection, in feminist fashion, of the development of feminist theories and methodologies within academic sociology, drawing on a range of international literature on feminist values of care. I reviewed these developments from their embryonic beginnings over three periods of what I call liberalism, namely social democracy, economic liberalism and neo-liberalism, contested though these notions may be.

I argue that the theoretical and methodological developments within sociology as part of the emergent social sciences and cultural studies are such that the 'boundaries' or distinctions between sociology *tout court*, sociology of education and policy sociology are now relatively porous and permeable. What constitutes each subject/discipline is highly contested and dependent upon changing theories and methodologies of which feminist theories were critical.

In particular, I am interested in the shifts around notions of 'personal and political' from 'second wave' feminist attempts to embed an innovative approach to learning and teaching around the centrality of women's experience to the ways in which, through transformations within the social sciences and cultural studies, especially with post-structuralism, and educational ethnographies, personal, subjective and qualitative accounts are now entrenched within sociology and/of education. Whether these perspectives and values can now be claimed as *feminist* alone is rather more problematic since a relatively recent approach to education and pedagogies is that of personal development through plans and portfolios.

The methodology of critical, feminist and personal reflections

The notion of critical and/or personal reflections has been gaining currency over the last decade or so within the social sciences and cultural studies within the global academy. These ideas emanate from several sources, but in particular draw upon feminist values, concepts and methodologies, as they have been developed within academic sociology.[162] They may also derive from ideas about reflective practice as they have been considered within educational theories, drawing upon Schön's work, the notions from psychology of personal construct theories and how this has contributed to 'personal development' as a method within the social sciences and even beyond.[163] More generally they also draw upon what has been called the 'social and cultural turn' or the 'biographical turn' within the social sciences.[164]

These all entail a methodological focus on notions of the subject and the self, known as 'the project of the self', including auto/biography, rather than on traditional and social scientific subject/object distinctions hitherto.[165] Giddens has also emphasised how the self in relation to a more reflexive society and its associated risks have become endemic to high or late modern societies.[166] However, these ideas have been highly contested even amongst feminist sociologists.[167] Nevertheless, they have led to changing practices in social and educational research methodologies and critiques of traditional approaches to social scientific knowledge and methodologies; away from positivism towards more experiential, ethnographic and qualitative approaches.[168]

At the same time, the rich diversity of sociology has also led to notions of reflexivity as an epistemological break with the past within sociology and extended developments in critical theory.[169] All of these trends have contributed to changes within the practices, theories and methodologies of sociology and of education. Moreover, the distinctions between substantive areas within sociology, such that the sociology of education has developed an approach that can be distinguished from sociology *tout court* is far more difficult to sustain. Nevertheless, it has become rather fashionable, within the social sciences, to develop personal, biographic and narrative accounts of personal experiences.[170]

Whilst this approach has become endemic within the social sciences extending the notions from purely feminist ones, as a part of the social and cultural turn, this has been particularly the case from the perspective of women of my generation internationally. We became involved in the academy and the social sciences, sociology and education as part of the generation who benefited from the expansion of educational opportunities in the post-war period. Many of these women in Britain became conscious feminists, valuing equality and have reflected upon their experiences more recently.[171] Oakley, whilst contesting the methodological developments has also contributed a rich and detailed analysis from her own feminist perspective of developments in academic sociology.[172] This is a phenomenon that has happened internationally with evidence from the Anglophone literature of such critical and personal reflections from *inter alia* Australia, New Zealand and North America.[173]

Personal and political: feminist theories and pedagogies

The notion of 'the personal is political' was a key to the second wave women's movement, as it developed in the late 1960s and early 1970s. It entailed the notion that personal, private and intimate family matters nevertheless were highly 'political' in the sense that they relied upon deep power relations between men and women. In other words, women's private family experiences were not unique but the product of wider power relations between men and women in society and ones in which women were subordinate and not equal. At first, these became ideas that influenced the burgeoning women's liberation movement as a political movement, but they later began to influence academic developments, especially in sociology as women entered the academy and became involved as academics.

The term 'feminist' was not in the lexicon of academe until the 1970s as such women became involved as academics, although it had been used in the late nineteenth century as a political concept. The ideas were highly contested as academic subjects such that women's studies initially developed outside of conventional undergraduate courses, and extra-murally, for mature women students, as part of lifelong learning. However, as more women became involved as academic sociologists, sociologists of education and social scientists they began to develop and transform the ideas based on feminist values and develop feminist theories, methodologies and/or pedagogy and 'knowledge'.

Indeed, the growth and development of such theories and methodologies within social and cultural studies reveals the complexities and transformations of these concepts.[174] A key transformation has been not only the shifts around notions of 'personal and political' in the sense that there have been moves from the centrality of women's personal experiences as being seen as deeply 'political' to the 'gaze' now being centrally focussed upon how the political is suffused with the personal. In other words, there has been a major shift from 'outsider' and objective approaches and accounts to more subjective and 'insider' approaches.

A hallmark, however, of these various feminist perspectives was the centrality of women's personal experience to understandings and the development of 'knowledge'. It is also a hallmark of feminist pedagogy.[175] This involves an exploration of personal experiences, reflections and narrative or biographical accounts of both professional and personal developments as part of the approach to learning and teaching, the 'curriculum' and the 'knowledge' created.

As higher education has also developed these ideas have become embedded in wider pedagogical practices and can be seen now also as a form of continuing/personal professional development (C/PPD). Indeed, they have spread to forms of professional education not only within the studies of education in higher education but wider forms of educational developments and practices of learning and teaching such that the notion of personal experience is no longer the preserve of feminist pedagogy and practice. There are also some key developments around personal development as part of professional developments and training and linked to lifelong learning. It remains important to account for these developments in both pedagogy and practices in sociology and educational studies by reference to the new 'knowledge society or economy'.[176]

The notions of personal and political have indeed become deeply embedded within the theories and methodologies of many of the subjects of the social sciences. The ways in which they have been adopted and adapted have also been associated with feminist and post-structural or post-modern theories and methodologies and with complex links to the three phases of liberalism.

Generation of feminists and feminist ideas: links with phases of liberalism

My general argument is that the three phases of liberalism, that is post-war ideological developments around social and political values, are linked with the changes in generations of feminists and their involvement in the academy as either students or academics. I associate the phases of liberalism with transformations in how perspectives on the personal and political have been transformed, together with transformations of generations of women as academics and students involved in higher education, especially sociology and/of education.

These three phases of liberalism broadly defined are:

1. *Social Liberalism*, associated with social democracy or socialism or individual political rights and with the 1960s and 1970s in Britain, Europe, Australia and the USA. One key characteristic was the rise of social and political movements, such as civil and political rights, and in particular the rise of the women's movement and movements for sexual equality.[177] This was also linked with economic growth and social changes in family lives and especially for women from middle-class families. In particular, women's involvement in education, especially middle class, was beginning to lead to the opening up of opportunities for employment, and social welfare changes also facilitated women's paid work (albeit often part-time) whilst married and raising children. The principle of equality of educational opportunities began to be extended to women, from the middle classes, rather than expansion for children from working class families.[178]

2. *Economic liberalism*, characterised by consumer choice, was associated with the political backlash in the late 1970s to such earlier forms of social liberalism. In Britain this was particularly associated with Thatcherism, in the USA Reaganism and the revival of a conservative approach to consumerism and market forces into public services and the rise of a market economy. However, during this period of the 1980s and early 1990s, there were contradictory forces at work, and changing family lives

continued, including with women's continuing and increasing involvement in education, including higher education, as both students and increasingly as academics. The era of economic liberalism is identified as contradictory in that it signalled the expansion of educational opportunities for all and the transformation to a mass system of higher education largely for undergraduates and emergent and attendant forms of control and regulation. However, this did not entail a transformation in terms of social class and educational opportunities, but rather an increase for all social classes leaving class distinctions relatively untouched.

3. *Neo-liberalism* is associated with the extension and enhancement of the market economy, during the later 1990s and into the twenty-first century, and characterised as 'the post-socialist condition' referring to the USA.[179] However, this is also the case for Britain, despite a return to New Labour in government, since it was committed to the politics of the 'third way', 'new managerialism' and 'the modernisation project' entailing transformations of public services through private and market forces.[180] Although higher education remains fundamentally elitist, the era of neo-liberalism is identified as the time when postgraduate education and doctoral studies moved to a mass system, with attendant forms of quality assurance standards and consumerism.[181] During this recent period, the economic, familial and social changes on a global basis are so great that they signal moves towards what have been called a 'knowledge society' or 'knowledge economy' characterised by the importance of forms of education to the society and to economic growth and development. Moreover, women's involvement and engagement with education, including higher education and postgraduate studies, has continued such that they are now the majority of undergraduate students, and they predominate in postgraduate professional education and academic women as feminists and sociologists are now a substantial minority.

I also characterise each period of liberalism in terms of the relationships between the personal and political and the forming and framing of feminist knowledge, theories and practices. Thus I elaborate on these briefly:

1. '*The personal is political*' relates to *social democracy or liberalism* and the initial 'feminist project' of embedding 'liberal' or socialist feminist ideas and practices about equal opportunities and critiques of past

'patriarchal practices' within a sociological framework, in an essentially elitist and traditional system of higher education. In Britain, the proportion of students in higher education was less than ten per cent, and they were all mainly from, or became, the middle classes. Moreover, women constituted an even smaller minority, although as social and economic changes began to be felt, women's opportunities for professional employment including in higher education began to grow.

2. *Personal and Political* relates to the period of *economic liberalism* of the late 1970s and 1980s, when feminist knowledge and practices had been firmly established within the academy, especially within sociology and its sub-disciplines such as the sociology of education and yet were subject to increasing forms of quality control in Britain. At the same time, there was a backlash from the New Right against new feminist knowledge, complex and diverse theories and practices within higher education. It also signalled the growth of women's involvement as students and as academics and researchers but it was a period of limited opportunities for women as academics and researchers, such that new movements for women in higher education were spawned in Britain such as *Women in Higher Education Network* (*WHEN*) and, for senior women as managers or administrators, *Through the Glass Ceiling* was born.

3. '*Political is personal*' refers to the most recent period of *neo-liberalism*, and shifts to a market and 'knowledge' economy, in which higher education has been transformed to a mass system, such that, in Britain, about forty per cent of the population participate in it, albeit that social class opportunities still prevail. Nevertheless, women have come to dominate as students, and feminist practices entwine with other social and cultural methodologies. The 'social and cultural turn' leads to a diversity of auto/biographic and personal, subjective theories and practices within sociology and the wider forms of policy sociology and/of education. In particular, the dominance of post-structuralism and transformations to critical feminist research ethnographies and the rise of 'critical realism' led to challenges and a rich diversity of feminist perspectives within sociology and/of education. However, a key is the ways in which 'the research gaze' is on the political and social as personal. Thus the transformation in theories and methodologies, associated with women's involvement in sociology leads to the possibilities of further methodological developments.

Conclusions

As women have entered the academy in increasing numbers and over the generations, the academy itself has been transformed. These changes over the last 30 years in British higher education have been associated with changing forms of liberalism and their justification in relation to technological and labour market changes and the economy. Developments towards a 'knowledge society or economy' have also entailed developments and diversity in women's education and forms of largely professional employment. A key feature, rarely noticed or acknowledged, has been women's contributions and engagements with such developments. What is particularly intriguing and important is the ways in which feminist values, theories, methodologies and pedagogies have contributed to the complexity and diversity of the changes, challenging future developments.

Feminist theories, methodologies and research practices have grown from within sociology and/of education to the social sciences more generally and have combined with other epistemological changes within social and cultural studies. This has happened over a lengthy 30 to 40-year period, in association with broader social and political changes, linked with transformations in forms of so-called liberalism. Thus there is now a complexity and diversity of theoretical and methodological changes to which feminist and critical theories contribute. Indeed, it can be argued that, as part of the 'social and cultural turn' feminists, within social and educational studies, amongst others, theorize the political as personal, and contribute to the pedagogical shifts towards the personal that is now relatively endemic in higher education. Moves towards personal reflections and reflective professional practices have influenced not only undergraduate studies and research practices, contributing to rich and complex educational research ethnographies but also developments in postgraduate and professional education.

Most recently, under neo-liberalism, whilst the majority of higher education changes have led to a massification of postgraduate and doctoral education and constraints on equity, originality and creativity through quality assurance mechanisms, at the same time there have been great opportunities for women's involvement and the development of feminist values and knowledges as part of the new knowledge economy.[182] Feminist values around the ethic of care and personal development are now deeply embedded in

115

pedadogical practices at levels of higher education. This seems to have been the case especially with respect to professional, doctoral education rather than in research training for traditional doctorates.[183]

Indeed, feminist values around an ethic of the personal and care, 'knowledge' and pedagogical practices, from the early second wave feminist political movement initiating feminist values, knowledges and theories, may have prefigured these developments in doctoral education in the new knowledge economy and feminist pedagogies may contribute to developing innovative practices in professional doctoral education. The development of feminist pedagogies within and across higher education and especially doctoral education, including personal and critical reflections, and experiences, have become embedded in the practices and pedagogies of higher education more generally.

On the basis of a personal reflection I have argued that feminist sociological methodologies have made, and will continue to make, important contributions to the development of new knowledge and innovative approaches to learning and teaching in higher education generally and in postgraduate professional and graduate studies in particular. The moves towards the personal in social and educational research and in pedagogical practices, such as personal development plans and portfolio assessment, in higher education have been critical to the wider transformations in higher education, such as widening participation and access to higher education. However, current changes in policies and practices may militate against such transformations for future generations especially in relation to postgraduate studies. Nevertheless, women's engagement in higher education, the changing work/life balance and the theorisation of the personal will continue to make important contributions for understandings in the future. Hopefully, there will be greater recognition of feminist ethics of care and concern in wider policy developments for education, and higher education in particular, modifying the class, race and gender imbalances currently in practice in the global society and knowledge economy.[184] Such concerns would ensure a greater commitment to how the personal and political are entwined in all of our lives.

8

Virtue and the virtual university

Christopher Megone

Introduction

It may not be widely known that the term 'the virtual university' is not another neologism attributable to the growth of the IT industry and the consequent possibilities for e-learning. In fact it was coined by Cardinal Newman in his famous lectures on 'The idea of a university', and applied by him to the University of London in virtue of the spatial dislocation of its constituent colleges. In Newman's view, the kind of community required for a university could not be sustained, at least at the time, in the face of such geographical separation.

My aim in this chapter is to defend the view that intellectual inquiry of a certain sort is best carried out within a form of community, a community which both requires and fosters certain virtues in its members. Thus I shall argue that a university, on at least one plausible conception of such an institution, depends upon, and needs to support, certain ethical virtues if its intellectual goals are to be attained. These ethical virtues sustain the university community, and that community in turn enables its members to contribute optimally to the achievement of its goals. In particular, though, I shall claim that the liberal value of tolerance, often supposed characteristic of a university in a liberal society, is insufficient to enable such an institution to flourish. In addition to tolerance, members of a university of this sort must exhibit and develop a much wider range of ethical virtues. This requirement in turn has repercussions for the structure of such a university.[185]

The structure of the chapter is fairly simple. I will begin by sketching out the relevant conception of a university, picking it out by contrast with two rival conceptions. It can be admitted immediately that each of these sketches is somewhat schematic. Nor is it my aim here to show that the favoured conception is to be preferred to the alternatives mentioned – it will suffice if it is at least recognised as a plausible account. In the second section, the focus is on the sort of liberal values that are sometimes supposed to underpin such a university, but I will raise doubts as to whether these are in fact sufficient to sustain its purposes. The third section focuses on the notion of a university community to which Newman alluded, and seeks to develop and defend a broader account of the ethical virtues it requires, by contrast to the liberal account. In conclusion some possible implications of this view for present-day universities are identified.

The idea of a university

In a recent review of contemporary philosophical discussion of university education Stephen Burwood asserts: 'In my experience…, by and large most practising academics have a perfectly clear [shared] idea of what [their academic] mission is…'[186] Although this might be true at some very high level of generality (but even that is arguable), once one reaches any level of detail this seems a rather implausible claim. Certainly even within one country, such as the UK, institutions sharing the name 'university' may vary significantly with respect to their practice in terms of teaching and research, the range of disciplines pursued, the nature of the teaching environment, the wider pastoral, social, and evaluative ethos, and so on. The diversity becomes broader still if the net is extended beyond national borders.

It may well be, as Gordon Graham has pointed out, that there is no need to restrict the label 'university' to a single type of institution.[187] If that is so, then a university sector could comprise several distinct types of institution. But then it becomes all the more important that any given institution is clear as to its own aims, and what is required to achieve them. In order to facilitate this it would be helpful to identify central features of possible types of university, and to consider what conditions might need to obtain for each type to best fulfil its goal (though in this chapter that latter task will be addressed only for one conception).[188]

As has been indicated, the purpose of this chapter is to focus on one favoured conception of a university, but for the reasons just given it cannot simply be assumed that there is clarity as to what form that conception might take. I will begin, then, by sketching this conception in contrast with two distinct conceptions. Even if the favoured conception is not the only 'right' one, it should strike the reader as at least as plausible as the alternatives. The argument of the chapter will then address this conception alone, identifying the values that are relevant to its obtaining its specified goal.

Writing more than fifty years ago, Sir Walter Moberly identified three conceptions of a university, and what follows draws on his work whilst adopting some minor changes in terminology. Thus I shall distinguish the favoured classical conception from what are here termed neo-classical and techno-democratic conceptions.[189]

The classical conception is essentially Newman's. It holds that the university is 'liberal' as opposed to 'servile', meaning by this that the university's primary goal is the enlargement of the mind, or the trained mind.[190] Such a goal is to be sought for its own sake, not in order to serve some further social goal, not for its further utility. It may well be that those with trained minds are better equipped to play other social roles well, and the university need not be averse to such a consequence, but that is an incidental side-effect, not the direct aim. What is central on such an account, is the trained mind, or intellectual excellence, and that is because such a mind is itself an ultimate good (or a component of the ultimate good).[191]

As Newman developed this view, undergraduates are central within a university. A university is concerned to train undergraduates (as well as graduates and academics) to think for themselves, and thus a university is not simply a research institute, even though 'any teacher worthy of the name is likely to advance knowledge of the subject'.[192]

In fact Newman himself thought research should not be done in universities, by and large, referring that academic function to Academies.[193] But an articulation of the classical conception need not follow him in drawing such a sharp distinction here. Indeed one might hold that whilst all education is concerned with the development of rational powers, or training of the mind, what is distinctive of the university's contribution to that training is that it develops the student's capacities to participate in a mature, independent way in intellectual inquiry. Thus the training of the mind at university is a training to participate in intellectual research, and thus necessarily requires to be conducted in a research institution. This reply could in fact be seen as congenial to Newman's outlook in that it still puts the training of the mind at the centre of the picture, as valuable in itself. What such a reply then holds is that research and teaching are here connected in their value because scholarly inquiry and the expansion of understanding are activities of the mind which are worthwhile in themselves, thus vindicating the value of the particular kind of training a university offers.[194] (This might contrast with conceiving of the university as a producer of research as an output, where that research is valued independently for itself, perhaps a conception that was the target of Newman's view in separating the activities.)

But although the undergraduates are central to the university, on this view, the training of their minds is not the same as the grading of minds, so the university 'is not [simply] a board of examiners, for certifying that young people have acquired a minimum of information.'[195] Each of these mistaken views, university as a research institute, or university as a grader of degrees, fails to grasp fully that the training of the mind, as a good in itself, is the central focus of the university.

Once that point is noted, other claims follow. Thus, second, university education is 'general as opposed to specialised,' in that one who has been trained to think will have the capacity to understand, and to make judgements, across a wide range of issues.[196] But, third, the notion of a general education here, which develops such a capacity for judgement, does not require a wide curriculum, but rather a depth of study in a demanding discipline. For the purpose of such depth of study is not to amass information, but to acquire the ability to organise and digest information so as to arrive at illumination, or the capacity to make appropriate use of that knowledge in the formation of judgements.[197]

In addition to these curricula requirements, if the trained mind of all its members is the ultimate purpose of the university, as this conception holds, then certain structural principles also follow. Fundamental here is that in order to achieve this aim, 'the university, as a community of teachers and learners, is to be regarded as a family.'[198] Or, in Newman's words, 'A university is…an *alma mater*, knowing her children one by one, not a foundry, or a mint, or a treadmill.'[199] To this we shall return.

This favoured conception can be further clarified by contrasting it with two alternative views of the university. The first of these is the neo-classical view. This shares some of the features of the classical view, but incorporates important differences.[200] Like the classical view, it holds that the university has its own proper concern, an internal goal that is good for its own sake, and thus quite distinct from the goals of the state or of business. So it is not servile, it does not serve the purposes of other institutions. This proper goal is knowledge, pursued for its own sake. The goal is similar to that of the classical conception, but knowledge may here be considered as a product, rather than a characteristic of the mind, so that the main objective is new discoveries rather than better developed minds. Thus this view sees research, here perhaps contrasted with teaching, as the university's primary purpose. However a more significant difference is the emphasis this conception lays on the freedom, or autonomy, of the university.

This freedom can be understood in various ways. First, since the university has its own proper concern, distinct from that of the state or business, academics must be left free to pursue their research and teaching as they choose. Similarly, given the goal is knowledge for its own sake, the university must protect its freedom to pursue that goal by being highly selective in the disciplines it adopts, choosing them for their intellectual value, not their social worth. A third aspect of the required freedom is found, on this view, in the demand that both research and teaching must be pursued by an open mind, free of assumptions; and to facilitate such an attitude of mind, the university must 'cultivate detachment…from matters of current controversy.'[201] Finally, just as the academics must be free in their inquiries, free from constraint and free from pre-supposition, so 'the liberty, initiative and adult status of the student are strongly emphasised' and '…The student belongs to himself, he is responsible to nobody and for nobody but himself.'[202]

This conception shares something of the first's ideal of knowledge as valuable for its own sake, despite the possible difference between valuing knowledge as an abstract product and valuing learning as found in a trained mind. But its emphasis on the autonomous academic inquirer, whether academic or student, leads to a rather different view of the academic community comprising a university, as I shall argue below.[203] However both these points of comparison help to sharpen our understanding of the classical conception.

The third conception, the techno-democratic, challenges much more forcefully the classical conception's view of the value of knowledge. This conception views knowledge as a source of power, and thus of purely instrumental value as a means to further ends.[204] So far as students are concerned, on this view, the knowledge provided by a university education is simply 'the avenue to a desirable job', so that 'success in examinations is...of dominating importance'.[205] By contrast with the classical view, the examining process is central here, because the university's purpose in educating undergraduates is to enable them to acquire the knowledge which makes them fit for the job-market, and to act as an assessor for employers of their fitness in this regard. So far as research is concerned, this conception views universities as capable, through research, of producing new knowledge, especially new technological knowledge, which has the power to facilitate social development. On both fronts, then, universities are agents of social change.

This view of the university as concerned with knowledge as a source of power in turn means that universities are in the relevant sense 'servile' as opposed to 'liberal', they serve wider purposes. Thus, for example, the reason for widening access to universities, on this account, is to further equality of opportunity in the pursuit of further goods, not to enable access to something that is good in itself. Similarly university research is not worthwhile for its own sake, but an agent of change, so can justifiably be directed to serve currently favoured social goals.

This conception again illuminates the classical conception by virtue of the contrasts indicated. The conception of knowledge adopted by the techno-democratic conception has implications for the relation of the university to other institutions such as the state or the business sector. And since the university's goals are not good in themselves, the structure of a university community can only be assessed by reference to its effectiveness in serving those further goals towards which its activities are instrumental means.

The three positions sketched may well be somewhat schematic in form. So, for example, the classical conception may happily make room for examinations as part of a university's role, though it may view their justification as lying in their role in the formation of a trained mind, and thus see their value to future employers as only a (desirable) side-effect. Furthermore existing institutions laying claim to the name 'university' may well overlap in form with more than one of these outlines, perhaps for the sort of reason given in the example just mentioned, perhaps because of confusion in self-understanding. (The latter might sometimes in turn be due to competing ideals held by distinct constituencies within a single institution.) For present purposes these points matter little since my claim is only that the classical conception of a university can be distinguished from the alternatives mentioned and is a plausible account of what a university may be.

The classical conception of a university and liberal values

Let us now focus on this classical conception of a university. For many, for example Rowan Williams in chapter 2, this remains the paradigm conception.[206] However I shall now argue that such a conception is at odds with the thin liberal educational values often assumed to be the basis of a contemporary university.

In brief, the liberal I have in mind supposes the central value of university education to be freedom of inquiry, in particular freedom of speech, and thus tolerance, that is, toleration of the beliefs, statements and acts of another even though one believes them to be wrong. Thus, on this liberal account, the goals of a university are best served if its members are free to pursue any lines of inquiry they wish (so long as these inquiries are not harmful to others), and to express any views they wish (so long as these statements do not harm others).

Two reasons may be given in favour of committing a university only to these thin liberal values, one negative and one positive. The first reason appeals to the idea that there is a plurality of values, a range of conceptions of the human good. Given this, it is supposed, a university has no right to try to enforce any particular ethical values, or traits of character, on its members. For a university is an institution whose role is the pursuit of intellectual goals. As such it may address itself to the development of intellectual virtues, but it should not concern itself with the ethical character of its members, or their ethical values. These, it is claimed, are a distinct matter.[207]

The second reason is more positive in tone, viewing liberal values in a Millian spirit as most conducive to the attainment of a university's goals. The reasoning here is that the pursuit of truth is best served if one allows a thousand intellectual flowers to bloom.[208] The more one encourages diversity of opinion, the more those opinions will be subjected to critical scrutiny, and the more likely it is that a true opinion may come to the fore.

It may well be that such liberal values contribute to the underpinnng of the neo-classical conception of a university outlined above. That conception emphasised the autonomous academic and the individual student each independently in pursuit of knowledge. But on Newman's classical conception, the university must be sensitive to a wider range of values if it is to flourish. The spirit of freedom and tolerance is not enough. This response need not challenge the second line of reasoning above – it need not deny the importance of freedom and tolerance as aids to the pursuit of truth. But the classical conception does imply that the values the liberal recognises are too thin a set to sustain a university as classically conceived. This is implicit in the assertion that a university must in addition be 'an *alma mater*, knowing her children one by one…' In that claim the classical conception challenges the first line of reasoning above. It challenges the idea that there is a sharp division between the attainment of intellectual virtue, or excellence, and the cultivation of ethical virtue.

To develop this challenge to the liberal position it will help to elaborate what is conveyed by the image of the university as a family. That will involve explaining why such a community is best equipped to achieve the classical aim of the pursuit of learning and the enlargement of minds. And that in turn will allow me to spell out the sort of ethical virtues such an institution needs at least to sustain.

The classical conception of a university and classical values

I begin this part of the argument by drawing on a report of recent developments in intellectual life in the Ukraine. The focus in this description is on the public sphere as a whole, but the point made can be transferred to a university environment. The reporter identified three stages in the development of the public sphere as the Soviet era in Ukraine ended. The first stage, in the late Soviet era, is perhaps not directly relevant here. It saw the public sphere developed not as a genuinely open forum for free debate, but simply as a space where the sole aim was to counter contemporary ideological assertions, so free expression had a very limited goal. Then came the second stage, the period of *glasnost* under Gorbachev, when the public sphere became a genuinely free space. Everyone seized the opportunity to express their views. But the immediate effect of the experience of freedom was that everyone talked and no-one listened. Ukraine, it was said, became a country of the deaf. Last came the third stage of development, the present condition of the public sphere in Ukraine, a modification of the second stage.[209] The public sphere in this third stage persists as a market place for ideas in which viewpoints, ideologies, and opinions are freely put forward, but the supply of such viewpoints continues to vastly exceed the demand. The result is that, although open discussions take place, the response to all viewpoints has now merely become ironic and skeptical.

The point of this anecdotal account is clear enough. The value of a free public sphere as a forum for rational debate depends on its participants being prepared to do more than merely freely assert their own views. That point can now be applied to consideration of a university. It seems quite possible that if a university is committed only to free speech and toleration, and eschews any broader concern with the ethical character of its members, then discussion in that university might mirror that found in the developing public sphere in Ukraine. Free inquiry and toleration would allow views to be freely expressed by university members, but not properly heard, or treated only with irony and skepticism. But that will be insufficient for the classical conception of a university, for that will be insufficient for teaching and research to be conducted in a way that leads to an enlargement of the mind. This points towards the insight in Newman's familial conception of the university.[210]

The line of argument here can be developed further by drawing on Aristotle's conception of human beings as by nature both rational animals and social or gregarious beings (the most gregarious of all animals), who flourish in a community, above all in a *polis*. Aristotle presents these apparently distinct specifications of human nature on the one hand in the *Nicomachean Ethics*, where the human function or essence is said to be rationality, and on the other in the *Politics*, where humans are said to be by nature, or essentially, political (or most gregarious).[211] But rather than seeing these as conflicting accounts, one can view them as mutually illuminating ways of presenting a single definition. Putting the two accounts together, one reaches the claim that the human essential potentiality for being rational (where rationality is construed in a broad sense) is best or fully actualised in a community, above all in a *polis*. This is because the complex range of powers (or potentialities) which are constitutive of each individual's potential for rationality must be actualised through interaction with others.

Aristotle's point can now be put together with that made by the Ukrainian example in order to develop the claim that a university on the classical conception must be a family-like community.[212] The development of a trained mind, valuable for its own sake, can be understood as a part, primarily the intellectual part, of the actualisation of our rational powers. This is something that cannot be achieved by a self-sufficient individual, but must be achieved through interaction with others in a community of a certain sort. But, as the Ukrainian example suggests, a community in which members only tolerate the freely expressed views of others, but do not really listen to them, or merely respond with irony, does not exhibit the kind of interaction which is necessary for fully developing rationality. When Newman suggests that the university must be a kind of mother to its members he is pointing to the need for those members to belong to a certain kind of community, one which both develops and is sustained by appropriate active engagement with the views of others. Only through such engagement does the development of each person's mind occur.

This in turn leads to the point that the university as classically conceived requires further virtues of character than merely the liberal virtues. For the active engagement just referred to requires that the members of the relevant community manifest certain ethical virtues in the way that they respond to one another. In what follows I will sketch the role of such a wider range of traits of character including, as examples, courage, self-control, truthfulness and an Aristotelian friendliness. I will then note how these virtues are connected with trust, the mark of a familial environment, and a crucial pre-requisite for the kind of rational interchange under consideration.

The relation of the university to these further ethical virtues must involve both their sustenance and development. This is because, as always with the ethical virtues, there is a bi-conditional relation between the community and its individual members developing and possessing those virtues. For the community is crucial to the sustaining and developing of those virtues, but at the same time those virtues contribute to and shape the nature of the community which sustains them.

Let me review this part of the argument thus far. On the classical conception the goal of a university is the development of trained minds. This can be construed as at least part of what is involved in the actualisation of an agent's rational powers. If the Aristotelian account of these powers is right, this is best achieved in a community, and Newman's suggestion is that it is a familial community, which has been contrasted with a thinly liberal community. The relevant community is not merely one in which views may be freely expressed and tolerated, but one which is more fully hospitable to reason. The latter sort of community requires that its members manifest and develop certain ethical virtues.

Consider first the virtue of friendliness, which shares with friendship the attitude of wishing another well for his own sake.[213] It is this virtue that is manifest in actively listening to one another, as it was termed above. In a discussion such listening is part of rational engagement with the views that are presented by others, and is itself a complex matter. It may involve the agent in an interpretative effort, in order to make best sense of what others have said, but also an effort of critical reflection in order to sift what is true from what is not. Furthermore, such friendliness will be shown in the willingness to challenge constructively what is said, rather than leaving questions unstated. Finally, in addition to such attitudes required at the time, friendliness may require that the agent make appropriate preparations for discussion beforehand. All these attitudes are part of the ethical virtue of friendliness in this context, in that they are constituents of wishing another well in circumstances of discussion. But it is discussion of this sort that actualizes rational faculties in a way that enlarges the minds of those involved.

But it is not only this virtue that may be required in actively engaging with a view expressed by others. Consider, as a second example, the role of self-control. In this context self-control can be manifest in restraint, a willingness to let others speak, and not simply to view discussion as an opportunity to put forward one's own views.

Such control may be necessary for active listening to others, but another ethical virtue may also be required in putting forward one's own views. Thus speakers may need courage to say what they really think. Finally, as a fourth example, the virtue of truthfulness will be manifest by those who take intellectual engagement with appropriate seriousness and say what they mean.[214]

It might be replied (by the liberal, for example) that since the behaviour mentioned as exemplifying friendliness, self-control, courage or truthfulness contributes to the development of intellectual powers, it is not in fact manifesting ethical virtue. However whilst it is not necessary to deny the importance of a desire to understand as an intellectual goal, the relation between the behaviour described and the achievement of intellectual excellence cannot be purely instrumental. On the contrary, what has been shown (in response to the liberal view) is that ethical virtues cohere, in a more complex way, with intellectual excellence. Thus, for example, the agent must exhibit the virtues of truthfulness or friendliness, in which he sees being truthful or friendly as worthwhile for its own sake, in order for there to be a community of a certain sort. If he does not view truth or friendliness in that way, but adopts truthfulness for instrumental reasons, or treats the other as a friend simply as a means to a further end, then he fails to exhibit the requisite virtues, and that kind of community is undermined. But that kind of community is the one in which, given human nature, the agent is best placed to satisfy the desire to understand. For the community in which rational intellectual powers are best developed, and truth is best pursued, is one in which agents interact appropriately with one another. Thus when agents manifest a wide range of ethical virtues in their intellectual pursuits they are best placed to achieve intellectual excellence.[215]

The importance of the ethical virtues here might be brought out further in response to another expression of a similar criticism. The liberal might now suggest that the only attributes that participants in an intellectual discussion in fact need are skills, not virtues. Their goal is truth or understanding, and what they need are inter-personal communication skills, for example listening skills or presentation skills. Given these, any ethical virtues, such as friendliness or courage, are superfluous.

Skills differ from virtues in that virtues are concerned with the judgement of goals as well as means, whilst when a skill is deployed the goal is given, and the skill is the capacity to optimally obtain that goal. Thus the skill of carpentry involves no judgement as to whether it is right to make a table. The carpenter is simply someone who has the means to make a table, given that is the set goal. So, the critic suggests, in the case of the university the goal of the pursuit is given – it is the pursuit of truth. The university community only requires, and is sustained by, its members' skills in attaining it.

But the possession of skills alone will not sustain the kind of community which optimally pursues truth. For what is actually required of the members of such a community is not merely skilled pursuit of that goal. It is judgement as to how it is right to treat the members of that community in the context of activities and discussions concerned with the pursuit of truth. What the ethical virtues will incorporate is the capacity to make that judgement as well as the ability (which might be a skill) to attain the end judged appropriate. Thus, for example, there may be occasions where it is not right to point out to someone an error in reasoning, or a blunder in presentation, even though that may facilitate pursuit of the truth. This recognises the fact that members of a university are not just pursuers of truth, but bring to their intellectual activities a bundle of other preoccupations, concerns, difficulties and goals. That is why they need to be known rather than merely numbered by their university. It is virtue that is needed to judge how it is right to treat them in the intellectual context, but the exercise of virtue requires appropriate knowledge of the persons concerned as well as the capacity to judge what is right in light of a conception of the good. The exercise of virtue in turn leads to the participants being treated in a way which enables them to be full participants in the intellectual community and thus to contribute optimally to its activity. Nor, again, is there some overarching skill here (as to how best to pursue truth). Rather the virtuous person will treat them appropriately because it is the right thing to do.

The way in which these ethical virtues are related to the existence of a familial community, can be brought out further by noting how they both require, in order to develop, and contribute to, through their manifestation, an environment of trust. The relevance of trust to the life of the university on the classical conception is discussed in Rowan Williams' chapter. As he writes, adopting slightly different terms, to have trust in a shared intellectual inquiry 'is to be conscious at some level…that your being there and your being who you are are not under threat; your existence and your identity have roots and solidity.'[216] Thus the existence of trust gives confidence to a speaker to express difficult or unpopular thoughts, or to attempt to articulate half-understood ideas, as well as to engage in a forceful or even vehement discussion, assured that such a discussion will only enhance mutual recognition, not undermine it. In other words such a community facilitates the kind of ethically virtuous behaviour discussed above.[217] But equally, as the discussion of those virtues indicated, it is the manifestation of friendliness, self-control, courage, and truthfulness that serves to develop and consolidate a trusting community. By contrast the adoption of an intellectual persona ('maintaining myself at your expense'[218]) serves to undermine the sort of intellectual community required for training the mind.

In sum, when Newman sees the university as an *alma mater* he points towards the sort of community required on the classical conception. It requires more complex interaction of its members than those communities sustained only by the liberal values of free speech and toleration. It is an intellectual community in which members trust one another in the way that both supports and requires the development of a broad range of ethical virtues.

Implications

I will end by exploring some implications of developing such an account of the virtues required on the classical conception of the university, first on the theoretical, then on the practical side.

The theoretical implication I want to mention can be addressed briefly. Three different conceptions of a university have been sketched in this paper, and the aim of the paper has been to investigate the values associated with one conception rather than to defend one conception against others. Nonetheless the discussion above might constitute the beginning of a challenge to some aspects of the neo-classical conception, in particular its somewhat atomistic approach to students and staff as each responsible to nobody and for nobody but himself. If the pursuit of knowledge (the neo-classical goal) requires the development of reason, and if the development of reason is best achieved in a certain kind of community, then such an atomistic approach at least inhibits the attainment of the neo-classical goal.

I shall say a little more about some practical implications. How might this discussion bear on the nature of a contemporary university? Some might argue that Newman's talk of the university as an *alma mater* is too maternalistic. Even if it is desirable that members of a university have certain attributes of character, the university is not equipped (nor has it the right) to attempt to determine the character of its members.[219] However when Newman went on to say that a university should know its members one by one, and objected to the University of London as too spatially dislocated to be a real university, he may have indicated a more subtle relation between an institution and its members' characters.

Character formation can be affected by structures and environment in a variety of ways. Most obviously character may be formed by means of explicit example or guiding instruction to the developing agent, and the opponent above might have been objecting to the university engaging with its members in such a directly prescriptive way. But structural matters can affect the development of virtues in less direct ways. Consider, for example, the virtue of friendliness. The formation of such a virtue will be influenced at least by the arrangements that exist for interaction between members of an institution. Thus in this case it will be affected by the way in which students interact with each other, and with staff, and by the way in which staff interact with each other. And other institutional factors, apart from geography can be relevant here in ways which contemporary universities might need to consider.

If, for example, students interact with university permanent staff only as members of a large audience before a distant speaker, then it is doubtful whether they are in any sense part of a community whose members trust one another, let alone whether there is any way in which friendliness can be manifested between the two groups. For whilst staff may eschew explicit prescription to their students, what has been said above shows that exemplifying the intellectual life to students is not simply a matter of intellectually polished presentations – rigorous reasoning, and incisive argument. What is also required are examples of patience in argument, self-restraint in listening to others, interpretative effort, and so on, which create the appropriate community for intellectual inquiry. And only certain kinds of teaching structures allow for such examples to be manifested.

Likewise if students' experience of seminar teaching is as members of a fairly large group with whom they do not interact on other courses, the opportunity for engagement with those fellow students in a way where friendliness can be manifested is minimal. They become merely ships passing in the dark. Finally, if staff are so busy that they cannot ever eat together, even with colleagues in their own department, and barely communicate except by e-mail, ethical virtues simply do not have the space (temporal or physical) in which to be manifested.

Why should these structural factors affect the development of ethical virtues? One reason is that although a social virtue like friendliness can in principle be manifested to a complete stranger, its manifestation in those circumstances is both more difficult, and necessarily very thin in content. It may be possible to make eye contact, or wish someone good day, but without more systematic interaction it is extremely difficult to know enough about those met to give more substance to what it is to wish them well. Equally, as has just been indicated, certain kinds of environment, such as the solitary lecturer before a large audience, simply preclude the possibility of certain kinds of behaviour that will both reflect and shape a community.

Many modern universities are now very large, with huge numbers of students and staff, and this growth in size means that if the classical conception requires a certain kind of community then a good deal of thought needs to be given as to what structures for teaching and pastoral interaction can optimise the opportunity for staff and students to become part of a familial community of the sort described. Many aspects of a student's (and staff member's) life at university may be relevant here, from the existence of a space within a department where staff and students can meet, to personal tutor arrangements, to accommodation and eating facilities, and sporting and artistic opportunities. For all these factors bear on the extent to which, and manner in which, students and staff may interact, and thus the possibilities for developing both the relevant ethical virtues and the associated communities.

In a similar way there are many constraints on the life of contemporary academic staff which inhibit the achievement of the relevant kind of community even at a departmental or faculty level. It will be all too easy for large modern universities to fail to reflect on how they can build intellectual communities, as substructures of the whole, which are of a size and shape to interact in the ways required to develop and sustain trust and its concomitant ethical virtues. If they fail to develop structures of the appropriate sort, then they will cease to be capable of achieving the classical conception's goal, training the mind.[220]

9

The rise of the rock dove [221]

Sue Vickerman

To my fledgling eye, Leeds was red-brick gullies,
crew-cut hedges, hard-faced trees, parks with frayed edges.
Today, when I glide in on an InterCity intending to visit
old roosts, I find instead chrome balconies, palms
waving from penthouses, sandblasted ledges

but there among the slender backs of bright tower-blocks
I spot some old-timers, the elderly chimneys along the canal
which haven't smoked since the fifties and look well on it;
the Town Hall in its helmet, and across from the jail's
tough nut, that monocled brain-box, the Parkinson clock.

It was hard, being part of the first pigeon influx.
Today when I hop on a Headingley bus
there are no second glances, yet I lived on campus
in times when pigeons received dirty looks; were dismissed
as chancers; were not even mentioned in certain bird-books.

We were treated by some as if we weren't birds at all.
But I was there for the transformation (some would say 'fall')
when we flocked in from pit towns, bog-standard quarries
and council tips to take up scholarships; created myths
of our past as 'rock doves' with a wild rural ancestry.

We were the first to wear nondescript colours
and hooded tops. We had red-eyed good looks
(if you like that type), but were written off by some
as scruffs, compared to those beautiful species
down south who resided in spires and turrets.

Yet we pigeons, though ordinary, though not all
the highest of flyers, had guts: we were the ones
who spoke out; the loud, feral townies. We taught
the southerners how to strut; how to conduct
their courtship displays on the Parkinson steps;

how not to be ruffled by complaints about squats
on the Great Hall's frontage, or the corrosive effects
of droppings. Soon, white streaks were as symbolic
as raised fists, and are now compared by sociologists
to the raised white streaks of self-harmed wrists

but see how our ways have been hijacked:
how other birds now scavenge for the best pickings,
flock into bars, get caught mating on shopfronts,
fly home at weekends. Meanwhile, ethnic pigeons
are wearing Nike to disguise their origins.

It's all a far cry from when we colonised Leeds 6,
rode bikes, picked through skips, shook buckets
to collect for the pickets, ate veggie, spent nights
doing soup-runs from St George's Crypt, marched
for other people's rights. We have been tamed,

pigeon-holed, allotted our place in the pecking order.
We have better-feathered nests; our status
is above the rest; our ethnicity has the respected
name and face of 'rock dove'. But remember this:
no bird-book, to this day, gives pigeons proper space.

PART TWO

VALUES and PRACTICE

10

Values and scientific research
– a practitioner's view

Tom McLeish

When questions of the nature and extent of public engagement with higher education are under the media's spotlights, when the impact of science and technology arouses sustained national debate, the contribution of broad social scholarship has clear advantages. Recent texts on research ethics exemplify how the social scientist,[222] the anthropologist, the historian[223] and philosopher of science, the theologian[224] draw on a perspective whose horizons of time and discipline naturally overtop the narrower and more local ethical viewpoints common to practising scientists and engineers themselves. However, it is just possible that a comment by those who engage daily in its minutiae on the ethics of that fundamental practice of the university – research – may complement this broader scholarship.

An additional potential of a view 'from the coal-face' that I hope to develop here is the identification of a more fine-grained set of ethical issues that might be missed in a wider assessment. My title naturally invokes the debates of boundaries; what might or must we research, what might we or must we not apply? Should research drive or be driven by a social agenda, and should the horizons of that agenda retain the national short-term interests implicit in current funding policy, or adopt global and long-term priorities? When our research allows us to manipulate our world to such an extent that it becomes within our power to manipulate ourselves, have we reached a rubicon? These large questions are certainly pressing, but their debate is not usually connected to the 'small-scale' issues of doing research: the preoccupations of running a research group supported on short-term resources, the pressures of regular 'quality' assessment exercises, the delicate balancing act of weaving the web of collaboration and competition across the uniquely global communities that represent scientific researchers. A close examination of some of these may even give us insights into the larger questions when they become bewildering.

We had better begin with one foundational question however: why do we engage in publicly-funded scientific research into the physical world? Without a teleology from somewhere, any ethical debate gasps for breath in an ontological vacuum. The current (and only) answer lodged in the UK Government remains the 1993 White Paper definition of the mission of our research councils to 'support wealth creation and increase the quality of life'. While politically understandable, and inheriting a long instrumentalist ethical legacy, such a purely mercenary view disquiets many within as well as outside the scientific community. The stalwart organisation 'Save British Science' exemplifies a focal point for counter-statements ('Newton would never have been awarded a research grant today' and suchlike). Yet an effective critique founded on such unease but without analysing its sources is of limited effect. The sources run very deep indeed, and spring from much earlier ages than the post-Enlightenment forms of science and scientific talk that we are used to. My first claim will be that a satisfactory exploration of research ethics in science will require an assessment of these ancient roots as much as an acquaintance with current technical potential. Whether framed as Euripides' benediction on those who 'engage in enquiry [into]…the order of immortal and ageless nature', or as Kepler's desire to 'think God's thoughts after him' or as the ancient writer of the Book of Job's teasing invitation to 'apply the laws of heavens to the earth', there are deeper motivations for scientific enquiry than those imposed by industrialised economy alone. Even these cursory examples indicate the antiquity of the idea that re-creating the structure of nature within our minds might be deeply characteristic of a broadly-defined human culture.

To note just one other highly suggestive example from a former period of intellectual flourishing, Gregory of Nyssa's remarkable dialogue 'On the

Soul and the Resurrection' contains a recognisable appeal to scientific process. Gregory debates with his sister (and 'Teacher') Macrina on the reality of the soul (we would surely employ the word 'mind' in a contemporary version of the debate). Macrina develops a lengthy supporting argument based on the human ability to deduce the solidity of the Moon, or, in the passage quoted below, the corporality of invisible air. These deductions are arrived at by thinking beyond mere appearances:

> It is by an abuse of language that a jar is said to be 'empty'; for when it is empty of any liquid it is none the less, even in this state, full, in the eyes of the experienced. A proof of this is that a jar when put into a pool of water is not immediately filled, but at first floats on the surface, because the air it contains helps to buoy up its rounded sides; till at last the hand of the drawer of the water forces it down to the bottom, and, when there, it takes in water by its neck; during which process it is shown not to have been empty even before the water came; for there is the spectacle of a sort of combat going on in the neck between the two elements, the water being forced by its weight into the interior, and therefore streaming in; the imprisoned air on the other hand being straitened for room by the gush of the water along the neck, and so rushing in the contrary direction; thus the water is checked by the strong current of air, and gurgles and bubbles against it.[225]

Of course, we need to accommodate our modern minds to the explicitly theological context of older scientific discourse if we are not to miss the ancient traditions that celebrate with stories, wisdom and song our exploratory relationship with nature. To expand on just one more example, it is worth recalling that the Biblical book most infused with questions of creation is not Genesis, but Job. It contains, for example, a haunting passage in which humans are contrasted to all other creatures in their unique ability to observe the structure of the world from the (literal) 'inside' (the miner 'dangles and sways' on his rope, glimpsing the precious metals and strata revealed only to his eyes). Wilson Poon and I have elsewhere attempted to articulate an Old Testament theology of science,[226] and it is not my task to develop these examples in depth here, but it is relevant to note that the core of a recognisable scientific process is as natural to the ancient Hebraic world as to the Hellenistic. In some ways the Biblical scientific writings are actually more accessible to contemporary readings, since they themselves do not have to bear all of the mystic weight that, for example, the Pythagoreans placed on their natural philosophy. Furthermore, its sources invite a more explicitly ethical exploration in the almost invariable context of human *suffering* in discussion of nature. Pain arises in either background or foreground almost whenever Biblical writers tackle comprehension of the natural world.

The Genesis story itself is a prelude to the pain of rejection from the garden; the deeply-searching questions of Job 39–40 hang ambiguously in response to Job's appeals against his own suffering; the achingly beautiful creation story of Proverbs 8 parallels the pain of a world without wisdom. In spite of the modern usage of the word 'science' itself, an enquiring engagement with the natural world has a recognisable place in Judeo-Christian theology. Now, if the narrative thrust of this tradition is towards a healing or reconciliation of broken relationships (as, for example, St Paul argued[227]), then we might explore how the scientific process functions within such a theology, rather than as counter to it. This is not a common approach to debates on the relationship of science and theology, but it is arguably more historically faithful than either confrontational or complementary viewpoints. It is certainly a suggestive starting point for an ethical discussion of scientific research. For the roots we have traced situate science as that part of the wider task of healing that enables the reconciliation of humankind with the *physical world* (in a parallel way to the better-trodden ethical grounds of reconciled individual psychologies, communities, and nations). The vision replaces a broken relationship of ignorant exploitation of the world on the one hand, and the threat of re-emergent chaos on the other, with a renewed husbandry of creation, marked by a shared wisdom. Science becomes part of *shalom*.

We have traced just one possible thread of an ethical theology of science in these relational terms through one tradition, but a remarkably similar pattern can emerge from treatments of Vedic, Islamic, Greek sources. The urgent demand for human activity and discourse that performs a healing role with respect to our relationship with the material world may even be drawn from a perspective of art criticism. George Steiner remarks in his hauntingly relational and personal assessment of language and meaning,[228] 'Only art can go some way towards making accessible, towards waking into some measure of communicability, the sheer inhuman otherness of matter...' Of course a scientist's reading of this claim can feel like a slap in the face (only art?), but it serves to help us evaluate whether or not our research really attains the level of communication of the 'otherness of matter'. Supposing that, for a moment, we have managed to identify a few of the shadows thrown onto our ethical preconceptions, the next task is to draw the lines of a healthy function and context for research that traditional roots such as these would project into a contemporary practice of science. Let us try to sketch a few outlines that suggest themselves.

1. The first must be that the natural timescale for a research project within a currently broken relationship with creation, is a long one. Deep wounds heal slowly, and require more than superficial restructuring of tissue. Or, to take a theological view, the double-edge of eschatology requires both action and waiting. Even though there is indeed reason to celebrate sudden, even decisive, entry of hope into the world now, that does not mean that its full realisation will not be as protracted and rich a process as the creation of the world was in the first place. The old 'wisdom literature' often repeats the theme of the long and difficult search for wisdom itself, and one aspect of the painful theodicy that so often accompanies Biblical contemplation of the physical world is that the 're-search' itself is to be a long and painful one. We will have more to say on what a juxtaposition of the ideas of 'contemplation' and 'science research' might mean later.

2. A second consequence of a reconciliatory context for scientific ethics would be a sustained communication and debate amongst the science community of its future direction and past account. The existence of such an identifiable community itself, tasked with informing and changing our relationship with the physical world, is by no means an obviously reasonable notion in a 'post-modern' world of individuals and private readings. Furthermore, it would be one in which individual achievement, though celebrated in the context of the whole task, would not be emphasised or accorded levels of 'prestige' that obscure the project's underlying motivation.

3. Thirdly, an ethical research community would naturally be highly multidisciplinary at its core. The heterogeneity of any theologically-defined community more than hints at this. If the medical metaphor of 'healing' can be sustained, then it is as natural to recognise that the process requires the co-operation of multiple agents as to assert, as Rowan Williams does, that academic disciplines site themselves in proximity because, in spite of everything, they know they have 'something to do with one another'. In another theologically-motivated lecture[229], Nicholas Lash, urging an academic grasp of the ultimately *connected* structure of the web of knowledge

that underlies all disciplines: 'Notwithstanding the accelerated fragments of specialised academic activities, we trample in each other's territory, sing each other's songs, whether we want to or not'.

4. Fourthly, the function of the ethical science-community would not be circumscribed by the narrow subset that is charged with tasks requiring long training. There would be, in other words, no elitist 'priesthood', but a publicly-shared project in which those with special roles were charged with listening-to and communicating with others. Drawing on the same tradition, we would find that, rather than a self-perception as a superior élite, the specialists would be advised to adopt a model of servanthood. In this regard it is resolutely non-Platonic.

5. Fifthly, the goals of the project would not primarily be associated with maximising economic return to a single group or nation. There is one world, one creation, and a relational ethics must recognise the global ownership of natural wisdom as well as global consequences of natural folly.

6. Finally, and to some remarkably, our situation of scientific research *within* rather than *against* a theological context does not immediately supply any pre-determined ethical boundaries for the subject of investigation or interrogation of nature. It recognises, even celebrates, the extraordinary ability of the human mind to sift the causes of phenomena, and also to alter them. The final Biblical vision of the 'new creation' of the Revelation to John is, after all, a *city* rather than some Arcadian vision of rustic simplicity.

By now, of course, it may be anticipated that such preparatory work will throw at least some of the actual practices of scientific research into sharp relief. But without it one can become so accustomed to the *modus operandi* of the social and political machine that supports and orders science today that any sort of ethical critique becomes at best groundless and at worst blind. The first shock that meets eyes now turned to contemporary research practice is the contrast of the anticipated long timescale of science with the relentless urgency that fuels the international research engine with increasing volatility. In his valedictory 'Festival Overture' lecture to the Edinburgh Festival in 1999, George Steiner typifies the 'noonday' cultural activity of science: 'Theorems will be solved, crucial experiments performed, discoveries made next week and/or the week thereafter'. He means to contrast a healthy community with a potentially-diseased one (that of the humanities), but to anyone within the scientific research community the remark is chilling. Increasingly, the pace of discovery is determined by the political lack of trust that drives the invention of the tools of accountability. Research activity and output is linked to funding, which is itself linked to assessment scores, which are linked to research activity and output... The analogy offered by Rowan Williams[230] with Scheherezade is exactly right. Every day new theorems will be proved because new stories must be told. The cliff-hanging hiatus of today's story becomes the grant proposal that fuels the tale of tomorrow. Without the next novel the axe falls on the continuity of the research group. An added dimension of concern at this issue of science as storytelling for survival is its palpable appearance at several levels. As individual researchers compete for the ear of the sultan, so do their universities. Even at a national level, the biennial (in the case of the UK Treasury) 'spending reviews' demand stories of promise from the entire research community (represented by the research councils). It is all too easy to equate success at these survival games with the maximising of financial return. There is dwindling political pressure to support research projects that run long, slow and deep.

The politically-driven pace of science has consequences also for its wider influence and perception. To take one example, the current critique of science as overly functional, and separated from 'human' values and aspirations, is by no means new. Famous cries against its assault on human and spiritual are present in Blake, in Keats, in Dickens, in Flaubert. The core of these complaints contains a voiced fear that science will actually destroy the means of our reconciliation with nature ('unweaving the rainbow') rather than nourish it. Jacques Barzun made the memorable analysis that 'science is not with us an object of contemplation',[231] an observation from the 1960s that is no less relevant now. It is still the case that research in universities is a surer route to professional preferment than the more contemplative activities of scholarship and teaching. I know of a few wonderful exceptions of scientists who are prepared to spend weeks working on pedagogical material that lets deep ideas connect, relationships assume their proper perspective and draws selflessly on the best work of others, but they are rare. Particularly when access and participation in higher education, and the necessary preparation for it are under reassessment, a rediscovery of both the pace and the depth implied by a contemplative research and teaching methodology is attractive.

One might be initially more optimistic about the ethical nature and standards suggested for the research community by a relational agenda. The integral activity of the conference, where a single research area is regularly discussed by the international practitioners who lead it, sustains social as well as professional relationships, welcomes young scientists, suggests new directions and celebrates the spoken word in debate and discussion. As such it has become an emblem of an underrated strength of academic research, namely the ability to build and sustain truly global communities that transcend cultural and linguistic boundaries. Furthermore, as Polanyi pointed out long ago,[232] these research communities are enabled to function because they do not impose on themselves the intrusive accountability we noted is increasingly imposed from outside, but instead recognise the essential currency of trust. This is why cases of 'scientific fraud' are so mercifully rare (but in consequence, of such high profile).

Yet there are reasons to suspect that the best of this practice is in danger of erosion. The last 15 years have seen the publication of an unprecedented number of nationally-commissioned reports on ethical and unethical practice in science.[233] Some of the pressures that arise from the increasing pace of publicly-funded science and that lie behind these voiced concerns we have already discussed. But there are others that are increasingly placing scientists in positions of conflicts of interest from which it is hard to escape, and that could induce fissures into the fragile nature of research communities. A heightened value placed on competitiveness generated by new systems of accountability and research funding is one. A scientist will find herself at one level urged to play for the prestige of her university, but simultaneously and at another level for a national research network. In the case of the European Union, funding channelled through the commissions in Brussels constitutes a third, higher, level at which suddenly one's rivals must become colleagues over and against other large global players. Moving in the other direction, micro-managed funding resource models within an increasingly large number of institutions threaten to set up artificial rivalries between departments in the same university. In this increasingly complex environment of externally-urged rivalries it becomes harder to sustain a vision of the globally-situated yet locally-cognate communities that embody a reconciliatory and contemplative research agenda. With whom, and at what stage of development should I share this idea or question? At what level of association do I declare a 'conflict of interest' in assessing or refereeing a publication or grant application? These activities in particular are at the core of the 'peer review' system that has evolved as a structural embodiment of the self-reflective task of the scientific community.

As equivocal peer-review is placed under increasing pressure, some of its inherent drawbacks become more tangible. In particular, there is an urgent need to address how to avoid suppressing the surprising, the innovative, even the revolutionary research programme under the double weight of accountability on the one hand and engineered rivalry on the other. Panels and committees tasked with ranking over a hundred ten-page research proposals before tea-time are unlikely to deal effectively with the very few that would fundamentally change or expand our vision of an area of biology or physics, let alone bring multidisciplinary patterns of thought together in new ways, however reliably they may compare incremental research comfortably within established programmes. In the UK, some tentative moves are being made at the national level to fund individuals and groups with promising records without a detailed dissection of their proposals. Yet even these, when they are not opposed by appeals to equality of opportunity, rely on the solid-and-reliable yet unimaginative peer-review process for approval.

A community over-loaded with these highly-formulated ethical processes in setting the research agenda is also tasked with policing the results of research programmes. So in the area of publication a similar set of pressures therefore arises. Financial and personal credit comes to those who publish, not just in quantity, but in those journals accorded with 'high impact factor'. Recent high-profile cases of series of papers in the journals *Science* and *Nature* have shown how a web of dysfunctional motivations and relationships within a research community can result in the publication of extensive accounts containing fabricated data. Large research teams working at speed under pressure from their director begin to economise on discussion and mutual checking of results. The journals themselves require a steady stream of novel and apparently cutting-edge research to fill their pages and emblazon their front covers. The potential instabilities inherent in such implicit collusion are obvious, especially when the governing pace of a research area has been accelerated beyond a respect for reflection, repetition, sifting and criticism. By degrees, attention is drawn away from the *contemplative substance* of the science, from establishing a firmer and deeper reconstruction of the physical world, to the epi-phenomena of visibility and prestige of the scientists themselves, and the publications that channel their results to the public. Remarkably, the pressure to publish a result before rivals differs considerably within sub-fields of science. A physicist colleague, used to an extended period of investigation of a problem before beginning discussion of publication was startled to find that the biologists in the same institution felt constrained to be thinking always of 'the next publication' rather than 'the next problem', lest their rivals publish on it first. These Scheherazades seem not to need the fear of a vicious sultan to spin their tales.

We have seen how pressures of this kind may affect the integrity of even science of the highest assumed quality. But it has another instantly recognisable effect on the quantity of publication: that of the multiplication of secondary or derivative results in great quantity. Even in the very narrow sub-fields of research typically constituting the domains of expertise of a scientist working today it is impossible to read the majority of the mountainous publication stream. A professor, now retired, on leafing through the many pages of yet another new journal muttered the response as frequently thought as it is rarely spoken: 'there simply can't be this many clever people in the world'! The scientist might therefore be puzzled to read a heartfelt criticism of precisely this phenomenon aimed but exclusively at the fields of the arts and humanities, by one of their own scholars, in deference to the 'primary' perceived content of the sciences. George Steiner, in *Real Presences*, imagines a 'Primary City' in which all writing is fundamentally art, and no secondary, derivative or parasitic forms are admitted. Crucially, this proliferation of the secondary in literature is related for Steiner to the breaking of the 'contract' of meaning, between words and world. One of the attributes of postmodern studies in literature – the centrality and self-justification of the text – becomes a force for the debasement of texts themselves in a proliferation of self-referential commentary. Steiner sets this movement, as we saw that he does the general pessimism of his field in the *Festival Overture*, against his perception of relative academic health in the sciences. But the grass really isn't as green as that when examined close-up. Furthermore the same pattern of proliferation in written output is hauntingly connected to a scientific version of Steiner's 'broken contract' – when science is superficial it, too, fails to connect with its object, and now the malady is palpably worse than its literary version. It is arguably academically legitimate in a department of English to write texts discussing texts. But a discourse among a scientific community that has lost essential physical referent, has also become a worthless heaping up of words. This is not meant to be a sweeping characterisation of the current scientific literature, but we may concerned when already the average readership of a scientific paper published today numbers less than one person.

If communication within the scientific community is already exhibiting the fault-lines that point to a failing grasp of a healthy relational ethic, it is perhaps not surprising that issues of public ownership, communication and trust in the scientific process are currently under serious scrutiny. In the UK, enquiries such as the House of Lords report on the public understanding of science, commentaries exemplified by Onora O'Neill's 2002 Reith lectures,[234] and the regular business of bodies such as the Advisory Committee on Novel Foods and Processes have identified a 'climate of suspicion' surrounding the process of science. This reflects in particular its perceived lack of independence from government. But, as Jon Turney has pointed out[235], it would be wrong to complain superficially of an 'anti-science' attitude that sets out to contain and to distance itself from scientists. More consonant with our working model of the fundamentally shared and public domain natural to science, is the analysis of Angela Tilby[236] (and Simone Weil before her) that scientists run the risk of becoming a new priesthood 'seeming to guard the key to knowledge, to have access to transcendental truths which the rest of us could never hope to understand'. These cries come from educated and intelligent people who feel shut out from a world of richness and truth, disappointed that the scientific community seems to offer no way in to a shared reading of its process or results beyond the superficial or patronising. The theological resonances are very strong, and a lesson from church history is surely of the latent social instability of such a perceived combination of power and exclusivity. Our media are very mixed in their positive and negative contributions to these and other public images of science, both negative and positive. This is even true of single broadcasting channels such as the BBC's Radio 4, which exemplifies models from a 'court jester' approach in interviews with scientists on its news and current affairs programmes to the personal, playful and engaging style of programmes such as *Material World*.

The consequences of a widespread failure to understand the process and context of research are widely-discussed, particularly in terms of the public perception of risk. Whether the issue is nuclear waste disposal, genetically-modified foods or animal cloning, we are beginning to talk of the validity of ethical viewpoints of scientists and 'non-scientists'.[237] Recognising valid and disparate grounds of choice in the challenging grand issues before us is an essential step, but in attempting to solve global issues rapidly, discussion restricted to this level sidesteps the *local* spadework of generating a shared recognition that science is at the core of human creativity. We need perhaps to return to Macrina's bedside to learn this afresh: there is a direct link between her playful, childlike and perceptive reasoning on the property of air to an appreciation of how an organism's genes change and may be changed. Both build on simple images accessible to anyone, while calling on a challenging degree of contemplation (one that, after all, pointed Gregory of Nyssa to identify the reality of independent mind). The language we use will be crucial. This is not the place to attempt an analysis of the way we currently educate out children, managing to excise this natural delight in questioning the physical world from so many, convincing them that is for the gifted (and freakish) few, but the linguistic baggage we inherit certainly hinders. It is not insignificant that the word 'science' carried Latin cognates of knowledge claims, overpainted by its relatively recent use in the word 'scientist' (unknown before 1832) in the dominant colours of Victorian industrialisation. I have sometimes suggested to people who react negatively to 'science' that they re-cast their thinking in terms of the older, Greek cognate of 'Natural Philosophy'. 'Love of wisdom of natural things' can germinate a fresh start to what science might be about, one that is also recognisably consonant with our working relational paradigm. It is the cause of immense joy just to see people able to smile when thinking about a realm that has previously generated fear or incomprehension. Such small steps as this can begin a personal reconciliation with common aspects of the physical world: a realisation of why a rainbow appears when it does, the reasons food smells nice when it is cooked. These examples, as much as Macrina's comforting her grieving brother by rehearsing the reason for the phases of the moon, point to the potential of a sort of 'science therapy' that might accompany 'art therapy' in rehabilitating and enriching. If a reintroduction to the activity of representing both inner and outer worlds in paint and drama can help to heal minds, what hope might there be for a participation in a gentle and contemplative science in restoring a broken or misunderstood relationship with the physical world? Both art and science have the wonderful power to render alienating environments human and homely, and the terrible potential to perform the opposite.

In suggesting that some of the more pressing issues in science research ethics are to be found in the undergrowth, rather than the top-canopy, of our public structures, we therefore return once more to the university campus. Wilson Poon and I have explored the interdisciplinary implications of the ethical path we are attempting to map in more depth elsewhere,[238] but we need here to make explicit the threads that bind disciplines together, however divorced they may seem to have become. In palpably sharing some of the maladies of Steiner's critiques, in a shared experience of the pejorative implication of the word 'academic', yet in promising at our best a publicly-owned project that is potentially therapeutic, both our arts and sciences have more in common than is commonly admitted. Returning once more to Steiner's haunting call to 'go some way towards making accessible, towards waking into some measure of communicability, the sheer inhuman otherness of matter', we receive an unrestricted task to which all disciplines are urged. In meeting it we might find the distance between us less if we were to recognise the shared experience of creativity with constraint. Again, terminology creates an unethical obstruction when use of empty phrases such as 'the exact sciences', and 'scientific proof' nonetheless serve to convince creative people that there is no room for imagination in the scientific process. No more does uncontrolled juxtaposition of paint, tones, words or forms produce good art, music, writing or architecture. Human minds seeking creatively to reconstruct the hidden processes below the surface of the natural world do so in a highly, but not overconstrained way, reminiscent of the channelling double constraints of form and idea in art. We will need more pliant disciplinary walls to create an academic environment conducive to ethical research programmes that encourage students to explore consonant interdisciplinary ideas such as this. Thomas Bender[239] connects the desirable disciplinary aspects of vitality, objectivity and democracy with an inherently interdisciplinary character that he terms 'weakness' (with no pejorative connotations). This is the openness to new movements and ideas that change the character of disciplines, but by evolving keeps them alive. He does not discuss the sciences, but his analysis applies both between them and more widely across our current faculty boundaries. The inherent 'weakness' of physics in his sense, for example, is clearly a strength that has enabled fresh views on such disparate and surprising fields as, for example, granular media (previously within the domain of engineering) and the molecular motors of muscle (previously biology). These movements are changing physics itself as well as re-seeding those other disciplines with fresh questions and approaches. The 'strength' (in Bender's sense of inflexibility) of the engineering disciplines, by contrast, reinforced by the prescriptive demands of professional accrediting bodies (in the UK), has impeded their development in such new directions. In looking for ways to realise 'creative weakness' in disciplinary boundaries, it hardly requires pointing out that even a minimal level of discourse between more widely-separated disciplines requires the 'contemplative time' that we have identified as one of our rapidly disappearing and precious resources.

This brief examination of value in scientific research is necessarily a personal one, but one that has allowed emphasis of a teleological and relational approach to science. Loosing sight of what science is for is the first step to stripping it of its values, and to losing a vital tool in the formulation of science ethics. The themes of reconciliation, communities of shared values and a primary engagement with the world are very ancient (this is why we have had to revisit some theology to unearth them). But at the same time they speak urgently to our present predicament of public unease with science. To realise the vision of an ethical research process, democratically shared, living and vulnerable, in the face of the severe challenges we have also identified, requires a faith in the academy that is increasingly hard to find. Yet the relational and reconciliatory task at its core I have identified needs just the form of faith proposed by Rowan Williams[240] in his own discussion of faith in the university: '…a commitment to the belief that our life is more than a struggle between a creative ego, individual or collective, and a lot of raw material; it trusts that there is a possible reconciliation ('atonement') between human selves and their world'. A 'love of wisdom to do with natural things' within that world would be a good travelling companion to take with us on that shared journey.

11

Assumptions and values in the production of knowledge: towards an area ethics of psychology and the social sciences

Hilde Eileen Nafstad

Medical doctors, psychologists, engineers, teachers, researchers, and others have become important agents in our everyday lives. This means that people in everyday life to an increasing degree depend on various professions as providers of development, for welfare and well-being and for mental and physical health. Hence, the well-being of the individual, as well as the positive functioning of society, is increasingly dependent on how these professions develop. Consequently, the production, dissemination and application of scientific knowledge have a fundamental impact on the modern human being. In turn, the ethical and value standards of the production of knowledge becomes an important issue, not only to the scientific community and the professions, but to wider society.

Ethics as a subject represents the systematic investigation of and arguments about good and bad, right and wrong. However, discussions of ethics within clinical professions, for example in psychology and medicine, very quickly get reduced to arguments about rules, prescriptions, and prohibitions for coping with clients. Correspondingly, discussions of ethics in relation to research are often reduced to questions concerning how to handle subjects, inform them, debrief them afterwards, cope with controls, and so on. Thus, research ethics seems more and more to involve only the issue of how to complete application forms in order to pass formal ethical committees and ensure future publication, while professional and applied ethics focus more on avoiding misconduct, negligence and how to maintain standards of professional behaviour. Additionally, university courses on ethics tend to deal primarily with codes of conduct and less with inquiring into values and ethical argumentation about what may improve positive functioning of society and well-being of the individual.

I shall explore a different type of ethics than this deficiency-oriented approach. We may classify this kind of inquiry as *area ethics*. In the Norwegian Ethics Program (1991–2001), area ethics is defined as, 'questioning into the values, perspectives and norms tied to a specific field of activity'.[242] Area ethics thus includes both applied and basic ethical issues relevant to a particular field, sector or activity.

Basic notions within this category of ethics will therefore not be misconduct, deficiencies and rules. On the contrary, its central concepts include values, virtues, norms, comparison of values, responsibility for full-fledged descriptions of the phenomenon one is studying, as well as ethical and practical implications of one's perspective and conceptual framework. Area ethics is also concerned with how to develop such ethical competence or sensitivity in students and researchers. This should include identifying and examining values and assumptions in their discipline and applied practice. I shall now use my own discipline, psychology, for illustrations.

Area ethics and the production of knowledge

Science may be divided into separate but related levels of activity. A pragmatic division of scientific levels of activity might be to distinguish between: (a) metatheory, (b) theory, (c) design, (d) methods of data collection, (e) data, and (f) phenomena.

Metatheory is concerned with basic presumptions; those ideas within the discipline that are generally taken for granted as the field of study's fundamental truths or givens. Moreover, metatheoretical positions are being created and formed at the point of intersection where general cultural values and ideologies meet the academic disciplines and traditions. As Krasner and Houts note of this interaction between culture and discipline: '...these discipline-specific assumptions function like 'value' systems within a scientific community and may be related to broader values shared by the society.'[243] Area ethics is thus an ethical and normative inquiry into the metatheoretical level on which the actual discipline or field of research rests. The horizons of understanding and the value-based starting points which lie behind the concrete research questions and form the actual research projects, are therefore central subjects of inquiry for area ethics. Moreover, area ethics is also concerned with which potential themes or aspects of the actual research field are given priority, and which themes are kept off or excluded from the research agenda.

Psychological researchers then do not operate apart from social contexts and conditions. On the contrary, each of us in our research is in one way or another an agent of our social and cultural conditions. Psychology as a science of human beings is thus composed of complex historically and socially constructed concepts.[244] Assumptions with regard to values – discipline-specific as well as culture-bound values – will therefore enter our research in psychology and the social sciences in a variety of ways: in our selection of areas worth studying; in what we actually conceive of as a problem; how we formulate our research question; in fact in every aspect of the research process.[245] Thus, a most challenging task for area ethics, not only in psychology but also in other subjects, is to develop in the researcher and the student an ethical reflexivity and sensitivity for the values and assumptions defining and influencing our projects as they are embedded in our approach to the problem, concepts, methods and theories.

However, contemporary mainstream psychology often views its assumptions about human nature as 'indisputable universally true facts'. Identification and critical evaluation of the value implications and moral consequences of the assumptions underlying current psychological research, is thus a task of great importance today.

Science may, in many ways, be considered what the philosophically and ecologically oriented psychologist Howard terms a 'witch's caldron' in which different *a priori* starting points, values, axioms and basic assumptions, as well as different concrete theories, 'boil' and vie for dominance.[246] Every position and concrete theory thus wishes to become the one recognized, become the one accepted as being the truth and an expression of reality. Another strong obligation of area ethics is therefore to identify and visualize 'losers' within a particular field of research; that is, to identify ignored, neglected or even excluded perspectives and positions about human nature. What kind of descriptions of humans, what kind of images of humanity would the 'losers' in this 'competition' have developed? As William James, one of the founders of modern psychology, noted, 'We have so many different businesses with nature... The philosophic attempt to define nature so that no one's business is left out, so that no one lies outside the door saying "Where do I come in?" is sure in advance to fail. The most a philosophy can hope for is not to lock out any interest forever'.[247] This task of identifying ignored or even excluded perspectives is thus another important challenge within area ethics. The different research areas at a particular time may be dominated by very few, perhaps only one grand theory with its accompanying empirical descriptions. If a discipline is dominated by some few assumptions, concepts and theories, the accompanying empirical descriptions may be reductionistic and consequently represent a dehumanizing psychology. A task for area ethics within science is thus to be reflective with regard to what kind of descriptions are missing or neglected within a particular discipline or subject to ensure more full-fledged descriptions of the phenomena.

I shall now give a concrete example on how to work in psychology to meet these obligations.

The individual as asocial and egoistic, versus the individual as a genuinely prosocial human being

The concept of relationship is one of the most used in psychology and the social sciences. As Noam and Fischer point out, 'Many of the most important classic works in social science, including psychology and philosophy, have recognized the foundational role of relationships...'[248]

As a researcher in psychology interested in area ethics, my task then is to inquire into the values tied to this specific research field. Concrete questions crucial to explore would therefore be: Which values are implied by the different definitions of humans as social beings? Is one particular definition of social relationships preferred by mainstream psychology at the cost of others?

Historically we may also identify three major philosophical roots of modern psychology: the Aristotelian or essentialist, the Marxist or cultural-historical, and the Darwinian or evolutionary model of human development and behavior. Thus, another question is which model(s) a particular field of research, tradition and project takes as its point of departure. Moreover, it is important to investigate whether or not certain theories may have negative consequences for humans.

Fiske, Herrnstein, Nafstad, and van Lange are among those today concerned with analyzing fundamental starting points or cornerstones on which psychology rests.[249] The anthropologist Fiske argues that contemporary assumptions are instrumentalist:

> From Freud to contemporary sociobiologists, from Skinner to social cognitionists, from Goffman to game theorists, the prevailing assumption in Western psychology has been that humans are by nature asocial individualists. Thus, psychologists (and most other social scientists) usually explain social relationships as instrumental means to extrinsic, non-social ends, or as constraints on the satisfaction of individual desires.[250]

A person is thus *a priori* defined as a self-interested, being constantly preoccupied by consuming, using or even exploiting the social, collective and material world with the goal of gaining benefits or the best possible result, physically as well as psychologically. Van Lange draws similar conclusions about the predominance of this idea in mainstream psychology.[251] As van Lange concludes his analysis:

> Within the domain of psychological theory, this assumption of rational self-interest is embedded in several key constructs, such as reinforcement, the pursuit of pleasure, utility maximization (as developed in the context of behavioristic theory, including social learning theory), psychoanalytic theory, and theories of social decision making.'[252]

This starting point forms the basis of central social psychological theories such as game theory; exchange theory; theories concerning cooperation, competition and general theories on interpersonal actions.[253] Mainstream psychology often assumes that when an individual acts socially, this is in the end merely motivated by the prospect of gaining advantages for oneself. Even 'prosocial' actions such as cooperation, altruism, solidarity, and helping behavior have the preservation and promotion of oneself as their ultimate goal.

This perspective of human nature will therefore guide studies in the direction of a theoretical approach to human motivation in which various positive and negative aspects of comfort or discomfort for the individual constitute the central concepts. The other in the relationship is only meaningful as tool or instrument for achieving better conditions for oneself. Other possible systems of motivation are regarded as various derivations of this single fundamental motivation – self-interest. Human beings' core nature is thus *a priori* viewed as a *for-oneself* nature. Thus, psychology often takes for granted almost a Hobbesian negative view of human nature.[254] Naturally, this assumption of individuals as beings guided in the end only by self-interest, calculating maximization or optimization of utility for oneself, constitutes most probably a very reasonable dictum about human nature as often humans are acquisitive and self-interested, in fact bad and sometimes even evil.

In sum, area ethics should, first be concerned with identifying and revealing the more or less explicitly formulated assumptions, concepts, and theoretical traditions which are influential in shaping current production of knowledge in the actual field. However, also as stated, area ethics should critically scrutinize and challenge the predominant axioms. We must therefore ask: What kind of knowledge about human beings will be construed from such and such a frame of reference? It is important to ask if the current axioms, for instance the axiom about human beings as asocial and self-interested, results in a description of humanity that 'reflects and reveres human nature in all its diversity, complexity and subtlety.'[255]

I argue that describing humans as by nature primarily designed to pursue self-interest, to conceive of the other only as a kind of storehouse of goods and benefits waiting to be used to improve one's own well-being, does not meet psychology's ethical obligation to revere human nature in all its diversity and complexity. Furthermore, clinical practices grounded on knowledge based on such a conception of the human being are questionable indeed. To reduce the individual to a simple, mechanistic cost-benefit being implies, for instance, that people seeking psychological assistance primarily need therapeutic help to become a more acquisitive consumer of one's social and material surroundings. Therapeutic help becomes in fact more a task of helping clients into the role of consumers in their social relationships. To trace all social relationships back to self-interest is, therefore, an implicit conception of humans that has to be questioned.

Area ethics of a discipline, as mentioned, also has the obligation to search for alternative paradigmatic presumptions. What if psychology, for instance, took as its starting point that the individual is genuinely a socially and morally motivated being? The idea of a moral and prosocial person has been proposed before, in philosophy by Rousseau, Hume, Smith, Comte, and in psychology by Spencer and McDougall. The social psychologist McDougall argued, for example, in favour of an independent prosocial instinct.[256] Currently, Hoffman, Batson, and Seligman and Csikszentmihalyi are arguing for such an approach.[257] Such a framework has never been accepted within mainstream psychology. As a researcher engaged in area ethics, however, my obligation is to argue that psychology and the social sciences needs the window on the human being as a moral, social, good, and positive being to be reopened. This vision of human social behavior may orient psychology more clearly towards the issue of what are good, worthy and meaningful social relationships. Thus, judging from this example, area ethics requires an ability to sift and contrast different points of view.

Area ethics as sensitivity to practical consequences of scientific inquiry

As area ethics researchers, we value the benefits of science. At the same time, however, one obligation of area ethics is to judge the consequences for society and the individual of the specific field's line of inquiry. Thus, area ethics takes as a point of departure that the pursuit of scientific knowledge also has to be judged by its consequences for society and the human being. Area ethics, then, involves being sensitive to and caring about the consequences of a field's research for society and human dignity. Today researchers are sophisticated when it comes to inquiring into and judging the consequences of the outcomes of their projects for their particular research field. However, they are rather unsophisticated when it comes to discerning and examining the consequences of their scientific advances for society. Let us, therefore, return to research on social behavior and ask more systematically what the consequences are for the individual and society of descriptions based on this idea of a rational self-interest motivation system.

As the psychologist Miller points out, 'Scientific theories, by generating self-knowledge and self-images, are always at risk of becoming self-fulfilling.'[258] Thus, people concerned with psychology and psychological knowledge may come to be formed by this description which psychology gives of the individual as an egoistic being. And Miller further concludes that psychology, by giving priority to the egoist position with its deduced theories and empirical knowledge, becomes an especially extensive and negative reflexivity problem, 'Nowhere would this risk seem greater than in the case of the self-interest assumption…'[259] On the basis of what is presented as scientific knowledge, people may come to believe that they must act selfishly, thinking only of their own gain: this is how the individual is, and should be. Consequently, such asocial motivation models may have extensive normative effects on people today. Descriptions – in fact prescriptions – based on these models may prevent people's development of prosocial values, virtues, and good or beneficial actions. Moreover, such descriptions might, in the long run, also lead to society creating or forming a certain type of person through the psychological knowledge which is produced on the basis of this current dominant perspective.[260]

As an area ethics researcher I do not of course argue that psychology should abandon empirical research on the various theories based on the self-interest axiom. However, area ethics should demand of current psychological research practice that they have a pluralistic spectrum of traditions or directions, each with its own values and perspectives on the individual's potentials and characteristics as a social being. If psychology does not put more emphasis on broad *a priori* basic assumptions about the individual and relationships between people, then the situation will continue as it is today: A single core vision, for example the idea of the individual as egoistic and rationally calculating, becomes almost absolute over a very long period, with the narrowing consequences this has for both the individual and society. In that case, a dehumanizing psychology would be in danger of developing. Thus, when psychology takes as its basis that the maximizing of utility for oneself is the core of human nature, it must also open up for alternative assumptions, such as independent prosocial motivation systems and individuals' genuine ability to support, help and comfort each other. I would argue then that in psychological research today there should rather be an overriding norm of pluralism in terms of underlying values.

Conclusion
Value perspectives within psychology focus today, as mentioned earlier, primarily on deficiencies in ethical standards, on immoral actors and misconduct or wrongdoing. Consequently, ethical issues within our university curricula are concentrated mainly on prescriptive rules and

potential misconduct in order to prepare the students for their future careers as professionals or researchers. Lists of prescriptions and prohibitions to be followed or rules formulated in terms of 'Thou shall/Thou shall not' aim to establish an ethical basis within our students and future professionals. Such an ethics is naturally important to protect society and the public by ensuring minimum standards of ethical behavior.

I argue, however, that it is even more fundamental to develop what we may call a moral and ethical sensitivity to the values embedded in our disciplines and in the individual student and researcher. What is needed is to create within the student a genuine interest for area ethics questions such as: What are the consequences for society and the individual human being of the research I am now undertaking or planning to undertake? Could it be that some of the assumptions underlying current research may be of detriment to society and the collective? Does predominant mainstream research give a too limited or reductionistic description of humans? Do the ideology and values in our culture ignore or reject particular potentials or aspects of humans?

To teach area ethics, therefore, is to develop in the student a genuine moral interest in shaping one's discipline so that it serves and improves society and human life. In my opinion, one of the most essential and necessary tasks in most fields and disciplines today is continually to develop and refine this approach.

12

Atrophy of the affect in academia
or
What next, after 40 years in the wilderness?

John Cowan

Introduction

In a much-quoted and no doubt apocryphal anecdote, Gandhi (although sometimes it is Chairman Mao) is said to have been asked by European journalists what he thought of Western civilisation. After a pause for contemplation, he replied that he thought it would be a good thing. I felt something of the same reaction when I was asked to make a 'wild card' contribution to a book dealing with values in higher education. For, in my considered, but admittedly passionate, opinion, it would be no bad thing if values and what I choose to label as 'the affect', were again to figure significantly in higher education.

I will argue the case for that view in this chapter, and will do so by posing, and suggesting answers to, six questions which feature as my alternative titles for the formally titled sections which follow. These questions are:

• What do I mean by the affect?
• Has teaching for the development of values been neglected in recent years?

• How much does it matter nowadays to feature values in higher education?

• How much does dialogue contribute to the purposeful development of values?

• How can teachers help learners to develop their own considered and reasoned values?

• What do these questions and answers imply for readers, and writers, of this text?

Defining 'affect'

I follow my ageing *Concise Oxford Dictionary* (1982). This tells me that 'affect' is a noun in psychological use, meaning *'feeling, emotion, desire, esp. as leading to action'*. Hence, in an educational context, I take the affective domain to refer to those learning activities, objectives and outcomes which centre upon feelings, emotions, desires or, as an amplification of the last of these, values.

A student nurse engages with affective matters when he has had occasion to disagree with a decision made by a consultant, with which he has had to concur; and when, in later reflection upon such critical incidents in his placement experience, he wishes to work out what he should have done – and why. A teacher who strives to persuade her students of the merits of ring composition in Homeric poetry, as a feature of the oral tradition, is pursuing an affective learning goal in so doing. A tutor who senses that one of his students is fearful about the possibility of making serious mistakes on the computer, engages with affective outcomes in making the overcoming of this fear a priority goal for his learning support, when that student aspires to obtain the European Computer Driving Licence. A congregational member, reading the preface to a new hymn book and noticing that references to battles and victory have been purged because they are no longer deemed to be politically correct, engages with an affective issue when she explores the validity of her belief that she has herself engaged in many battles in which no blood was shed or weapons of war brandished, and that she has on occasions won victories – over prejudice, racial discrimination and her own weaknesses.

The affective domain in education is, then, that part of educational practice, theory and goals which concerns itself with feelings, values, emotions, and the sound handling of these in a mature, defensible and purposeful manner – aims whose choice and review, of course, themselves call for reasoning and thinking in the affective domain. Thus, I differentiate education within and concerning the affective domain, with affective outcomes in mind, from the recently popularised focus on 'Emotional Intelligence', which has the worthy but distinct goal of raising self-awareness of emotions, and the handling of them in self and others.[261]

The atrophy of the affect *or* Has teaching for the development of values been neglected in recent years?

In 1956, Bloom and colleagues published a taxonomy of educational objectives in the *cognitive* domain.[262] This excited great interest, and rapidly became a success. It has been much used, much quoted, and (even when criticised) has earned and enjoyed an enduring place in the educational literature.[263] However the prompt attempt to follow this up with a similar taxonomy of affective objectives immediately ran into considerable and well documented problems.[264] These writers cited several causes for what they described as the 'erosion of affective objectives' from curricula. The reasons they identified included lack of wish or willingness to assess or evaluate the achievement of affective objectives; and the declaration of objections in principle to contravening the democratic right of individuals to formulate, and to retain in privacy, their own beliefs. The latter recalls Newman's advice to Mrs Froude (1848) that 'We can believe what we choose. We are answerable for what we choose to believe.'[265] However, it places rather more stress on the first than on the second part of that standpoint.

Be that as it may, atrophy of deliberate activity regarding the affective domain is indeed still evident in higher education, 40 years later. I assert here that this is so – while recognising that the *absence* of anything is more difficult to demonstrate than its existence. With that in mind, I consulted those books on my shelves which are often included in the reading lists for educational methods courses offered nowadays in the UK to lecturers on probation. From a sample of nine such texts, I found that seven made no mention in their index of the affective domain. These are (in order of apparent popularity) – Ramsden, Biggs, Ketteridge et al., Bligh, Brookfield, Rowland, and Knight.[266] Of the remaining two, one (MacDonald) offered only the one-sentence aside that 'Bristol women reported that the learning group afforded the opportunity to share struggles in learning with others, (especially women), to confront crises of identity, to develop confidence and to link affective and cognitive learning.'[267] Even in this particular programme, it seems that affective outcomes had hardly been afforded much attention in planning, teaching, assessment or evaluation.

In the ninth text, and in the writings of the ever-scholarly and comprehensive Heywood, I found acknowledgement of the failure of the taxonomy by Krathwohl et al., and mention of a subsequent, 'relatively unknown', but perhaps more usable, taxonomy by Kaplan, of which more later.[268] Yet even Heywood, who is meticulous in directing his readers towards examples of good and stimulating practice, could quote only one exemplar. This was the innovative and extremely unusual curriculum of Alverno College, where the importance of the affective domain in education for personal growth has long been well appreciated.[269]

Unlike Newman,[270] who had a holistic view of values education, and simply assumed that this will happen for a student, if the university arranges appropriate collegial experiences, the Alverno approach goes further. It maintains that, if you wish a student to have a commitment to the values inherent in the curriculum, then you must do something – formally – about it. Such formal efforts are rare today. There are some who have devoted attention to methodologies for moral education and training for citizenship, mainly in schools.[271] At university level, and in the context of ethics and philosophy, the lone voice of Collier has reported valuable thinking and practice.[272] Recently Barnett, probably the foremost authority on the purpose of higher education in the UK, has written about communicating values.[273] Perhaps higher education is awakening to the importance of the affective domain?

Nevertheless I submit with respect, which as usual means the opposite, that relatively little has happened in these 40 years in higher education to advance the teaching, assessment and evaluation of affective outcomes. As in 1964, there still seems no 'systematic effort to collect evidence of growth in affective objectives', whether for the purpose of assessment of the students, or evaluation of the programme.[274]

The present importance of affective outcomes and capabilities *or* How much does it matter nowadays to feature values in higher education?

162

The first reason for learners and teachers to engage thoroughly with affective outcomes and capabilities is probably their historical place in the disciplines which constitute higher education.

We have long provided education in areas such as the performing arts, where values feature centrally in goals, desired outcomes and teaching methods. We nowadays offer education in areas such as the caring professions, where values in respect of patient care feature strongly. Even in our heavily cognitive subjects, all judgements made at the highest level on the Bloom Scale must be assembled by setting characteristics of performance or of product against criteria which reflect disciplinary or personal values – which are thus far from private matters. Hence, certain values are an explicit part of each of the disciplines we study and practice, since they are used in critical appraisal and especially in self-appraisal. Consequently disregard of the affective domain can scarcely be justified by the oft-argued need to respect the individual's democratic right to regard their beliefs and values as a private matter, into which neither education nor any other agency should seek to intrude.

It will often, of course, be argued that an *apparent* and almost hypocritical profession of adherence to values can seldom be differentiated from genuine belief in the underlying principles. But in response it can be equally argued that the formulation and explanation of such lip-service, as soon as it moves beyond routine and well-drilled behaviour, calls for at least an understanding of the complexities of the values to which the lip-server strives to be seen to adhere, even if not to embrace.

A second, and more immediate, reason for educational engagement with the affective domain stems from the current social and educational situation. In 1980, the *Education for Capability Manifesto* was published.[275] This document was signed by over 200 prominent personalities of the time, most coming from outwith academia. They professed themselves perturbed by what they saw as the disregarded need for education to prepare people 'for a life outside the educational system'. They stressed the need for learners to 'improve their **Competence**;… to **Cope** better with their own lives and the problems that confront them and society; to develop their **Creative abilities**; and, above all, to **Co-operate** with other people.'

Amongst the criteria *(sic)* which the Committee believed and stated should underlie any programme designed to provide this 'Education for Capability', was one that stated, 'Learners are encouraged to get on with other people and to initiate and engage in co-operative activity'. This recommendation is, of course, in accordance with a finding, some ten years earlier, about the importance of interpersonal capabilities for engineering graduates. This was reported in a paper of which I am afraid I have kept no record, other than in my memory. The writers described research to the effect that, while engineers on graduating would spend 70 per cent of their working time communicating with other people, their degree and training programmes, on the whole, would have devoted none of their time to developing the necessary interpersonal abilities.

I turn to the neglected taxonomy by Kaplan, part of which I have paraphrased in the appendix to this chapter.[276] I find it difficult to conceive how someone can engage in co-operation – as the Manifesto (to which I was admittedly a signatory) defines and encourages that behaviour – without displaying and probably developing to a considerable extent, some of the items on my selection from Kaplan's taxonomy for the affective domain. Society would surely expect graduates to be able to:

• Openly defend the right of another to possess a value.
• Seek the value of another.
• Attempt to identify the characteristics of a value or value system.
• Clearly express a value.
• Compare one's own value to that of another.
• Attempt to identify the characteristics of a value or value system.
• Show the relationship of one value to another.
• Try to convince another to accept a value.

A third argument for the importance of values (which I have already mentioned) centres on their vital role in the making of all judgements, whatever the discipline and including cognitive judgements.

Defensible judgements cannot be made in any discipline without comparing performance to accepted, predetermined criteria; and there is no situation where the choice of these criteria is not in itself a value judgement, made by people. For example, there have been striking changes over the past thirty years or so in the syllabuses for Geography (in schools) and Technology (in the Open University). These have not come about solely, or even principally, because of the advance of knowledge. Rather have they occurred because of overt and developing agreement amongst bodies of teachers, in which women were increasingly represented, that the values which underlay the design of curricula in the past should be abandoned, or at least radically modified.

The role of social constructivism in education for the affective domain *or* How much does dialogue contribute to the purposeful development of values?

I confess to encountering a semantic problem (in this section especially) in that experts dealing with issues in higher education may write variously of abilities or capabilities or skills or competences. For my part, I shall try to adhere to the term 'capabilities'. I will (almost) adopt the standpoint of Humpty Dumpty, who in *Through the Looking Glass* maintained arrogantly that 'When I use a word, it means just what I choose it to mean, neither more nor less.'[277] I hope my readers will permit me to take a capability as my *Oxford Dictionary* does, as a 'power to do something'.

With the advent of information technology, the past half century has seen a striking change in education. Today's graduates emerge into a world where most of the tasks which were undertaken by their predecessors as human operatives are now carried out more effectively, more economically, and often more creatively, by computers. Even medical diagnosis has succumbed to this technological takeover, as many papers will testify.[278] In consequence, graduates today and tomorrow face three types of high-level demand. First, they must concentrate their education and training towards the higher end of the (admittedly cognitive) taxonomy, which nevertheless centres there on capabilities; secondly, they must develop interpersonal capabilities in what Romiszowski[279] tellingly called 'the missing domain'; and, finally, they must prepare themselves with capabilities adequate to enable them to take full charge of their ensuing personal and professional development, of which much will be demanded during their lifetime in a rapidly changing environment.

Capabilities are certainly not developed because they are passed from teacher to student, like a parcel of accrued wisdom. Yet, until now, it has been assumed, perhaps implicitly, that development of capabilities will occur through either osmosis or serendipity. However, we know that they are rather more effectively developed through a constructivist experience. This approach (Fig. 1, p. 175), following a model ascribed to Kolb,[280] sets out to develop capabilities purposefully. The teacher structures activities in which the learner reflects upon relevant experiences, generalises therefrom, and should then plan to actively experiment with, and test, each generalisation in the next similar experiences which are encountered. Teachers who have structured constructivist activity for their learners in this way, myself included, have reported evaluations showing worthwhile successes.[281]

Nevertheless issues of educational effectiveness, and of cost-effectiveness, are increasingly prompting innovative academics to move on from relying simply on constructivist learning and development, to explore the potential of social constructivism. Herein there is explicit and purposeful recognition of the undoubted role of others, and especially of peers, in learning and development. Thus all are, as learners together, drawn more and more out into what Vygotsky has called their Zone of Proximal Development (ZPD).[282] The ZPD is that area of achievement which is within a learner's potential, but which the learner will only realise when nudged forward, facilitatively, beyond what they can manage on their own.

In this model (Fig. 2, p. 176), interaction with peers, structured in different ways at different parts of the cycle, facilitatively enhances the effectiveness of the process for learners. Yet such interactions with our peers call for conversations and discussions. In these, differences in their and our value frameworks become apparent, should be appreciated by all concerned, should be explored objectively and should be catered for in a productive manner. All of these are demanding the exercise (and development) of capabilities, often affective or partly so. Consequently there is a further and growing need to concentrate on the capabilities in the affective domain, on which we will inherently depend during such social constructivist interactions in which effective dialogue will be vital.

Facilitative teaching for affective outcomes *or* How can teachers help learners to develop their own considered and reasoned values?

I have defined teaching elsewhere as 'The purposeful creation of situations from which motivated learners should not be able to escape, without learning or developing.'[283] I differentiate, then, between the undoubtedly worthwhile learning and development which often happens outwith the context of education; and that which ensues as a consequence of a purposeful effort by a 'teaching person'. I will also concentrate here on 'teaching' in pursuit of higher level outcomes, for which instruction and didactic methods are inappropriate.[284]

Around the time I entered academia as a university teacher, Rogers had published a book which advocated *Freedom to Learn*.[285] This was tellingly sub-titled 'A view of what education might become'. For many teachers, myself included, this book was a rallying call to embrace a different set of values for education. Rogers set out to promote an approach in total contrast to the behaviourism favoured by such as Skinner.[286] Rather was it based upon the principles which had served Rogers well as a counsellor, before equally serving him and others, in various capacities including teaching. He forcefully advocated three essential conditions for facilitative teaching – empathy, unconditional positive regard and congruence – of which more later.

Some 20 years later, Rogers published a book under much the same title,[287] but now analysing the successes which so many of his disciples had convincingly reported to him. By following Rogers' three principles, then, we have known for 20 years or more that the facilitative teacher can provide, not instruction, but 'scaffolding' – with whose support each constructivist learner reaches further forward into their Zone of Proximal Development than they could otherwise have managed.

In addressing the question posed in my sub-title for this section, I now venture into territory for which I have no authority, in the form of papers or textbooks written by others, although I acknowledge that Collier outlines an approach similar to what follows.[288] Otherwise I draw merely on my own experiences, and invite you to test *your* own experiences against the conclusions which I tentatively draw.

From the successes of the examples I will describe (and failures of others of similar form), I have formed the view that:

1. The purposeful transfer of values usually depends on the creation of a bridge of a meaningful relationship between teacher and learner, across which values can be exchanged, declared, described and discussed.

2. In such a relationship, it is vital that the person from whom a value or belief is acquired is someone who is respected and valued by the person assimilating and possibly (but not inevitably) then accepting the value or belief.

This view I invite you to test out, first in four personal examples.

Example 1: As an undergraduate, I was taught mathematics by someone

I regarded as a very gentle gentleman. On occasion, and without being tedious about it, he was ready to explain to any of his somewhat stolid engineering class why he found joy in his mathematics. Sometimes I would ask him questions after class, and he would patiently explain to me, for example, why he valued elegance in a mathematical proof. First he had to explain and I had to understand what he meant by elegance, and then why he valued it. And so it was that I gradually came to value elegance myself, as part of the lifelong joy in the study of mathematics with which he infected me. These important affective learning outcomes, for me, came about through a relationship in which a teacher whom I came to respect deeply was willing to declare, explain and discuss values which mattered to him, and which, through that relationship, came to matter to me.

Example 2: Over a period of three years or so, I worked intermittently on curriculum development projects in Saudi Arabia, One of my collaborators was a devout Turkish Muslim, with whom I grew quite close. I taught on some of his surveying classes, and he came to many of the events which I and my colleague arranged. Often Baha and I discussed how we should tackle learning and teaching challenges, and why. Quite naturally, this entailed declaring and explaining the values on which we each hoped our teaching and teaching practices were founded. Some of these values were disciplinary and secular; some, for both of us, stemmed from religious beliefs. From Baha, I learnt to respect, but certainly not adopt, his intense Islamic stress on the importance of taking important steps right foot first. This would lead him to reject any measurement taken by a student surveyor who did not set off on the right foot, as he and his partner 'chained' a distance, marking out one hundred-foot chain length after another from the starting point to the end point. From Baha, in addition, I learnt both to respect *and* to assimilate, many approaches to what I would call 'loving your neighbour', in which I found the Muslim faith to be subtly more demanding than the Christian one, into which I had been recruited as an adult. I have never forgotten what I learnt from and with Baha, and hope that it has enriched my own value framework. Across the bridge which was central to our working relationship, a fine man whom I came to respect enormously for his staunch adherence to his principles declared his values. He explained them and their implications to me, and helped me to 'try them on', and to find over time that many of them fitted me more comfortably than their predecessors.

Example 3: As a practising structural engineer, I cared intensely about anticipating and avoiding danger on construction sites, and did so long before legislation attempted to prescribe safety. At first I would declare this value to my classes – with little apparent effect; I soon came to the conclusion that I might as well save my breath to cool my porridge. So I changed my tactics. I tried to make my point to my students by telling two rather gruesome stories from my own site experience. On each occasion, it had greatly disturbed me that, when I went to bed, I was still hearing a man's screams in my ears, and still not knowing if it was I who had been responsible for that anguish. [Fortunately for my peace of mind, I later learnt that each of the injured men was responsible for his own injury.] I presented the cases, and my reactions, before I found out where responsibility lay. I suggested that my students should do all that they could, when *they* went on site, to anticipate and avoid danger to others as well as themselves. In so doing, I would finish by simply expressing the wish that *they* would never have the experience of going to bed, still with a memory of screams for which they might have been responsible. I tried to build upon, but not exploit, what I saw as an established relationship, in which my students had come to trust me. I hope I passed across that bridge for consideration, a value which mattered to me, by declaring it, and my reasons for holding it, in a relationship within which students could question, and discuss. Some students would talk to me or write to me confirming that they had come to share my concern – weeks, months and even years after.

Example 4: I became a university teacher in 1964, and gave myself five years to do a better job than most of those who had been my teachers (other than in mathematics!) In 1969 I was far from satisfied with my performance, but anxious to justify my continuing in a job which I had come to love. I was attracted by the publicity for a course at UMIST for university teachers. It was to be run by a certain Professor Bill Morton, who puzzled me by asking us to accept the condition that, while we were resident for a fortnight in Manchester, we were to have no engagements outwith the course.

For Bill Morton, supporting worthwhile student learning was what a teacher in higher education should be concentrating upon. He was a man whom I would describe as an educational evangelist. He wanted to convert people like me, to take our emphasis away from trying to teach well, to concentrate instead on how and what our students would learn. But he never preached to us, or at us. In our two weeks together, he created a little community – in which we worked, where visiting teachers taught, to which very assorted visitors came to speak to us after dinner and discuss their experiences with us. All the while Bill lived in with us, and spent lots of time with us, as we digested the experiences of each day, and then of each week, in informal discussions.

A massive shift in my values, which has since endured and has been refined over the ensuing 45 years, came about in the context of a very special relationship. It was a relationship with someone whom I had quickly come to value for himself as well as for his achievements, someone who tabled his values and principles, and answered our questions about them – but who first painstakingly and with sincere interest listened to *our* values and views, and engaged in ever-deepening discussions in which he never attempted to indoctrinate us. He explored with us the value which most of us at that time put on trying to instruct as effectively as was within our power; and he allowed us in turn to explore his own values. He carried the conversation into consideration of the implications of applying both sets of values. And he left us to decide what value framework we would work within, thereafter. These exchanges, which brought such a change in my teaching and the values on which it was based thereafter, took place without Bill being regarded as, or feeling himself to be, an expert with a message to pass on. I was far from the only member of that group to return home, determined to tear up my old lecture notes, to stop concentrating on my teaching and to focus instead upon on supporting student learning. This came about within a collegial relationship in which the discussion and informing took place as between peers, albeit peers with different experiences and outcomes to share. Bill Morton, and his style with us, exemplified the perceptive analysis by Rogers of 'Realness in the facilitation of learning', in which prizing, acceptance and trust in the teacher feature importantly.[289]

My examples, you will note, have taken us somewhat beyond Rogers' three original basic principles,[290] which have subsequently been helpfully illustrated by McGill and Beaty.[291] Nevertheless these principles are, I suggest, our best starting point from which to answer my subtitled question: 'How can teachers help learners to develop their own considered and reasoned values?'

The first quality, empathy, is intellectual or emotional identification with another. We display empathy when we understand (or show that we are wishing to understand) the position, values, circumstances and emotional state of others – as does a Christian who is willing to understand what matters to a Muslim colleague, and why; or as does an experienced teacher who takes time to explore the standpoint of a young teacher who thinks in terms of teaching rather than learning.

Rogers, in an extensive set of statements about empathy, included such helpful phrases as:

'...entering the private perceptual world of the other and becoming thoroughly at home in it...

'...being sensitive, moment to moment, to the changing felt meanings which flow in the other person...

'...frequently checking with him/her as to the accuracy of your sensings, and being guided by the responses you receive.'[292]

Rogers' second quality is unconditional positive regard. This goes beyond empathy, in that it entails wholehearted acceptance that a learner's questions and aspirations, however difficult to locate relative to the immediate learning task, are genuinely of importance to that learner. According to McGill and Beaty, it is...

'...a non-possessive caring for the learner, an attitude which believes fundamentally that the other person is trustworthy and worth caring for. It accepts the feelings of the other person as relevant to their learning.'[293]

My teacher of mathematics displayed unconditional positive regard for the naïve position from which my questions to him arose. I hope I had unconditional positive regard for the slight concern which my students displayed for safety on construction sites.

Rogers' third quality is congruence, which entails matching ourselves up with the other person. Bill Morton displayed congruence when, in his discussions with us, he recalled a time when he himself had held the views we were expressing. Rogers talks of congruence in these terms: 'There is a close matching, or congruence, between what is being experienced at the gut level, what is present in awareness, and what is expressed.'[294]

I now offer a combined example, in which all three qualities were, I hope, displayed:

Example 5: Some years ago, within a personal development planning module, I required my engineering students to set and work to their own worthwhile educational objectives, criteria, assessment scheme and study plan. Three students of Chinese extraction, newly arrived from Singapore, called at my staffroom, to speak with me. They approached me formally, with a spokesperson. They brought me the news that, coming from the directive educational culture they had experienced, they had chosen as their aim for personal development, to learn to be self-directed learners. I enthused. 'How will you do that?' I asked. Their spokesman replied 'We would like you to teach us to be self-directed'.

I found little difficulty empathising with their aim. In this case, empathy entailed having an understanding on my part of the world as these students saw it, and trying to communicate to them my understanding of their feelings, experiences and behaviour. I found I could summarise to their satisfaction their reasons for setting a high priority on adjusting to studying in a department with a powerfully learner-directed ethos learner-centred learning, coming as they did from what I knew of their prior experience in Singapore, as they had described it and as they now perceived it. We could begin from a shared standpoint. I believe I also showed an unconditional positive regard in identifying with these students' decision to begin on their search by what might occur to some of my colleagues as the nonsense of being taught to be self-directed learners. We thus not only began from a shared standpoint, but continued with a purpose to which we all subscribed.

I then tried hard to be the true me, in a congruent manner, while tackling the Singaporean remit, which I would certainly not have chosen for myself. My memory of the experience at UMIST, which had led to such a value shift in my own case, played a big part here. I discussed the dichotomy with the trio. We considered ways of resolving it. Eventually, we negotiated an arrangement in which I would 'teach', as they called it, for half of the time; this on the condition that they would take charge, as best they could, for the other half, and try then to work out how to direct their own learning. Thereafter, I did not quite operate in the somewhat reactively facilitative manner of the counsellor or the classical Rogerian teacher. I went rather beyond that, into the somewhat collegial relationship which I had learnt from Bill Morton, and of which I did not find Rogers writing, until much later.[295]

My 'teaching' therefore took the form of a number of small seminars, in which together we explored the students' values and mine, and their implications and outcomes. We did not overtly compare. After some twelve weekly meetings, their spokesperson approached me to report, in a delightfully courteous manner, that 'We do not think we need your assistance any longer, Professor Cowan. We feel we are now ready to take charge of our own further development as self-directed learners.'

Notice, in relation to my assertions earlier in this chapter, that teacher and students had entered into a relationship of mutual respect, a relationship which depended upon the construction of a metaphorical bridge between them. Across this bridge, values and aspirations were volunteered from each side to the other, being declared, explored and discussed. Rogerian principles featured throughout this relationship – but in many ways it had moved from the counselling to the collegial style. I did not merely facilitate their development; I offered contributions to that process, which came from my own experience and knowledge, in a relationship in which the discussion and informing took place as between peers, albeit peers with different experiences and outcomes to share. It certainly seemed to achieve the desired outcome. One student wrote, years later, and described to me how, with some difficulty at times, he had remained a self-directing learner on his return to the East.

The consequent challenges for us all *or* What do these questions and answers imply for readers, and writers, of this text?

It is often said that any fool can ask a question which it takes a wise man *(sic)* to answer. So I feel it behoves me, in response to my invitation to provide a wild card contribution, to pose a few closing questions which focus on the challenges we should all be facing – readers of this volume as well as writers, myself included:

• Is it reasonable to be concerned that we have neglected the affective domain in our scholarship, curricula, learning, teaching, assessment and evaluation?

• Do we take our value frameworks for granted? Are we unduly reluctant to reconsider them?

• Have we an adequate basis, in academic disciplines and in matters of spiritual faith, for the rigorous questioning, review and development of our thinking about values and the handling of them, at a higher level in the affective taxonomy? If so, do we make sufficient use of it?

• Do we have an adequate pedagogy, upon which we can found our attempts to share our values with others, in the hope that they will choose to sign up to them? Is it based upon sound theory and proven practice? Do we put it to good use?

• Can we continue to endure the atrophy of the affective domain in our scholarship, curricula, teaching, assessment and evaluation? Should this issue become a top priority for us?

I ask these questions in the context of what I trust is a collegial relationship, with those readers who have remained with me to this point. I leave you to decide what your answers to these questions suggest to you. I take it that my own answers can be discerned within or between the lines of this chapter.

Appendix: Extracts from Kaplan's taxonomy of affective behavior for the classroom.

3.00 Valuing
3.10 Preference for a Value
25. Seeks the value of another
26. Defends value of another
27. Clearly expresses a value
28. Defends own value
29. Openly defends the right of another to possess value
30. Tries to convince another to accept a value
31. Agrees with value of another
32. Disagrees with value of another
4.00 Organization
4.10 Conceptualization of a Value
33. Makes deductions from abstractions
34. Makes judgements (implies evaluation)
35. Compares own value with that of another
36. Attempts to identify the characteristics of a value or value system
4.20 Organization of a Value System
37. Compares and weighs alternatives
38. Shows relationship of one value to another
39. Ties a specific value into a system of values
40. Synthesizes two or more values into one value
5.00 Characterization by a value or value complex
5.10 Generalized set

41. Revises judgements based on evidence
42. Bases judgements on consideration of more than one proposal
43. Makes judgements in light of situational context

Fig. 1

**Current
pedagogy**

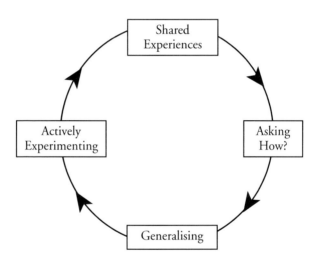

Fig. 2

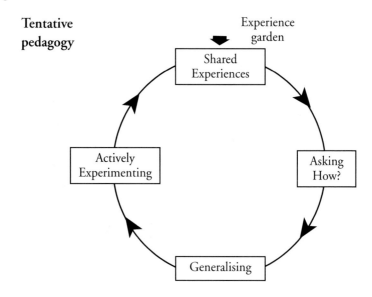

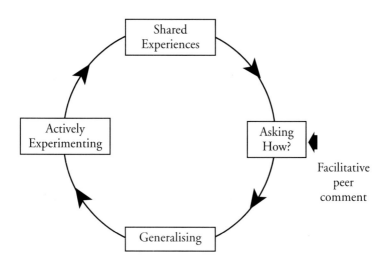

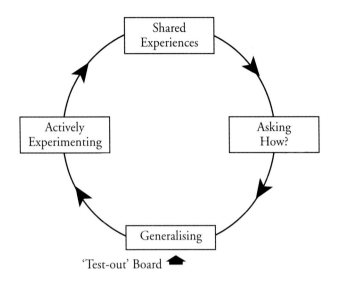

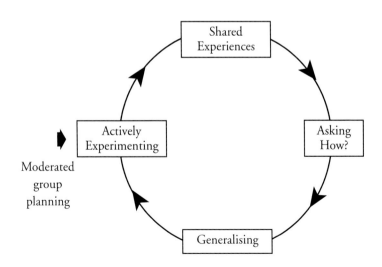

13

Values and student support

Nigel Humphrys

Over the last 20 years there have been seismic changes in the British higher education environment. Indeed, if we look back as far as the Robbins report, the higher educational landscape is barely recognisable. Then only one person in eighteen entered full-time education. In 1962–3 the student body consisted of barely 200,000 students. In the early 1960s women made up only 26 per cent of students in higher education. Mature students only accounted for 41 per cent of the student population. The Dearing Report in the mid-90's described how the numbers of woman students had increased to 51 per cent and mature students to 58 per cent. Dearing also underlined the significant rise in ethnic minority students, with a proportionate representation greater than their share of the general population. Recently the Disability Discrimination Act (DDA) 1995 and the Special Educational Needs and Disability Act (SENDA) 2001 have produced an environmental change that is now more encouraging for disabled students providing them with the basis to compete equally with peers.[296] The recent White Paper has encapsulated these changes and has called for further advancements in addressing the need for higher education to attract students from under-represented groups particularly from lower income families. Indeed the government target of 50 per cent of individuals between 18–30 benefiting from university by 2010 will be largely made up of this group.

The above changes, the widening participation project, and the importance of student retention has given student support an unprecedented national profile, placing the sector at the centre of government and institutional thinking. This is emphasised by a recent UUK (Universities UK) report, on student services and student retention, which states that,

> … these functions (student services), however they are operationalised in particular institutions, should be given a level of priority comparable to other key institutional activities, values – such as research and teaching and learning.[297]

Now clearly the values of, for instance, the University of Leeds, have not fundamentally changed as we are formally committed to critical independence and academic freedom; lifelong learning; inclusion; responsiveness and openness and transparency. However the nature of the student profile has changed and will continue to diversify to meet government targets.

A recent report by The Association for Managers of Student Services in Higher Education (AMOSSHE) for the UUK summarises these changes:

> The significant increase in the proportion of the UK's population, particularly in higher education over the last decade has changed both the nature and the expectations of the student body. Students who might previously have been effectively excluded from higher education by reason of their social and/or ethnic background, their prior educational experience their age, their gender or their health or disability, are now increasingly able to take advantage of the opportunities provided by HEI's. In addition, UKCOSA (the Council for International Education) reports that international students currently make up 11% of the UK higher education population. At the same time, the abolition of maintenance grants, the introduction of fees and the development of a more clearly defined legal framework of rights and responsibilities have raised the expectations of many students in respect of the educational opportunities and pastoral support offered by HEI's.[298]

The final sentence of this statement underlines a major shift in the nature of the relationship between students and their university. It is clear that the payment of fees has created a different legal relationship, which is largely untested, but is likely to be a major source of strategic interest to institutions over the coming decade. There is at least a change in expectation about what may be provided academically and pastorally by universities. The duty of care issue is likely to be placed higher on the agenda of most institutions and legal areas that may be tested could be breach of contract, liability for negligence, standard of care, breadth of statutory duty and judicial review.

179

In light of the above it is not overstating the case to say that student support could become as important as learning and teaching, research and academic services. It is a probability that student support will be at the sharp end of the relationship between the student and the institution offering an 'aftercare' service to an increasingly sophisticated and legally aware consumer.

What this chapter will explore is the value system within which student support operates; the nature of the universities support responsibilities; how support might be structured and organised; and the evolution of support at the University of Leeds.

It could be argued that philosophical thought about values and student affairs has its origins in American universities in the early twentieth century. In 1924, Herbert Hawkes, the first Dean of Men at Columbia University USA, stated that his college 'should educate the whole (student)...the physical, the social, the aesthetic, the religious, the intellectual aspects each in its appropriate manner'.[299]

In 1949 the 'Student Personnel Point of View' stated that the major focus of student affairs practice was 'the development of students as whole persons interacting in social situations'.[300] As Young states, 'This assertion implies the two central values of early student affairs work – individuation and community'.[301] Individuation describes the process by which the individual functioning self is developed. Community is the environment within which this process occurs through social and learning relationships. In essence, the university becomes an organic reflection of its students.[302] Young further suggests that two other related values have come to the fore in recent years, equality and justice. It is no accident that the huge increase in female student numbers between the Robbins Report and Dearing happened at the same time as the women's rights movement of the 70's and 80's. In its train followed increases for other disadvantaged groups, such as ethnic minority students and disabled students via DDA and SENDA. Justice is linked to equality, but is about the institution and is encapsulated in the procedures and practice of the university.

In essence, the value system as described above still underpins the offering of support to a student community that is multicultural, class diverse and broad based.

Clearly any support offered to students by institutions has to be largely appropriate for the university student population as a whole. Furthermore, whilst it is important to ensure that study skills programmes, academic techniques and information are accessible to students coming to universities via the Widening Participation route, it could be argued that all these initiatives are as pertinent to the needs of the 18–21 year old student population.

What institutions need to also guard against is being *in loco parentis*. The payment of fees may change the expectations of students (and parents), but at present university provides a secure and creative place for students to experience and achieve their developmental goals. Services should not try to take responsibility for student problems, but seek to get alongside students to support them through personal, financial, academic, disability, cultural and spiritual concerns. Furedi[303] has been critical of the way universities are supporting students and specifically argues that Counselling Services are pathologising 'everyday' difficulties and not allowing students to use their own resources to overcome difficulties.

If this was happening student services would not be fulfilling their purpose. However, the kinds of clients that counselling services attract are those whose previous history, relationships, bereavements, sexual experiences, eating issues, have led them to have difficulties concentrating on academic work, often compounded by anxiety, depression, suicidal thoughts and other disabling concerns. Chaplaincy will see a wide range of students with religious, spiritual or pastoral needs or problems. The International Student Adviser will see those students whose immigration, cultural and financial issues are usually quite complex and intractable. The financial adviser will see a broad range of students, from those who need budgeting advice to those seeking complex information about benefits and bursaries. Disability Services will often know what support students will require in advance of admission, but will still require an assessment report or carry out an assessment early in the students career. Depending on the disability a student may require, technical and funding advice if they have a learning disability, information re brailing resources or, if the student has a significant physical disability, advice about voluntary help, accommodation and a support plan for the duration of the course. Most students will require information re employment or further study post-degree. A significant proportion of students are likely to have contact with at least one of the support services during their academic career. The crucial work that student services do, however, is to 'facilitate' students facing complex difficulties. To be there to offer specific and professional help if required, but not to take away from students developing their own resources. Ostensibly support services are about helping students, regardless of their physical, economic, social or psychological history, achieve their academic and personal objectives.

AMOSSHE, in the paper *Responding to Mental Health Issues: Duty of care responsibilities for student services in Higher Education,* recently published a set of guidelines advising institutions how to deliver Student Support Services. The guidelines acknowledge that

> the growth of a mass higher education system and wider diversity of the student population has required a refocusing of traditional pastoral support structures.

In the AMOSSHE paper, some telling points are made about how institutions should respond to students with mental health issues, but it also makes some important comments about student services generally. It states that because of the prevailing climate outlined above, that there needs to be a revaluation of what support provision is offered to students. Importantly, boundaries need to be clearly stated, explaining the limitations of the support provided. Any service offered, should be provided with 'reasonable care and skill'. Significantly, the relationship of the student to the university can be seen in contract terms and potential claims for breach of contract may ensue, if information set out in institutional literature is not fulfilled. Claims about provision should be accurate, precise and fulfillable. Referral systems to specialist services in the community should be established. Procedures for students who have to suspend studies should be developed and publicised widely.

The necessary concentration on the legal aspects of duty of care means the emphasis in the AMOSSHE document is inevitably, less on individuation and community and more on equality and justice. The nature of this document, however, underlines the changing nature of the universities contractual relationship to its students. The 'Principles of Good Practice' in the delivery of student support services outlined in the above document, suggest that a balance needs to be kept between the responsibilities of the student, institution and staff, but also mindful of the expectations of community and professional bodies.

How student services are managed differ from institution to institution, sector to sector. I draw this distinction, as a consensus now seems to be emerging about how student services should be co-ordinated and managed. Before 1992 most 'new' universities had a centralised system, usually with a Head/Director of Student Services. The Head would often be responsible for the budgets and co-ordinated the development of policy and professional practice in consultation with service heads. 'Old' universities often had free-standing services, who answered to a Registrar or a Pro-Vice-Chancellor, but were largely self-managed with the Head of Service responsible for policy and practice. It is interesting to note that many 'old' universities are now opting for Heads/Directors/Deans of Student Services (e.g. Cardiff, Liverpool, Newcastle, Royal Holloway, Bath, Hull, York, Nottingham). To complicate matters further, Oxbridge and other college-based universities may deliver certain support services (especially academic and pastoral) at a local level.

Student services as a given entity have been in operation for at least 20 years, yet there is still a sense that the sector is very much (especially in the older universities) in a state of evolution. The sector, however, as is suggested above, seems to be moving towards, centralised, one-stop services under the co-ordination of a single senior manager.

Student Services at the University of Leeds have gone in a different direction, but with many features in common with the models mentioned above. Simon Robinson identifies three key principles that drive the student support services: autonomy, equality and community, echoing the founding values in the USA.[304]

In the first instance, services work towards developing and enhancing the autonomy of the student, as discussed above, ensuring that they develop the resources to make the best of their student experience and achieve individuation. The second principle largely speaks for itself, but services should work towards offering responses that are appropriate to each individual and need. It is the final principle of community-based support that perhaps marks out the Leeds model as being unique in style.

Annie Grant, Director of the Education and Development Support Centre at the University of Leicester, recently stated that:

> we must acknowledge the very significant role that can be, and in many institutions is being played by Personal Tutors, other academic staff, library and computing staff, students' unions, other students and employment and community activities that promote student self-esteem and feelings of self-worth.[305]

In essence this is what we have been trying to do, to engage staff and students in a dialogue about student support and thus integrate these considerations into the centre of the university's thinking.

Prior to 2003 Support Services were co-ordinated by the Student Support Network (SSN) (founded in 1994) at a practitioner level and by the Student Welfare Committee (SWC) (founded in 1995) at a policy level. In 1998 a Dean of Students was appointed to develop an overview of services and provide a link to senior management. Once this link was established, it soon became clear that student affairs needed to be managed at a more strategic level within the university especially as the issues of student retention and widening participation were becoming paramount and the 'Student Experience' needed to be managed. As a result a Pro-Vice-Chancellor for Student Affairs was established.

The membership of the SSN and SWC were combined into a new grouping called the Student Support Committee chaired by the above PVC. It now has full responsibility for policy and practice within the university. The SSN, formally a group of student support practitioners, meanwhile has been extended to include any staff (academic, clerical, administrative), hall wardens, union, with a responsibility for supporting students. Presently the membership is about 150 staff (including staff and sabbaticals from the Leeds University Union). We hope to further extend this by having a representative from every department and service, a probable target figure of 500.

The cement for this network is a mail base, where information is disseminated (e.g. reports, minutes etc.) and discussions take place; lunchtime training sessions on student support issues; two formal business meetings a year and an annual conference at the end of the summer term.

So far the events have been very well attended and a university-wide awareness of student support is starting to emerge. The SSN launch event attracted over 100 staff, training sessions have attracted between 35–40 staff and the annual conference (which has been running for five years) has attracted attendances of over 120 staff. The hope is that the network will mirror the established collegiality of the university and develop in depth discourse about issues that affect all staff and students such as pre-information, course handbooks, induction, referral, service delivery, retention, evaluation and monitoring. There will also be an established forum to discuss the challenges, pitfalls and opportunities of government projects, such as widening participation.

The consultative nature of student services will also become further established, where staff will feel less awkward about seeking advice and guidance about students experiencing problems. One of the first actions of the newly formed network will be a survey of departments, which will seek feedback from management and representatives about services and their practice and ask for suggestions about how practice may be improved.

In short, the new arrangements will provide a fertile environment where ideas will be exchanged, information disseminated and training provided. The ideas that emerge will be passed to the policy and practice committee where responsibility and action will be taken and, if appropriate, funds allocated. The Pro-Vice-Chancellor for Student Affairs with his place on the Strategy Group and links to teaching and learning, will be a crucial facilitative element in this process.

Two other areas the university is seeking to develop are appropriate: communication with students, and liaison with outside agencies to ensure services are not duplicated and referral channels are established. Whilst this project is in its early days the university has sought to establish informational tools that primarily use the internet as a means of communication. Research is presently being undertaken by individual services to see how email and text messaging may be used. Clearly we do not want to establish a caricature of the way students communicate, but at the same time do not want to ignore the media they use.

An example of the way the internet is being used is the Ahead4health website[306] which is a mental health resource, largely set up as a result of the UUK Guidelines (2000). This website offers a series of scenarios detailing student experience in a movie form, definitions of mental health/illness, workbooks and a list of internal and external referral sources. This site has been advertised via a screensaver on university computer clusters. At its peak the site received 25,000 hits a month.

Recently established is a website called Student Personal Development[307] which has centralised all courses, seminars, workshops offered by Student Counselling, Careers, the Union, Disability Services, Chaplaincy, the Skills Centre, Library and Computing. This site is designed to provide an easily accessible resource for students seeking training or support in virtually any area from, how to use the library, CV writing, preparing for exams to coping with loss, anxiety and depression. In its second phase students will be able to know how many spaces are available and register for courses on-line. The hope is that the site will be as useful for staff engaged in working with student progress files, as it is for students themselves. In the first two months of operation the site received 2000 internal hits.

In terms of email, all students received a message from the PVC for Student Affairs at the start of the academic year when first entering their mailboxes. It listed all student support services with website links and the above websites and asked all students to save the message for future reference. Our feedback from the Leeds University Student Union is that this message has been well used and received by students. Whilst it is unlikely that student services will be centralised in the near future, by 2004/5 a one-stop information desk will be established offering basic information and advice as guidance about referral to services.

Liaison with community agencies and the development of external referral routes is another priority for the university. An example of this co-operation is the Group on Student Mental Health issues, set up largely to work with the issues raised in the UUK report. This is an attempt to further extend the notion of community to include external support and provide a close link between the universities and NHS services.

The membership of this group comprises the Head of the Student Counselling Centre (Chair), Leeds Student Medical Practice GP representative, a Consultant Psychiatrist, a member of the Community Mental Health Team, Leeds University Union representatives, Head of the Equality Unit (Disability Services), Academic representatives, Chaplaincy co-ordinator, Uniquol (University Quality of Life Survey) representative, Primary Care Trust Mental Health Worker representative. This cross-sectoral group has been responsible for writing a booklet entitled *Helping Students with Mental Health Difficulties*, which has been given out to all members of staff and published on the Ahead4health website mentioned above. However, the most important aspect of this group is the fact that most of the major players in the field of student mental health citywide, are represented, which enables us to operate and negotiate as a united group.

One of the major areas where we hope this will bear fruit is enacting the recommendations of the recent Royal College of Psychiatrists Report[308] which suggests that where numbers warrant it, NHS Trusts might consider establishing student mental health teams and Primary Care Trusts might consider developing student mental health strategies. There are also recommendations about developing University/NHS networks. Clearly we already have this in place which we hope will ensure joined up services for students.

To summarise, the push within Leeds is to involve as many staff who have responsibility for supporting students in a collaborative network, that works closely with professional practitioners operating at the centre. The hope is that every department, through their representatives, will thus be considering student support as a crucial element in their thinking and policy to meet the current challenges of widening participation and student retention. There have also been attempts to integrate support within the curriculum which has to some extent established an academic importance for the notion of support for staff and students. Attempts have been made to utilise the media available that is currently used by students and finally attempts have been made not to replicate services available within the community, especially the NHS, but build strong links so that the university has a dialogue with important stakeholders and university needs are considered.

The development of thinking in the delivery of student support services has changed hugely over the last 20 years. Also the impact of professional groups, such as AMOSSHE, HUCS (Heads of University Counselling Services), AUCC (Association of University and College Counsellors), AGCAS (Association of Graduate Careers Advisory Services) has been extremely significant in the development of policy papers from groups as diverse as the UUK and the Royal College of Psychiatrists. The changing nature of our student population is likely to push these changes even further. Presently services are usually freestanding and available to the whole student population. The offering of specific services to disabled and international students may be a pointer to the future. It could be that various groups within our communities could ask for similar services. A good example of this already happening is the University of Hull where specific support is now offered to mature students.

McNair, in a DfEE briefing paper, emphasises the view that guidance (used in its broadest sense to include counselling advice, tutoring, careers and informational advice) will become increasingly important and therefore is a need to focus support:

> Expansion (in higher education) in some form is likely to continue and with it a continuing diversification of students, demanding more individualized

responses, precisely as institutions struggle to cope with larger numbers… while a shift towards funding through the learner rather than the institution will force institutions to become more sensitive to the needs of individuals who will be more like clients and less like beneficiaries![309]

Finally the idea of student affairs being heavily engaged in the notion of individuation and community, still holds true to this day. In its various forms, student services help students develop the skills and qualities needed to achieve academic and personal potential. What support services offer is that no matter what the students' concerns and challenges, they can stay at university, work with their concern and complete their course. Whilst student support practitioners in the UK might not have the breadth of responsibility experienced by their American counterparts, particularly in the area of residential life, it is still a primary aim to help the university develop a community where development of the whole person can take place. At Leeds, this aim and responsibility has broadened out through training and networking to move beyond practitioners and include all staff who support students. The hope is that staff are fully aware of and connected to support services and build appropriate support structures within their own departments.

Equality and justice are major driving forces in the provision particularly of targeted support services. Also increasingly students and the requirements of the law are pushing universities to explicitly state their position in terms of equal opportunities policies, provision for disabled students, and mental health policies. Higher expectations resulting from fees and the intense pressure of the market place will place student support at the forefront of an institution's relationship with its students, especially in an increasing litigious atmosphere.

Student support services can no longer be seen as being on the margins of the institution, but operate at its centre, interacting with students, staff and managers to develop policy and create a dynamic and challenging learning community.

14

Diversity, values and international students in higher education

Clement Katulushi

Introduction

There are as many universities as you can wag a finger at! Universities are certainly a world-wide phenomenon. Almost every country has either at least a university or an institution of higher education. *The World Higher Education Database*, complied by the International Association of Universities (IAU), lists close to 9,200 university level institutions from 184 countries, plus a further 8,000 university-level institutions of higher education. Thus there are more than 17,000 higher education institutions worldwide, offering an array of some 2,000 degrees and diplomas. Numbers fluctuate from country to country. Zambia has only two universities whereas in the United Kingdom alone, there are over 171 universities and non-university institutions of higher education.

In literally every country in the world today, there are graduates working or in the service of their country in some way. Scholars of globalization are pointing at possible implications regarding the role of universities in general, and how they relate and inform the values and practices of a global community. Indeed, the IAU, in their introduction on the subject, argues that globalization influences many dimensions of higher education such as quality assurance, accreditation and the recognition of qualifications – especially when qualifications are earned through transnational education.[310] Just as there are many universities the world over, and many ideas, both new and old, about what universities are and what higher education is, the idea of a global community in higher education is not one that can be encapsulated in any single argument. To do so is to restrict its global nature, but to fail to try to do so is itself not in the spirit of higher education. It is with this in mind that the values of international students, the global community, and higher education are debated.

In this chapter, I will explore the relationship between the global community and higher education on the one hand, and the values of international students within the community of scholars on the other. I will focus on an appreciation of diversity as central to the substance of university communities. I will argue that higher education in general and universities in particular, have a duty over and above any one notion of community, that they are communities in constant redefinition according to the demands of an ongoing and continuous pursuit of knowledge, and ways of knowing, and a 'being-ness' in the post-millennium world. My argument accepts the challenge of change but appreciates those standards which seek to transcend their own limits. From the outset, I want to present the premise that diversity is a crucial element of higher education, that a university is not too big as not to be informed by its local setting – the values and cultures therein – nor can it be too small as not to benefit from engagement with the global community, and be informed and inform the values and cultures thereof.

> *As a South African international student in his first year of a Masters degree in Education, Zulu spent some time adjusting to life in a new city, trying to understand a new culture as well as getting used to life without his family, relatives and friends. He was also spending some time in the Education department, going through material which lecturers had marked as essential reading. His life was experiencing an upheaval of changes, besides the mass of handouts issued by lecturers and other staff, bar the numerous fliers from all sorts of officials, nobody was quite sure what his needs were and who was going to help him meet them.*
> *Zulu's subject seemed dull, boring, except when he was doing the core module and the other two modules which he had chosen. His core*

module seemed linked to his professional interests in South Africa. It was related to curriculum development in an emergent democracy, education and the Anti-Apartheid Movement, and one topic was concerned with development of girls' education. This module was the basis of his work in the re-structured Ministry of Education back home and merited more time than other modules.

Zulu's dissertation supervisor on education sector management, Dr Whiz Shortfoot, was full of enthusiasm. 'Think of a doing a Ph.D. next year – there must be something exciting you can contribute to education in South Africa', he said.

Widening participation

The debate on the UK government's intentions to widen participation by facilitating and enabling a greater range of students to access higher education cannot be fully complete without considering the admission, place, and role of international students. In its broadest sense, widening participation includes the attraction, recruitment, involvement and retention of students from all over the world. It should not only attempt to engage with those students outside the élite circle of powerful and wealthy parents but attract those to whom the opportunity for higher education is denied by reason of funding. This requires new measures, new initiatives and refreshing of existing ones to include widening participation. The nature and diversity of global communities invites global cooperation. This is unavoidable because student mobility either online or across continents, continues to be a core means of cultural education.

Nevertheless, international students form a critical part of institutions of higher education in the UK. Indeed it is inconceivable to think of the British university as completely devoid of some international presence or link either through its staff and students or in its reputation and resources. According to Warwick, 'In 1997/98 the UK attracted 209,000 international students to study in the UK'.[311] The desire for any university to attain accolades such as first-class world status is undeniably intended to convey an impression of high standards in learning, teaching and research quality. There are perpetual pecuniary initiatives which influence and sometimes determine the place of international students in higher education. For example, government guidelines have cut funding to research departments rated 4 in the 2001 research assessment exercise and deemed to be doing research of national but not international excellence.[312] Thus in order to survive, higher education in general and universities in particular need to perform at a world stage, for very high stakes indeed. To enhance such performance, it is increasingly imperative for universities to strive for global cooperation.

However, how does a university conclude that it is offering a higher education of international repute? How can a university be said to be enjoying first-class status? Whereas secondary schools have been pitted against each other through a system of league tables, for universities at an international level, benchmarking seems to be the means towards achievement. Student perceptions, scholarly citations, research and even the availability of resources and facilities may contribute to the acquisition of such a status, if so desirable. Often, it is the case that the presence of a culture, both of learning and the range and diversity of its clientele, informs the identity of a university, and attest to its standards, world-class or otherwise. The world's oldest continually existing institution of higher learning, Al-Azhar University, at Cairo in Egypt, founded in AD 970 as a school of Islamic studies, is as much a part of Muslim heritage as it is of a culture of learning. Makerere University in Uganda, once one of the most prestigious and historically significant universities in Africa, was a place for presidents and kings. Makerere, the Luganda for 'the place where dawn breaks', still evokes affection in its former students. Today, that affection is tinged with sadness and grumbles as newer universities challenge its place. At stake here is the reputation of the university as embodying learning and diversity. Partly, this is the trail left by its one-time Chancellor, the illiterate dictator General Idi Amin Dada.

Without doubt, most universities see themselves as part of a global community, or at least, strive to achieve standards and offer services, recognisable at a global level. Thus, for example, for the University of Manchester:

> The vision for the University of Manchester is to be one of the finest universities in the world. The University will be the largest in the UK and will have teaching and research in more subjects than any other single-site British university. Our vision is the creation of a twenty-first-century university that will become the preferred destination for the best students, teachers, researchers and scholars in the world.[313]

The University of Manchester boasts more than 3,000 academic and research staff, many with international reputations in their subjects and an exceptional record of generating and sharing new ideas and for producing graduates who are always in demand from the world's top employers. Size seems to matter and perhaps serves to assert a higher education institution's global aspirations.

Diversities of international students

An important aspect of higher education, in both its historical settings as well as future make-up is the presence of international students. The term 'international student' needs unpacking. In British universities, a distinction is made between various categories of students using a 'fees' criterion. According to Seddon, international students 'usually have to pay full-cost fees for their courses, often amounting to several thousand pounds'.[314] Thus home students are students, generally British nationals, whose fees are subsidised or paid in part by the tax-payer. However, this is not a blurred criterion since non-British nationals may qualify to pay the 'home student' rate if they meet a certain criterion. For example, a non-British national living in Britain whose initial purpose of entry into Britain was for a purpose other than education, may qualify after three years, to pay upon admission fees at the 'home student' rate. Also, students coming from EU member countries may or may not be considered as international students. This is a factor created by political developments in which moves towards greater European integration and unity challenges national identities.

Some students coming from outside the European Union and commonwealth countries are required after the first few weeks of arrival in the UK to fill out an alien registration form. This requirement is reminiscent of the Alien Act 1905 passed primarily to prevent refugees seeking refuge in Britain. By 'aliens' was meant people who were not from any part of the British Empire.[315] However, use of the term 'aliens' does not imply that such students hail from outer space! In fact, it is perhaps politically incorrect to refer to international students as aliens, although it is puzzling that this term still appears on official stationery. Another popular term is 'overseas students' which connotes in a sense the explorer who has come from far-flung places, crossing the seas in search of the best of British learning. Thus by nationality and not necessarily the fees determination, 'international students' is a term encompassing a broad diversity of students for whom the country in which they pursue their studies is not their native or 'home' country.

Within British universities, international students may also be identified by other factors including whether or not they qualify for 'home student' fees. Where international students are required to pay full fees, UKCOSA has consistently worked towards the establishment of a coordinated, positive and coherent policy on overseas students and lamented the omission of overseas students in earlier major strategic policy documents in higher education.[316]

Recent changes in visa requirements have highlighted again the precarious status of international students in the UK. The UK government's introduction of a fee for visa extensions for international students indicates the economic realities which international students often have to face. It is not far off the mark to assume that these students are seen as contributing little to the UK's intellectual base, indeed, the value of their knowledge is worthless, assuming worth only 'by being put in a context'.[317] The ability to pay consequently means that well-funded international students can study anything they wish as long as the value(s) set they have established is met. For those international students on Spartan budgets, it is more often the case that other factors and interests may have to be considered. In the 1972 debate marking the requirement for international students to pay full-course fees, it was a view in some quarters of the British government that international students were a burden to the tax-payer, that students from countries such as Iran and Nigeria, and similar 'outer space' did not benefit Britain in any way. However, the payment of fees is as contentious in the UK as elsewhere. Only recently in 2004, university students in Malawi fought running battles with the police on the subject. In Zambia, the Copperbelt University and the University of Zambia have experienced disruption of classes and forced closures owing to student protests against fees. However, international students in the UK are less likely to engage in protest as home students for reasons that this chapter is not able to explore at length.

Cultural values

A pertinent mark of identity for international students is culture. Indeed, the fact that an international student leaves her home to undertake a programme of study in a British university and will therefore engage with a totally different culture is reason enough for most universities to embark upon induction programmes designed to minimise the 'culture shock' such students may experience. However, are such inductions desirable? Do they 'dumb down' or show a disregard for the international student's own culture and values? How does the university influence the values of an international student, and how does the presence of international students contribute to the culture and established values of a university? I submit that a genuine experience of higher education is that which enables interaction between and among the diversities of learning communities, respecting their idiosyncracies while at the same time holding true to the tradition of university education, helping individuals and societies to transcend themselves.

Induction programmes are designed mainly to enable international students to fit into the local culture. In short, these students are inducted, through some form of annual ritual of leafleting, speeches, city tours and comedy-drama, into the civic culture. This should help them make purchases in the local shops without being offensive, attend lectures or tutorials without looking too much out of place. Induction programmes and 'culture-shock' plays are also intended to outline the potential curve of experiences an international student is likely to undergo.[318] In all these well-meaning initiatives, it is often the case that these students are not provided with the facilities and opportunities to negotiate their own values and the values of the host community. Thus culture-shock induction programmes prepare students to fit into, to adapt to, or to manage the shock and awe of a new culture, but it does not provide for a means of a dialogue between those contesting and perhaps collaborating cultures. When this happens, most induction programmes are simply a means through which one culture is enabled to dominate and inhibit another. It may also happen partly because international students are made to feel that the only way they can achieve is by way of holding their own cultures and values in abeyance.

Culture shock

The term 'culture shock' is in itself a generalisation. A number of inferences can be drawn from this term, among them the notion that culture is capable of inducing 'shock' or trauma in somebody. It is not in dispute that for some individuals moving from one culture to another causes difficulties. However, it is equally important to consider what a particular international student has already done to prepare herself to make that move. Often, most of them will have an idea of the implications of their decision. They will have some information about the culture they are moving into and therefore likely to expect to live in a totally different culture to their own. Further, most of these students will be mature, and some of them will have their own families. Yet it is true that the new culture will take some adjusting to. Addressing culture shock however should be from the understanding that some international students may need help in negotiating their values with those obtaining in their new environment. This should be a part of the learning process rather than a one-off event during induction or 'fresher' events.

In itself, induction of international students ought to be seen within the context of education, either as nurture or as nature. But this must also be within some understanding of what is meant by higher education. The danger is to view universities as another aspect of schooling and the induction of international students as a way of getting them to learn the rules for survival. Induction in its lower sense attempts to enable an international student to 'fit in' and so avoid standing out, like an alien. Induction as a truly educational opportunity should go on all the time, allowing international students to explore both the new hosting culture, as well as themselves. In this way, induction is not reduced to a few days of leafleting, talking at international students and explaining to them the culture shock they must be experiencing. Rather, induction should be an education, an exploration, part of the continuous learning process the students seek. This means that those who seek to offer international students a welcome and to make inductions a real educational experience should also strive to learn something about the culture of the students being admitted into their universities. It means equipping professors, tutors and support staff with the necessary skills and offering them the opportunity to truly engage with different cultures. Such an 'induction' is consequently on-going and it is my considered view-point that it should be integrated in the deliberate learning processes of a university.

International citizenship

The presence of international students in a university also has implications about citizenship. This subject is explored to some length by Fryer[319] in this book. In simple terms, citizenship may affect international students in terms of 'them' and 'us'. There is a divide represented by rights, social, political and otherwise. For some international students, citizenship seems not to apply. Their involvement in the university community stretches as far as rights to education exist, and their recognition may also be enhanced or limited by their economic rights. However, citizenship may not affect international students in negative ways only. Like academic and other staff in a university, the global community, which transcends and permeates university communities in a variety of ways, creates its own citizenry. This community embraces that which higher education is or should be about. Here, the practice of *viva voce* comes to mind. The doctoral *viva* which embodies a lively debate points to an aspect of higher education inviting communities to a spirit of discovery, testing and challenging. The *viva* as either a teaching method or a tool for assessing a doctoral candidate is but one aspect of assessment in higher education. However, in a deeper sense, it is a meeting of minds or a market-place of intellectual discourse, the gauntlet is thrown not as the mighty challenging the weak, but as peers opening the door to debate, testing and delighting in an opportunity to excel. Further, it is within the *viva* that skill negotiation is tested – did the international student engage with the culture of the university adequately as to reveal a passion for his pursuits?

At the core of universities lie communities. As Elliot et al. observe, '...the modern university professes to be in tune, indeed arm-in-arm, with all manner of "communities".'[320] How true this is remains to be seen in part at the level of individual universities. However, it is the engagement of various stakeholders of the university with communities in diversity, both in the cultivation of a presence of communities of international students and in the appreciation of their values, which mark the university as truly a safe home of learning excellence of truly world first-class standing. International students represent a community of communities, cultures in constant jostling, filtering, refining and re-firming. These cultures are in engagement both with the home culture in which the university is established,[321] and the culture of the community of scholars. Consequently, it is in this process of re-culturation that international students find the university a place in which their values are re-shaped the result of which intellectual reflection and knowledge is crucial. In turn, this leads to further networks of relationships, values and abilities. What the university does is to facilitate such networks, to enable clarity and clarification, dissection and discernment as well as critical reflection. This is how a university communicates to and interacts with the global community. This is also part of what may be deemed the tradition of university education. At the heart of a university community lies communication, the publishing or making public its debates, research, ideas, skills and values to a community far beyond academia.

Fellowship of learners

Universities, as essentially communities in which societies entrust the pursuit of higher knowledge and advancement of technology, need the involvement of international students as critical to the global search for excellence, indeed of knowledge without frontiers. When this becomes the key reason for the cultivation of international students, there is a danger that the values of such students may be subsumed. However, there is also the alternative of recognising and appreciating 'glocal' values, the values shared by universities and their towns, and also the international communities that are to be found in these universities. On a grand scale, glocal values are much the same as the *United Nations Declaration on Human Rights*, accepted by all nations and of importance to individual persons and communities. As essentially being a community of scholars or a scholarly fellowship, whilst acknowledging that this is but only one of several other independent, even autonomous communities in a university, it is incumbent upon higher education institutions to provide an environment in which respect for the values of its constituents is evident.

The idea of fellowship or community is a varied but may be seen to be one based on a sense of identity, meaning and values.[322] University communities are dynamic – recognisable communes or *kibbutzim* in the sense of shared values such as freedom, justice, truth, excellence and equality. There are other types of communities which espouse similar features, but at the heart of universities is the desire and habit of learning, and unlearning, and learning to learn. The global community with which higher education identifies is no longer satisfied with asking age-old, sometimes even mundane questions, such as what is life, or what is development, how best can we feed the starving thousands in Sudan's Darfur, and so on. Whereas these may constitute genuine enquiry, they are inadequate if all they do is reflect a reproduction of a body of information, a repetition of detail handed down over the years. Higher education is not just about learning to ask questions but also learning to answer questions, to find answers and to *enable different types of literacies* as opportunities allow.

Whereas universities tend to have their physical existence rooted into a town or city within the grounds of a campus,[323] their ambitions often betray a penchant for bringing together a band of men and women pursuing titles which are recognisable in almost every education system in the world. Despite the use of similar or familiar titles or degree awards, higher education institutions indulge in a form of competition or rivalry, as is the case in the UK with the advent of league tables. Universities compete for students and reputations, for generous endowments and grants. Sometimes, rivalry is indicative of 'belonging' and 'owning'. On one level, a university may be seen to be owned by the citizens of the country or town in which it is located. On another level, students attending that university, regardless of their origins and backgrounds, identify with the university and hence entertain a sense of 'belonging'. In this respect, the university is *alma mater*. Some African universities, among others, are keen to stress their nurturing contribution in the lives of illustrious alumni, such as Nelson Mandela and presidents Thabo Mbeki and Robert Mugabe from South Africa's Fort Hare University.

Where the university loses its *alma mater* relationship, detachment follows and student numbers drop. For example, the establishment of the University of Zambia in 1966 and the University of Malawi was mainly owing to dissatisfaction with the regional University College of Rhodesia and Nyasaland in 1963. Among the reasons cited for this dissatisfaction was political tension in Southern Rhodesia (Zimbabwe) and the fact that the university was situated in Salisbury (now Harare). Sometimes, universities may put aside such rivalry and cooperate. This could even lead to universities merging. Examples of this include the merger of Fort Hare with Rhodes University in 2003 and in the UK, Manchester University and UMIST. Even the partnership between Strathclyde and Glasgow Universities established through the Synergy initiative, reported to be worth an extra £20 million in research funding, has the underlying bulwark of international pre-eminence.[324] Whatever the reason for rivalry or cooperation, the existence of a university, physical, virtual or otherwise, is deeply linked to the reasons for its establishment. Often, these reasons indicate a local or national need[325] as well as a yearning for standards which would be acceptable by the global community. This requires creative and imaginative partnerships among universities. In reality, this global community is the academic community in its diversity.

In the case of international students, their education is not only the interest of the individual students. There may be various identifiable stakeholders such as other individuals or groups providing scholarships. Consequently, an international student's values may be expressed within the context of other competing values, such as the pursuit for truth, the desire for excellence or the acquisition of particular skills. In as much as 'pursuit for truth' may seem to be an overused phrase if not a cliché, it nevertheless is indicative of the hound trait of the international student, a seeker trait. The overseas student is a seeker after knowledge and skills which are for one reason or another to be traced in a foreign country. It is this process of searching, exploring and learning that higher education engages with different ways of dealing with Pontius Pilate's question, 'What is truth?'. Higher education makes it possible then to ask whether there are other questions that need to be asked, and whether today's hyper-modern university seeks not the truth but truths. As Reeves observes, 'Wonder and awe are the Alpha and Omega of the activity of knowing'.[326] This process of probing, questioning, reflecting and scholarly testing has different translations but for most international students, the reasons for undertaking such a process in a foreign land demonstrates a confidence and trust of far greater importance than could be stated here.

Within the university community, international students are expected to show a commitment to academic values, which mark them out as ambassadors of both their home countries and their university. Academic values may mean a number of things but I would like to use the term to refer to values which underpin and influence scholarly learning. Such values bolster the attitudes behind a student, tutor or researcher's desire to explore an area of study. A university provides for the student an evaluating forum which acknowledges and legitimises for the sake of the broader society the student's knowledge and skills. Notwithstanding the generalisation about international students and their values, at the heart of global communities is diversity and plurality. Often, this might mask confusion about expectations and roles. Teaching styles are not necessarily the same. Students from Asia, for example, might expect closer guidance and model-type teaching than American students. Where these expectations are not understood and addressed, uneasy learning is likely to occur.

International students study in foreign universities for a variety of reasons. A study undertaken by Hall et al. reveals that students chose Scottish higher education institutions mainly on the recommendation of friends and/or other students.[327] One strong reason is that these universities offer a quality of higher education not readily or easily available in the home country. This is not necessarily so in all cases. Indeed, when university education was first being considered in most African countries, it was beset with conflicting agendas. For the British colonial office in the 1940s, it was 'necessary to clear the native mind of any suspicion that African universities were a sham, designed merely to sidetrack native ambitions by ensuring that the degrees and diplomas granted by African Universities were as good as those obtainable outside'.[328] Consequently, part of the strategy involved academic marriages and collaborations between African universities and universities outside Africa.

A number of African universities, such as Nairobi, Dar-es-salaam, Khartoum, plus several others in West Africa, trace their historical development to British universities. For example, the University College of Rhodesia and Nyasaland (UCRN) in Salisbury (Zimbabwe, then Southern Rhodesia) was first a college of London University. However, even those African universities that have not began their origins as colleges of British universities have tended to benefit from British higher education expertise. Prior to its establishment, the University of Zambia benefited immensely from the Lockwood Commission, a committee of British and American HE experts led by Sir John Lockwood, then Master of Birkbeck College and formerly Vice-Chancellor of London University. In their report in 1963, the Lockwood Commission were anxious 'first, that the university must be responsive to the real needs of the country; secondly, that it must be an institution which on merit will win the respect and proper recognition of the university world'.[329] These sentiments are similar to those expressed by Dearing which are stated thus:

• To develop the person's potential to be well equipped for work and to contribute to society.

• To increase knowledge and understanding for their own sake and for the economy.

• To serve the needs of the economy at all levels.

• To help shape a democratic and civilized society.[330]

Indeed, many international students in UK universities will be familiar with the expectations of their home governments, that they will acquire a higher education which upon their return will enable them to meet the real social, economic and even political needs of their countries. A country's real needs may be interpreted differently by successive governments and generations. The economy is but one aspect of the country's needs and its performance may or may not be influenced by higher education. However, for most countries, the nature of global capital movements and business, in short, globalization, requires that a country has to invest in some form of higher education for its citizens. This regards students in higher education as having a certain worth or value, which may or may not be rewarded with hard cash or an elevated social status.

A large number of students from African countries will have undertaken their undergraduate degree programmes in their own home countries and seek postgraduate study abroad. Like other students undertaking higher education outside their native countries, they are a community set apart but yet not entirely divorced from home and host communities. Whatever the reason, international students cultivate within universities the opportunity of living-out and establishing a truly global community. Such a community comes into existence mainly by the recognition of key values, such as respect, equality and diversity. As stated by UKCOSA, 'an institution which is seen to be working as a multi-racial and multi-cultural establishment will hold fewer fears for local students from ethnic minorities who wish to pursue courses of higher education...'[331] Whereas various communities are the beneficiaries of a multi-ethnic community, its place in higher education should be much deeper than a mere understanding of different cultures. It should lead to a more mature engagement made possible by an on-going educational process. Higher education institutions contribute to informed debate about the new world order, and its attendant issues about terrorism, war and peace, conflict resolution, global financing, ethics and cultural dilemmas and tensions, through reaching out and embracing engagement with other institutions across the world. Such contact ought to lead to fora of mutual learning and exchange which in turn helps lessen distrust and suspicion of other cultures. An example is that of the continuous tension between Western and Islamic cultures.

However, it is the twin engagement of teaching and research available in a university environment which appeals to international students. A taught degree programme provides an environment for excellence in learning enhanced by keen exchange between lecturers and students. Teaching as an integral element of university education is an opportunity for students to benefit from the expert referral resources of the lecturer and in some cases a way to tapping into the lecturers' seemingly extensive network. Thus, it is not uncommon for some international students to seek out 'the best teaching method' as opposed to a variety of teaching methods. Research is the means by which the student delights into an opportunity for unique scholarly engagement of discovery.[332] On the wider society level, this discovery may have service implications, which may be linked to commercially viable results, while on the individual or personal level, it may lead to Maslowian feelings of self-actualisation. In this way higher education is seen to possess a common good, even a global good. It contributes to a global ethic of responsibility, engaging policy on wide-ranging issues such as global-warming or international development, and enabling the further development of skills and resources.

> *Student A was disappointed with the quality of supervision provided by his department. His supervisor had already 'lost' one of his draft chapters for his dissertation. Then it seemed that there just wasn't an opportunity to meet the supervisor because he simply wasn't anywhere to be seen. Thrice, he had agreed a meeting with Dr Longtooth, thrice Dr Longtooth had failed to meet him. He sent emails suggesting alternative arrangements. He received a reply once telling him to 'get on with it'. Student A felt cheated. People within the department spoke of Dr Longtooth in whispers and hushed tones. There was awe in the mention of his name as his numerous citations were listed. He had an enviable reputation within and beyond the university. Student A was not impressed. It seemed Dr Longtooth was had lost touch with his core responsibility towards him. 'A' wanted something more from his supervision, more quality time with him, more input on his writing, more guidance about sources of evidence and references, help with identifying and recommending conferences. Further, Student A was also disappointed that as his supervisor, Dr Longtooth never expressed interest in his personal life style, well, at least in his family and health. 'A' felt a university programme taking longer than one year warranted a closer relationship between tutor and tutee if only to build up a meaningful educational experience. Student A's tutor was not just somebody who strolled in and out of the university – he was a guru. He had to be seen*

> and not just heard! 'A' put much store in relationships, his family, faith community and learning community. These were relationships that were to be forged by the close ties of loyalty, respect, commitment, and hard work. He wanted to see these things in his family and he expected to see them in his university communities.

International students, and indeed foreign staff and academics, by putting themselves in the position of vulnerable learner and explorer, reveal their strongest trait. They posit themselves in such a way as to suggest they are prepared to have their culture, beliefs, knowledge and sense of being challenged. They expose themselves to the influence and effect of a culture and cultures and sometimes at the mercy of structures which maybe suspicious of their presence. Yet it is in this vulnerability that their strength lies. For universities as safe places of learning means that the communities of international students genuinely become centres of world-wide learning and diversity. Communities of learning are only learning communities when they are open to enquiry, and when they ferment respect for mutual, active and passive learning amongst their members and the wider society. In so doing, universities inevitably push back the frontiers of knowledge.

In the cases of Student A and Dr Longtooth and the South African student and tutor Dr Shortfoot, there are clearly identifiable values, which need to be worked through, not least the sense of familial support and guidance alongside autonomy and responsibility in learning. Such conflict can be lead to great anxiety when the student's family, home institution or community may be depending on his success. Generally, international students are a transient community. They are displaced in as far as their programmes of study dictate a period or length of study or research. This change in circumstances may create apprehension in a number of students, which may be referred to as culture shock. Failure to succeed may lead to loss of face for the family and significant others not least a financial crisis.

The geographical displacement of various communities does not necessarily entail the abeyance of cherished values. These values may even be further entrenched by transition, diasporic experiences and higher education. All the more important then that the values underlying the learning relationship be articulated and worked through, so that anxieties can be recognised and the different aims of the learning be respected. The interplay of diverse communities in higher education institutions may also serve to inform these values. Teaching and research in universities should not necessarily be divorced from the values of learners, teachers and researchers. For some, these values are the motivation behind learning, teaching or research. For example, the Ph.D., sometimes regarded as a lonely, isolated and expensive experience, is often described as a programme of study, of at least three or four years, perhaps involving a piece of original research. The doctoral student may have a personal reason and focus for research, but this may have far-reaching implications. Dr Longtooth and tutor Shortfoot are not necessarily representative of academic staff but in these cases, they reveal certain values to be found in members of university communities. Dr Longtooth is an illustration of those academics whose work often involves participation at various fora – national and international. The work some academics do concern the welfare and quality of life sometimes on a global scale.

The academic in global engagement

The work of Carolyn Baylies is an example I would like to draw upon. Born in Texas, Carolyn Baylies graduated from the University of California, Berkerley in 1969 and the University of Wisconsin, Madison in 1971. She then undertook her doctoral research and taught at the University of Zambia from 1973 to 1978. Her work at the University of Leeds embraced the local history about the Yorkshire miners but even then, she still kept a finger on political and economic developments in Zambia. Her output was borne of a professional ethic as well as personal values. Whereas her professional interests were distinguished in projects of economic and political interest to governments and scholars alike, her personal interests were equally professionally distinguished and of interest on a global level. Thus *AIDS, Sexuality and Gender in Africa: Collective strategies and struggles*[333] is not merely an academic publication but the embodiment of glocal values – values criss-crossing the globe, from Texas to Lusaka and then Leeds. Like Dr Longtooth, Carolyn Baylies was a sought-after speaker at local and international fora, but unlike Longtooth, she was available and accessible to her students.

Areas of global interest such as HIV/AIDS affect the lives of international students in various ways. Although as communities which often adopt a duty of care ethic, the cost of providing medical care and attention is one which presents difficulties for higher education institutions and health authorities. HIV/AIDS is a complex issue which does not only require medical intervention but demands in addition social, legal and educational support. In those countries where stigma is a stumbling block to the care of people living with HIV/AIDS, the British university may seem to offer acceptance and sanctuary necessary to undertake a demanding programme of study. Hence social acceptance in the communities of learning may serve to provide confidence and a model for social acceptance into the wider society. Bearing in mind that in some societies, people living with HIV/AIDS have suffered some form of discrimination, if we consider the fact that some societies feel that providing university education to people living with HIV/AIDS is a waste of resources, human and otherwise, universities may have to provide leadership in this area, just as has happened in the provision of equal opportunities and disability. In dealing with discrimination of people living with HIV/AIDS, the values enshrined in various instruments concerned with human rights is a legal consideration going beyond the groves of academe. However, it is also the case that the prevention of the further spread of HIV/AIDS and the treatment and care of those people already infected by HIV/AIDS, is not only of concern to higher education, but rather of all education. Thus the dangers of HIV/AIDS lurk not only in international communities, nor are they spread by international students only. Rather, the HIV/AIDS spectre overwhelms both the local and the global and resources directed to dealing with it require the tenacity and commitment equal to any shared understanding of what it means to be human.

It is the case nowadays that the costs involved in the care of people living with HIV/AIDS tend to be high, and consequently most governments, including the British government, are wary of international students adding pressure to any already harassed national health service. In such cases, it is most likely that those international students living with HIV/AIDS are likely to find that obtaining a visa to the UK is an uphill battle. The duty of care towards international students is not only embedded into care offered to home students, although in some cases care for international students may be conditional upon whether or not public funds are used. Care for international students is continuously challenged by international or external circumstances, often changing and unpredictable and involving a complex web of diverse needs. This may ignore intrinsic values which characterise higher education: originality of mind, critical judgement, enquiry, learning, freedom, loving relationships, educational influence in others' learning and in the education of social formations. Whitehead considers these as values of humanity.[334] And humanity is the one denominator common in all types of university communities through which universities in turn embrace and are enveloped by global communities. The twin functions of universities, that is, teaching and research, are both activities of humanity transcending cultures and boundaries. To participate in higher education is therefore a willingness to challenge the mundane and obvious. This is partly the quest upon which international students embark.

Values of care post-'September 11'

Higher education still exists in a world bestride with strife, poverty, epidemics of violence and disease. Recent history has presented a number of events with direct and indirect implications for international students and the global role of universities. For example, to boycott or not to boycott the Israeli academic community is an indication of the political activism obtaining in some universities. Israeli academics such as Mirriam Shlesinger of Bar-Ilan University, Oren Yifttachel of Ben Gurion have been boycotted in a bid to force a change in Israeli policies regarding Palestine. The 1999 war in Bosnia, the tragic events of September 11 in New York, and later the 2003 war in Iraq, created complex difficulties for a number of international students. For example, the horrible incident of the September 11 terrorist attack has led to a backlash of tension and hostility which challenges the values of tolerance, difference and diversity. In most universities, some international students felt alienated by various quarters of the university community. They were at times seen as representative of the perpetrators of these crimes, and were thus liable to subtle and even overt forms of hostile behaviours.

My earlier discourse on HIV/AIDS, like SARS, requires further input from HE, although here it should be noted that the Association of Commonwealth Universities has already began to provide guidance about this.[335] It is a discourse that challenges the duty to care, just as those challenges posed by September 11 and continuing troubles in various parts of the world. The experience of major trauma which international students may feel, owing to any number of causes and factors, inevitably affects the nature of higher education. The way it meets these challenges is an indication of the value a university places on its international citizens. However, the duty of care was never one completely shirked by universities. Responding to the 2003 war in Iraq, for example, the Vice-Chancellors of the Universities of Leeds and Leeds Metropolitan University wrote letters of assurance and guidance to international students in their universities outlining forms of support available to affected students. These letters were published in the student newspapers and produced on university websites. The effectiveness of the processes involved here has not been determined but it is clear that crises such as these which affect certain sectors of the international student community often receive little priority in the wider society.

Responses to dealing with such issues tend to be knee-jerk reactions, from both government and university central administrative structures as well as student union support systems. Concern for student welfare in general, and about their health in particular, has always been expressed in a number of ways in most universities such as Cambridge, Leeds Metropolitan University and the University of Leeds, by establishing some form of student health service. As far back as 1948, the Council of the University of Leeds accepted responsibility for a student health service and made a requirement for compulsory medical inspection on entry.[336] Even then, the values that underpinned such a decision were those of inclusion and fuller development rather than discrimination. This is indicative of the nature of the place of the communities of international students. It is worth noting that the obligation to care, for many institutions, was translated into establishing welfare services which began with special provision for overseas students and spread outwards to benefit the generality of students. For some universities, their primary client is town and country first, and global whenever opportunities allow. This is especially the case where universities are funded mainly by national governments, and therefore are seen to play a national role, and sometimes funded by a benefactor, and consequently seen as driven by that benefactor's hidden agenda. The duty to care is one that invokes universities to ensure that care is integrated into every level of university operations, and that HE should enable staff and students to respond to global issues ethically and responsibly. In both the situations given above, that is, September 11 and HIV/AIDS, rooted deep in the responses of universities and the global community is the issue of equity – the move to striking a balance, redressing inequities.

Being part of the global community places requirements on the role of scholars, researches and teachers. A noticeable characteristic of university communities is its large composition of academics engaged either in teaching, research or both. Academics, it may be assumed, are guided in their activities by a code of practice and values which perhaps make up an academic policy. When explaining what is meant by academic policy, E. Margolis writes that 'a project that necessarily starts from a definition of what the university is or what higher education is.'[337] The project, while embedded in what may be regarded as university tasks and their social insertion lead to a wider universe, that is, to what society is and should be. The values of academics should inform their project, and such values and such project are in turn an aspect of what the university is about. The values of a university, given, for example, in its mission statement or charter, enshrine that university's place in society. It also points to a mission which transcends its immediate locality. As long as a university continues to aspire towards some form of excellence, in academic pursuits and in service to society, it does so mainly by exacting upon itself engagement with the global community. This is borne out in Whitehead's comment:

> What passes as values in higher education is possibly to be seen and identified in the substance or core of higher education. To be acceptable beyond the immediate confines of one society, or culture, and to be seen as underpinning the shared view as to what it is that informs higher education on a global level, may be expressed in these sentiments: 'I am saying that the form of my explanation is disciplined through the process of learning to live values of humanity. These values are embodied in who I am and what I do. They are not static. They are living. I clarify their meanings in the course of their emergence in what I am doing as I research my own practice and learn to live these values. The meanings of my embodied values of humanity cannot be validity communicated through interconnected sets of propositions.[338]

Partly, this explains why universities desire world-wide recognition, why they seek to be considered world-class and to be counted among the top-most universities. It is also the reason why universities, like football teams, seek to recruit top academics, high-performing managers, the best students and so on. Whereas football teams play to strict regulation, determined by bodies such as the World Football Organisation (FIFA), regional and national football organisations and enforced by a referee, universities are almost autonomous and varied in how they function. Self-regulation occurs at various levels of teaching and research. For example, the manner in which research is conducted within a university may be guided by a research ethics committee or an appropriate body within the university itself. Ultimately, however, responsibility lies with the individual researcher. Yet even the individual researcher or lecturer is subject to rules and regulations which universities have established. It is the values which universities embody which sets out the standards of practice. As to what values these are, Ellacuria's words are apt:

> The starting point of our conception of what a University should be consists of two considerations. The first and most obvious is that the University has to do with culture, knowledge and a particular exercise of intellectual reason. The second consideration, which is not so obvious and commonplace, is that the University is a social reality and a social force, historically marked by what the society is like in which it lives and in which it should live...[339]

Ellacuria's idea of a university can be reduced into the understanding that universities are a cultural phenomenon. As cultural institutions, they exercise influence within and outside their immediate localities. Groupings such as Universitas 21, a global network of top universities, exists in order to exert influence far beyond the civic precinct. This is the same with other similar groupings such as the Association of Commonwealth Universities and the International Association of Universities. The development of organised bodies which incorporate a number of universities, from regional groupings of collaboration such as the Russell group in the UK, to global networks such as Universitas 21. Such networking and linking is made much easier by information and computing technology. Information technology is in itself a feature of culture and intellectual reason, and in the global community, a social reality. This has been realised into e-learning.

Another type of transience is the fact that e-learning has become a strong complement if not supplement to the displaced away-from-home international student. The doomed e-university managed by UKeU with initial funding from HEFCE is an example of another type of the global community. Based on interconnectedness through computing technology, the e-university focuses on the idea of community as shared interests. In essence, it is the signing up of students from all over the world for online study. The Open University is an example of an institution which has taken full advantage of advancements in information technology. Of course, virtual universities and e-learning may revolutionise the delivery of international education and re-define the character of international students in higher education. For a number of universities, one response has been to franchise overseas courses, a business boasting some 140,000 students and raking in some £250m. a year.[340] Virtual universities and e-learning are rather more global in that they appeal to students across geographical borders. Virtual universities take a step further the tenets of distance education. Time and space are not priority issues since the cyber-class is not constrained by either need. Virtual universities bring closer access to higher education in a widened sense.

Global community

Global communities, to be understood, require a perception of what globalization means. Reflecting on the meaning of globalization, Sacks finds John Donne's expression memorable:

> All mankind is of one Author, and is one volume... No man is an Iland, intire of itselfe; every man is a peece of the Continent...any man's death diminishes me; because I am involved in Mankinde...'

Sacks sees globalization as the interconnectedness of the world through new systems of communication.[341] For Held, globalization is thought of as a process or a set of processes 'which embodies a transformation in the spatial organization of social relations and transactions – assessed in terms of their extensity, intensity, velocity and impact – generating transcontinental or interregional flows and networks of activity, interaction, and the exercise of power.'[342] The semantic field of globalization includes words such as global poverty and debt, multinational corporations, global market, world religions, global ethic(s), capitalization, HIV/AIDS, modernity, global élites, and so on. The *United Nations Charter on Human Rights* provides an attempt at encapsulating a common vision and values for the global community.

Roger King observes about globalization and higher education:

> Historically, universities are more global than national in their academic and intellectual orientations. Science and rationality tend to chafe at territorial limitations on knowledge, while inter-country exchange and mobility are critical aspects of university work.[343]

Michael Gibbons acknowledges that globalization is touching the heart of the university – the research process, suggesting that universities should

> move from the production of reliable knowledge to what may be termed socially
> robust knowledge which is increasingly in demand in the world…through
> closer engagement with the wider research community, universities will be able
> to maintain their integrity and impartiality as institutions that serve the public
> good, and remain truly critical participants in the process of globalization.[344]

For me, this is the core of critical engagement, a sense and keyed-in involvement with the world entire.

Globalization in higher education is not just internationalism, as is the case when a university engages with another university in another country. Rather, it seeks engagement, the cross-pollination of learning, across the continents of the world. The idea of a global community reflects elements of globalization, an interconnectedness of peoples, communities and cultures from the major regions of the world, including their attendant discontents and strengths. Thus the global community is dynamic and in tune with issues that affect and have an impact transcendent in nature and outlook. The global community is not a threat to the local communities, instead, it is a complement to that the local. Universities in particular, and higher education in general, are at the core of the global community. JANET is but one piece of evidence in which universities have exercised interconnectedness through technological advances.

University communities generally characterise complex interconnections enveloping cultures, experiences, truths, traditions and difference. But at the very essence of the university as a global community, a community which speaks not only to its locality but seeks to render its voice to all kinds of communities, is an interconnectedness through knowledge and truth(s). Often, this knowledge is marked by the activity of teaching and learning and research, with varied emphasis according to individual institutions. The more knowledge a university embodies, the more power it wields, for knowledge is power and businesses are prepared to pay huge amounts of money to access and utilise that knowledge. On one hand, however, knowledge is not necessarily aligned purely to monetary gain. For some universities, courses on peace and conflict resolution may be a way to deal with issues which are seen as possessing global ramifications.[345] Whereas it is possible that curriculum considerations may simply be altruistic or utilitarian, on the other hand, it is also the case that some courses are planned mainly to meet an agenda which guarantees funding. When this happens, quality in terms of teaching and resources are the least of priorities. Here the courses are seen merely as a product offered often to overseas markets as a business venture.

Wealth generation

Universities cost money: buildings have to be maintained and staff and academics have to be paid.[346] In some cases, universities are entrusted, even as repositories, of priceless artifacts, instruments or objects which in turn require financial support. The business created by universities through the franchise of overseas courses, the wealth-generating[347] function of universities on the global scale can be seen in two ways; the local impact and the wider global implication of higher education. Nottingham University is an example, with a campus in Malaysia and building another one in China. It has set up a China Policy Institute and opened an office in Shanghai. It has 5,000 international students of whom 1,000 are Chinese. This is indicative of a flurry of business activity possible in higher education. Generally, the student population contributes to an economic activity which is needed in the city. Whereas the university and country relationships sometimes entail tensions between increased sales owing to a high student clientele, and perceived down-marketing of residences where students take up multiple occupancies,[348] it is also the case that universities, in their own way, create multiple communities which in themselves require sustaining in a number of ways.

The labour market is an example of universities contributing to job creation. Some universities employ over 5,000 staff and have some 30,000 students on their roll. Universities have to be managed. This often involves huge amounts of money coming from a variety of sources. University budgets are also high. While £2 billion of public money goes on university research each year, only £90 million is spent on third-stream activity.[349] This is in the context that there is an increasing link between universities and industry. For example, in health research, GlaxoSmithKline has committed £44 million to a £76 million venture with Imperial College London whilst AstraZeneca is to pump £74 million in drug and advanced lead discovery facilities. The higher education industry in the U.S. boasts some reputable names, such as Harvard, Princeton and Yale. Competing with these universities requires that UK universities both acquire much more funding in order to conduct their business as efficiently as is humanly possible. Whether this funding is acquired by top-up fees and/or increased public funding, there is also an expectation that the benefits will always far-out weigh this funding, with more wealth generated. While it is important that universities are financially robust, the use to which this money is put, or intended to be put, acknowledges the values underlying higher education.

Wealth-generation maybe expressed in immediate, local returns, (the education budget in the UK currently exceeds defence!)[350] but the basic purposes of university education and research continue to have global appeal and influence. The identity of universities is intricately linked with its communities, and the corporate wealth of society ought to invest in the networking of these communities. Thus universities contribute to national, and indeed global wealth generation in the literacies of its communities composed of a diverse student and staff profile.

Conclusion

I revert to the football parallel. Football clubs such as Arsenal Football Club, Liverpool and Manchester United are seen as English clubs. The strength of these clubs is in the ability to combine both diversity and talent to such a balance that they consistently stay at the top of their game. The English premiership increasingly reflects football as a global phenomenon. International players raise skill levels, enable success, and bring with them a cultural diversity that relates to local clubs through the practice of football, and increasingly through club/community initiatives.

In the same way higher education has become inextricably linked to the global dimension. Some universities are faced with similar doldrums. In terms of recruitment, there has been an influx of students from China and less so from other countries. This may be good for economic reasons but the long-term implications point to an imbalance in cultural diversity and lop-sidedness in what it means to be a part of the global community and to have world-class standards. Recently Ivor Crewe, president of Universities UK, urged universities to promote UK higher education abroad. Crewe warned that 'it will not be long before leading American universities establish campuses, including graduate schools, in London – especially now that U.S. entry visas for international students have become less available in the aftermath of September 11'. He added: 'The presence of international students and faculty is no longer an optional, mildly exotic, welcome ingredient of campus life. It is quite simply what makes it possible for the academic enterprise to continue.'[351]

Universities will continue to attract international students, but those universities with an enriched and delighting global community will be those with an appreciation of multi-cultural, multi-racial and multi-educational communities. Higher education is not only about engagement with diverse cultures, but also enabling investigation of questions of single-focus detail as well as devotion to those issues that have global importance or ramifications. Without attention to these elements, the values they embody and the dialogues they demand there runs the danger of simply seeing international students as, at best, consumers, who have to be adapted to our way, or at worst, a commodity that enables our survival. To genuinely embrace the global dimension demands effective partnership at the level of learning, and management, in terms of global collaboration and global responsibility.

This can only happen with clear, deliberate planning and thinking, putting in place policies that have a global perspective, and standards which are truly world-class. Of course, this requires financial support and astute management. Further, the values and motivations of academics play an important role in articulating the global perspective and vision any university may lay claim too. Such academics influence global issues in their work and networks through which diversity and learning transcend their individuality. How can we identify a world class university? By its articulation of and commitment to the global community, by its devotion to responding to global issues, and through its expression of integrity.

15

Only connect

Gwen Collins

This chapter outlines the findings of a small research project into academics' understanding of the meaning and purpose of their work, and whether they identify connections between their work and pressing contemporary global realities. It indicates that the academics interviewed derive much personal and professional satisfaction from their work. This is primarily expressed in terms of commitment to developing the potential of students and of intellectual interest in one's subject area or its application in industry or commerce. Of some concern, however, is an apparent sense of powerlessness to effectively address wider global issues through the educational process and a lack of any clear overview of a global public service role for our universities. The research findings prompt the question as to whether there are ways in which the intellectual and material resources of higher education (HE) could be more effectively harnessed to meet these challenges. This question echoes those posed by leading educational theorists. The chapter ends with a brief overview of a global perspectives approach to HE and suggests that this offers a framework for making the necessary connections between academic disciplines and global needs.

Research project
What motivates academics? Why are they doing this kind of work? How do they view their work in relation to the big global issues of our day? Working

as a university chaplain I was very interested in these questions and I decided to embark on doctoral research to try and find some answers!

Thirty-two women academics volunteered to participate in the research. They were invited to tell their story, within the area suggested by these questions. They were informed that I was interested in both internal and external factors. In what terms do people understand and talk about their own sources of energy? For what purposes is that energy then used, and why? How do people perceive their own work and its value within the wider sphere of the university and beyond?

Each individual interview consisted of three sections: personal narrative; interpretation of a diagram; focused questions. In this last section I asked each person to reflect on the relationship between what they consider to be the pressing issues of our day, and the reality of what is learnt and taught, in their experience, in our universities. When they think and speak about HE and their own academic work do they think in terms of HE making a real contribution to building a more equitable, peaceful and sustainable global society, or do they not?

The interviews were recorded and transcribed, producing over seven hundred pages of negotiated text.[352] There is not space here to describe either methodology or findings in detail.[353] However something may be deduced empirically about values in HE from the rich mass of data relating to these academics' personal histories, attitudes towards work, self-understandings regarding what is the driving force in their lives, and perceptions of the role of the university in the world. Some key points that are emerging in this research are presented in the following sections under the headings 'Meaning' and 'Purpose'.

Meaning

The most frequently cited factor that gives meaning to work and results in job satisfaction is the opportunity to help students to develop their potential, both intellectually and personally. Every person but one attributed importance to this. Even those who seemed on balance to feel negative about their work spoke of this area positively. The following quotes give a sample of this widely expressed view.

> The motivation now is to make a difference with the students, to enable them to fulfil their ambitions and I think that's tremendously rewarding and hugely motivating.[354]

> I believe that the contribution I can make to students…is helping them to develop themselves through their opportunities and one of the main things that I can do that through is placements… They are so well developed when they leave here, both cognitively and personally and that's great really, that you've been part of that process. And you can see them when they first came and you see them when they go out and think, 'I don't believe that's the same person.'

Several people spoke specifically of the satisfaction of teaching, or of facilitating learning. Phrases such as 'to see a light click on' or 'to press the right buttons' were used to express how meaningful people found it to have helped someone else to understand. The person quoted below, though, was not alone in finding that much more achievable with final year or Masters students than with first or second years!

> I do love working with students, standing in front of students and actually trying to develop their minds and encourage them to learn… sometimes they aren't highly motivated in the first year with lots of other influences…and in the second year they tend to be a bit bogged down by so much work and they get a bit grumpy I find, but in the third year… You get more from them, more give and take.

People's experience of where the balance between motivated and unmotivated students lay in their own courses varied enormously. But several expressed considerable concern about students' attitudes to learning:

> The culture…is more about working out what I've got to do to get 'x' – very results driven, and I think that pervades the whole of university life.

> All I know is that with my own students, who are confronted with such horrendous injustice[355]…their main concern is about their careers… I've only at the moment got one student…who gives me hope. But maybe one out of twenty-five is as good as it gets [laughter]… The others, it's about their careers. And I know they're really just expressing the culture they live in. Materialistic.

The pastoral role was meaningful for many.

> …if you have managed to stop them going into a deeper abyss than they were going, then I think that's probably the most satisfying and that's the part I'd miss most…

> …I seem to act as a bridge and that is something that I value, not because I am nosey particularly knowing everyone's problems but that I feel that it is important that students have somebody that they feel can talk to within the academic framework.

Everyone whom I interviewed was interested in her subject. Some were also passionate about the importance of its applications. For a few this amounted to a sense of purpose which was a driving force in their work, but more common was a deep personal and intellectual interest that made their academic work satisfying and worthwhile. This embraced both teaching and research:

> I'd never thought about that area before… It just opened up doors in my mind that I had never realised were shut… I could see the theories, how they connected with my past experience and I thought, 'I really want to teach in that area'…and I've directed everything to that.

> …intellectually it's very, very stimulating because of the interface between the disciplines…there's lots of energy going in all directions in terms of research and the way things can be planned in different disciplines, so…the intellectual side can be quite challenging.

Thus although attribution of meaning, significance or importance to particular aspects of life and work varies from individual to individual, there are also commonalities. For some of these women work was the centre of life's meaning. For many it was in a subsidiary role to a primary focus of meaning in the family. Others expressed alternative primary foci, or held several in balance. For all of them their academic work provided some degree of satisfaction and there were several aspects of the job in which many clearly delighted. Primary amongst these was the opportunity to help individuals to develop and achieve their goals.

Purpose
What about the bigger picture? Is the 'what is it all for?' question one that people customarily ask themselves, or not? Do they think about the way in which their work relates to the global contemporary context in which humanity finds itself in the 21st century?

I am interested not only in *what* people said in answer to the questions summarised as 'Why are you doing what you are doing?' but also *when* in the interview they said it. If a particular sense of purpose was habitually uppermost in their self-understanding they might be more likely to mention this early, within the first third of the interview, the part in which they were given free rein to say whatever they liked in an unstructured way. If a sense of purpose was present but not primary, it might be mentioned later, in response to questions.

Table 1 summarises, in my words, individuals' comments about their own work in this regard.

Table 1. Sense of purpose: when and how expressed[356]

	I Clearly articulated, unprompted	II Articulated in response to questions	III New connections appeared to be developing
It is my purpose to… make a difference to the future	1	6	6
It is my purpose to… educate individuals	4	8	3
It is my purpose to… equip individuals for their careers	2	3	
It is my purpose to… add to the body of knowledge	1		
It is my purpose to… help develop my industry or profession	4	3	1

Table 1 shows that a substantial minority indicated, as they told their story unprompted, a clear sense of purpose in work (column I). One person stood out as having a strong external imperative, feeling that her work was making an important contribution to a better future. Most included comments in response to questions that showed a wider vision than simply meeting the needs of students and institution day by day (column II). Nevertheless this wider vision was patchy and weak compared with the strong significance, to most, of the nurture of individuals referred to in the previous section. Some said either that the interview was making them think of things they had not considered before, or that is was causing them to make new connections (column III).

Table 2 summarises, in my words, what people said about shaping the future and whether the university as a whole and their own courses in particular have a role in this.

Table 2. Shaping the future: does the university have a role?

	I Profound questions about the future are largely untouched. The status quo accepted.	II Students as individuals are encouraged to engage in critical thinking.	III Global social and environ- mental responsibility is considered.
I. In my course	6	6	13 (see note 1 below)
II. In the university	4	2	2
III. More of this should happen		1	10
IV. This is not the realm of HE.	1		3

Note 1: Most people qualified these statements by saying something like, 'in a small way, for example, part of one unit in a level 3 module'.

To understand this table it is important to remember that participants were all asked whether they thought the university had a role in addressing the big issues of our day that they themselves had identified. It was up to them, then, as to how they chose to reflect on and expand this question. All but one said that the university did have such a role, but it became clear that most meant 'should', or 'did in a small way', rather than 'did'. Six people emphasised the development of critical thinking skills in their students as a way in which these issues are addressed in their courses. For some of these, and for others who mentioned this but gave it less prominence, it seems that critical thinking is not necessarily seen as a useful tool for shaping a better world, but more as a tool for developing intellectual integrity in an abstract way, leaving the global status quo substantially unchallenged. Thirteen spoke of consideration of global or environmental responsibility, but also made it clear that this was a minor component in their courses.

Connections
None of the participants in this research had any trouble in identifying issues facing the human race that they considered serious, pressing and having

major implications for the future as well as the present. There appears to be a consensus that we live in an age of momentous significance. Perhaps 'the present moment' of past ages has very often felt like that too. Nevertheless a cogent case can be made for the critical nature of this present moment in shaping tomorrow.

There are indications in my research that people feel they are part of an educational system that is moving in a particular direction and that they have little power, if any, to influence that movement. There is little expression of active hope that things can or will be different, but neither are there expressions of hopelessness. There is a disconnectedness, a compartmentalisation perhaps. There is little evidence of concerted, serious thought across a wide canvass in regard to HE's contribution to building a more equitable, sustainable and peaceful world.

What challenges does this present to HE? Can it embrace a philosophy and a practice of learning, teaching and research that gives top priority to creating a healthy global, social and political framework that works for the sake of the whole planet and all of its people?

As long ago as 1996 the Review of the Toyne Report recommended that responsible global citizenship should be regarded as a desired core learning outcome.[357] Since then other analysts have identified the radical challenge that global realities present to H.E. Barnett (2000), in his comprehensive reflection on appropriate philosophical models for HE in our day, asks:

> What is the likelihood that concerns about teaching performance might give way to a serious debate about the curriculum and the need to transform it into an experience for new modes of being?… In the longer term I believe that universities will move in the required direction because…there is a societal, and even a global, call for it to come about. The writing is on the wall.[358]

Maxwell (2001) writes from the rather different viewpoint of the philosophy of science, but one can hear, in his words, similar concerns:

> At present, academics show few signs of recognising the need for the required revolution. Will no one take responsibility for creating traditions and institutions of learning intelligently designed to help us become civilised?[359]

Brundtland (2000) spells out the challenge facing humanity in terms that relate directly to the realm of HE.

> What is new to our generation is that we also have the knowledge and technical capacity – for the first time – to choose to leave, for posterity, an inhabitable

planet. Our challenge today is to organize our knowledge, and our tremendous scientific and technological potential, and address the survival issues of our times.[360]

My research suggests that there is only a fragmentary and fragile engagement of individuals and of the institution with this reality. It is perhaps no wonder that in the face of the enormity of such challenges many academics respond by focusing almost exclusively on their immediate area and their own students. The scale of the task means that it needs to be addressed at the institutional and sector level. Universities and HE funding and policy-making bodies need to create an ethos that actively encourages academics to explore radical approaches to learning, teaching and research to meet these challenges.

The concept of global perspectives in HE is one approach that does, in my experience, begin to address this need. The values underpinning a global perspectives basis to education are that every person is of equal worth, wherever they live and whatever their economic status, and that the well-being of the earth's ecosystem, now and in the future, is a primary good. It regards higher education worthy of the name as an education that enables people to understand the global impact of their actions, professionally and personally, individually and corporately, and empowers them to share responsibility for building a better future.

This applies to the sciences as much as to the humanities. Let me suggest what this might mean, for example, in medical ethics, multi-media technology and pure mathematics. I do this tentatively, but in order to put some flesh on bones, and with the hope that people from within these subject areas will pull my examples apart and construct their own more appropriate applications.

• Thirty million babies a year are born with stunted brain development because of maternal malnourishment in pregnancy.[361] A global perspectives approach to medical ethics gives at least equal weight to the ethical issues and solutions involved in the plight of these thirty million as it does to the surgeon and society's dilemma over one pair of conjoined twins.

• A multi-media technology course embedding global perspectives gives in-depth consideration to the values, both implicit and explicit, that are conveyed and reinforced through the 'product'. As part of the design process it poses the question, 'In what way does this product contribute towards a better future for all?' On the technological side, of course, it includes sustainability of production and disposal. It encourages creativity in relation to technological possibilities alongside an awareness of the digital divide.

• Pure mathematicians educated through global perspectives graduate with a full grasp of mathematical principles enhanced by an informed understanding of the inequity in the provision of education around the world. They have pondered on the possible mathematical geniuses lost to their academic community because millions of children do not get beyond primary school or even that far.

A global perspectives approach is, in this, no more prescriptive than a 'traditional' approach which channels its students, like it or not, through a course that takes no account of these global realities. It refutes the notion that any academic discipline is value free, and invites academics to explore the sometimes hidden values and exclusiveness that underpin their practice.

Conclusion

Is this a diluting of the academic ideal, the pursuit of pure knowledge for its own sake? Thomas Bender's essay in the first part of this book sets this ideal in a historical context and draws our attention to the enrichment of both academic disciplines and civic society when academics take seriously the pressing issues of their day, be it DuBois or Dewey. In the second part of this book individual academics and others working in our universities describe how their values inform and 'earth' their work. Katulushi has argued that higher education has to engage with global issues, and especially with creating policies which help clarify the contribution of academics as stakeholders in the learning, teaching and research process. Citizenship in its broadest sense demands a global outlook, global responsibility requires global action, and global action is possible only through global partnerships and networking.[362]

Whilst the research project outlined in this chapter indicates serious shortcomings in HE's response to global realities, my professional involvement on the ground with global perspectives networks and projects has convinced me that there are many pieces of good work being done.[363] When the academics involved come together this can help to generate a more globally responsible and proactive institutional ethos, which in turn creates more possibilities.

Global Perspectives in HE project: generic themes, skills and dispositions

Generic themes	Generic skills	Generic dispositions
Ethical issues, questions, problems	Critical enquiry, analysis and reflection.	Commitment to promoting global responsibility
Cultural difference and diversity.	Active learning and practical application	
Sustainability debates and solutions.		
Connections between local and global developmental issues		

Global Perspectives in Higher Education, DEA (2003)

16

Religion, spirituality and higher education

Simon Robinson

Half way through the three hour seminar on Engineering and Ethical Decision Making, the lecturer turned back to the over-head and asked the third year class of about 120 students, 'And what else would you have in a moral decision-making process?' It was a warm day and they were all ready for the coffee break. So when the lecturer heard a shout from the back of the class, 'doctrine!', he didn't really take it in. Indeed, for a moment he thought he was back in his Student Christian Movement days…those glorious days when you could watch cricket at the Parks and discuss matters of import with the keen theological students of Oxford.

Just in time he woke up to the enormity of the situation and turned to face the class. There sat not an enthusiastic Christian but a rather matter-of-fact Muslim student. The lecturer asked the student to clarify what he meant. The student carefully noted how doctrine was the basic life meaning that he found in his religion, and how his view of judgment at the end of time affected how he would take ethical decisions as a professional engineer. The beginnings of a dialogue on integrity and the relationship of private and professional ethics and worldviews were then swiftly interrupted by a keen evangelical Christian. A former member of the Christian Union executive, he noted how he too had a doctrine and how this affected his decision making. A self-declared atheist sprang to the attack at this point, wondering whether he was in an engineering seminar or religious studies, 'It is surely not relevant to talk about all this'. Another atheist then stood up and said, 'I'm also an atheist, but I have *my* doctrine, something about the belief system and worldview that underpins my life, I can't see how they don't affect my professional practice'.

There followed an intense 30-minute debate, involving several students, on the values behind professional values, about different life meaning, personal and professional, and the ground of faith and hope, be that theistic or not.

The assertion of doctrine was one that shook and surprised both students and lecturer. What did this student mean? Was it relevant, or just an embarrassing assertion? How was the lecturer going to handle this? Respectfully listen, ignore, put down or brush off? Where are the boundaries between personal religion and professional practice, and once crossed how are they to be policed? Did the student have a right to bring his faith into the discussion of professional practice or should he keep it to himself?

These are not unlike the kind of questions that have been asked by universities themselves over the past twenty years, and this chapter will look at the strange, numinous world of religion and spirituality, and how universities have handled that, and how they might handle it in relation to the whole reflection on values. The first section will look at the gradual liberation of universities in the UK from the yoke of religion and then the reappearance of religion through human and legal rights and community agendas. The second section will look at the emergence of spirituality as a human universal, related often to certain professions, and how this contributes towards a richer reflection about meaning and values in higher education.

Religion

A number of universities in Britain at the close of the twentieth century have been unsure how to handle religion. The history of the university in the UK has been dominated by the Christian church, and in particular, the Church of England. The original universities were church foundations, with the exception, before 1824, of Edinburgh. The Anglican church dominated proceedings, forbidding access to members of other faiths and denominations. Even by the late 1850s Bebbington notes that in Oxford University

> all heads of house except one were in the Anglican ministry; virtually all tutors
> were clergymen; and about 80 percent of undergraduates were intending to

pursue a clerical career. Students had to subscribe to the Thirty Nine Articles of the Church of England on admission to the university; they took an obligatory test in Greek New Testament and attended compulsory college chapel.[364]

Because there were so many clergy around, there wasn't even the need in many colleges to actually employ a chaplain. Much of the subsequent history of higher education in England is about widening participation in response to this kind of religious dominance.

In the late-nineteenth century the Anglicans began to lose their grip, with new universities establishing secular or non-conformist charters that began to end the Anglican domination. In the twentieth century a mass of new universities rose from a genuinely secular background, ranging from the new green field sites to the former polytechnics. Religion simply did not figure in the value systems of these universities and the Anglican church for the most part withdrew to simply providing support for student accommodation. Religion had lost its seat at the table of power and being unsure of its role accepted simply the task of looking after Anglican students. In a belated attempt to engage this new population of students and with no privilege position, apart from the Anglican foundations at such as Oxbridge, the Anglican church in the 1950s and 60s tried to establish chaplaincies for these new universities, and since then has been trying to work out how to relate to higher education in collaboration with other Christian denominations and faiths.[365]

Universities, for their part, have looked somewhat quizzically at the religions on campus. Gilliat-Ray[366] notes many different perspectives, including:

• *Anti-religious.* One older civic university, for instance, makes no space provision for any religious groups in campus, and its statutes explicitly forbid the teaching of theology. Having ousted privileged religion they have no intention of letting it back in again.

• *Tolerant.* Some provisions are made for worship space on campus, with a minimum of maintenance, but there is no attempt to promote these activities in any way.

• *Anti-denominational.* Some so-called secular universities happily accommodate religious groups, provided that they collaborate and none is seen as dominant.

• *Multi-faith pragmatist.* Such universities note the validity of religious needs, especially of Muslims and Jews in relations to space and to exams, and try to ensure that there is some pastoral or worship space for all the different religions.

A number of things have led to universities responding in these different ways. Firstly, many university charters are clear that they do not want to be dominated by religion again. Secondly, religion, and especially the Christian religion, nationally has lost its position of a privileged narrative. Whatever one's view of the theories of postmodernity it is clear that we are in a world where the major narratives which gave some meaning structure to society are no longer relevant.[367] Side by side with any postmodern developments has been the rise of the New Age. The New Age is really a number of different movements who share certain key ideas:

• Spirituality as acceptable, whatever the form, unless it harms an other. Hence there is a tolerance of a great range of spirituality. Indeed, all existence is seen as a manifestation of some greater Spirit. All religions are seen as an expression of this same reality.

• Everyone is free to choose his or her own spiritual path.

• Spirituality is to do with the 'other worldly', stressing the mystical and even magical. This seems a conscious attempt to locate spirituality in the numinous, that which is beyond and greater than oneself.

• Spirituality as largely anti-rational. Feelings and experience are paramount.

• All life is interconnected and human beings work together with the Spirit to create reality.[368]

The effect of these movements has been to stress the rights of the individual to their own spirituality, but also to further develop the private or group view of religion and spirituality. Religion is a matter for private groups, with no shared public discourse. After all, by its very nature religion is confessional, i.e. demanding personal commitment. Religions have become confined to either the private sphere or the sphere of the religious community. It is not easy then to see religion on campus as other than the object of a particular interest group, no different from the ball-room dancing society in the student union. Religion is thus quite separated from the public ordering of the university. It may of course be part of the discourse practiced by the discipline of theology. But this is first and foremost not confessional but an academic discipline in dialogue with other disciplines.

Thirdly, however, whilst the Christian religion has lost its dominance, especially in higher education, the issue of religions per se has moved into the area of rights. The increase in different cultures led to an increased awareness of the religious needs of others and the need to respect religious rights. This is exemplified in the *Employment Equality (Religion or Belief) Regulations*, 2003.[369] A section of this applies to higher and further education, making it unlawful to discriminate against a student because of religion or belief, in admissions, through refusing access to benefits, by excluding him from the educational establishment or by 'subjecting him to any other detriment'.[370] The last of these opens a wide field of interpretation. In addition there has been increasing attention paid to responding to religious needs. The two major areas are in terms of examinations and worship provision. For many Jewish or Islamic students the timing of examinations may cut across religious festivals, necessitating special consideration. Many campuses are looking to ensure the provision of worship facilities so that students can attend to their faith practices during the ordinary week. It is not quite clear whether this falls under religious rights, respect for religious practices or customer care. Some universities see this service as an important part of the recruitment drive, especially for international students.

Fourthly, alongside a concern for religious rights and practice, universities have been uneasy about the more oppressive and intolerant role of religion. In the 1970s, for instance, the National Union Students (NUS) was put under great pressure to equate Zionism with racism and to ban Jewish and Israeli societies from campus. The Student Union at some campuses did pass such a motion. In addition to this the 1980s and 90s saw a great increase in high profile cases of new religious movements (NRMs) or the so-called 'cults'.[371] A good example of this is the London Church of Christ. It began as the Boston Church of Christ, operating on Boston University campus. Such was the fear of its methods of recruiting that it was excluded from the Boston University campus. The Church of Christ then developed a series of new identities in London and elsewhere. Such groups are characterised by:

• An aggressive evangelism which targets new and vulnerable students at key points on and off campus, such as halls of residence or local coffee houses.

• Claims to have the status of an established denomination, thus especially confusing international students.

• Use of mind-altering techniques such as 'love-bombing', with the aim of making the person's well-being and sense of identity dependent on the group.

• Driving a wedge between student and family, and in some cases turning them away from their studies.

• Strongly literal view of scripture, leading to a narrow definition of orthodoxy, and polarisation of views with those outside the group.

• Strong dependence on the leaders, often with intrusive policing of disciples' behaviour and beliefs.

Such groups would often locate themselves close to more formal faith or denomination groups in order to gain respectability, with the result that the formal groups would often get the blame for any problems caused by them.

In response to such movements, the then Committee of Vice-Chancellors and Principles (CVCP, now Universities UK or UUK) commissioned a report on *Extremism and Intolerance on Campus.*[372] The report limited its remit to a consideration of the legal obligations that the university might have to maintain order and protect the rights of students (*Public Order Act 1986*). It noted that inter-religious, multicultural and interracial harmony are not part of the report's remit but might well be explored in their own right. The report therefore looks at the legal views on issues such as racial hatred, incitement to violence and so on. In particular it looks at the implications of the *Education (No. 2) Act* of 1986. For a university campus, this involves issues including freedom of speech, unlawful speech, codes of discipline, allowing or banning public meetings on campus, and the distribution of literature. For some universities this simply means that any voice is allowed, providing that it does not lead to incitement to racist or religious hatred and harassment. Others, including the National Union of Students, have taken a more assertive response, banning certain groups from the Union or university property. For the most part universities have chosen to respond to such groups not in terms of their religious beliefs or practices, but rather in terms of any adverse effects that they may have on students. For instance, if an NRM is phoning possible student recruits several times a day this could constitute harassment, and thus be dealt with under harassment procedures. There is also an increased stress on raising awareness of NRMs and their problems and enabling students to think and respond critically to them.

Universities then have been concerned to support freedom of speech, to recognise religious rights, and at the same time to provide some guidelines about how to deal with intolerance and intrusive recruitment and evangelism on campus. Religion has been kept very much at arm's length, whilst recognising that some customers, especially international ones, find it important. This embodies an interesting mixture of values and principles, from respect for belief, to freedom of speech, customer care, and protection from intolerance or harassment.

In more recent years universities have begun to explore more creative ways of dealing with these issues, than simply relying on rights and directives approaches.

• Some universities have chosen to deal with the 2003 regulations on employment equality under the head of the Equality Unit. Many of these have begun to develop a very different set of values, looking at the roles of religious groups on campus and how they can both work together and work with wider cultural groups to build up community. Major annual festivals such as One World Week provide the basis for working together towards a community of inclusion, stressing collaborativity and co-creation.

• At the same time there has been a move amongst the religious groups themselves to begin to collaborate through the development of interfaith groups. This has quite often arisen because of major public events that might cause a backlash on campus, such as the Palestinian/Israeli conflict or September 11. Ideally, such groups involve the major religious groups on campus and representatives from the university management and the Student Union. Such groups have become the basis for dealing with religion on campus. They are very often the group with the most intelligence about problem NRMs on campus and are better placed to raise any issues about religious need and rights.

Interfaith groups can also act as the means of developing policy statements on religion which provide a framework within which the university can handle religious issues. The University of Derby, for instance, has an institutional statement which does the following:

• Welcomes the variety of religious groups as a 'positive enrichment' of university life rather than a 'source of problems'.

• Requires that religious needs and obligation be sensitively responded to. This includes examinations and food contexts.

- Requires sensitivity to religious dress.
- Assures all religious groups that where possible rooms will be made available for their meetings on campus.[373]

Recent examples of Islam fundamentalist groups, with major political agendas and often an anti-Jewish perspective, have been dealt with successfully by interfaith groups or networks or in the light of Institutional Statements. One mainstream Muslim Society wished to distance itself from an extreme group's political agenda. This was best achieved through working with the campus interfaith network, and the university and Union. This same society then also decided to host a debate on the Palestine issue, outside which they intended to have placards depicting Palestinian babies killed by the Israeli army. They brought this issue to the faith network and together agreed that such images would be likely to cause offence, leading to their withdrawal. In all this, the university is finding that whilst codes or protocols are important, such issues demand a community and collaborative response.

The campus then becomes a place where major issues in the wider world can be worked on at a local level.[374] In fact it becomes a place where debate and negotiation around religious pluralism and related political issues can be modelled. A further example of this is the debate within the Christian churches on homosexuality. Whereas this has often been a debate leading to simply polarization in the wider church, the university campus provides both a direct experience of ethical pluralism and a safe place in which to hear all the different sides and work through the issues.

Hence, far from the university 'privatising' religion, i.e. ensuring that religion remains private, it provides the environment within which religion can develop real dialogue both within the religion, between religions and between religions and the wider community. This openness of religious sharing can also be extended to raising awareness of religions on campus and what they stand for. A good example of this is one university's development of a Faith Awareness Week. Annually the different religious student groups who make up interfaith networks can organise a week-long series of events, detailing the nature of the different faiths and how they relate on various issues.

University chaplaincy

Alongside much of this there has been an increased sense of the religions finding a functioning place within the campus. This can be partly through the student religious groups working with the Student Union and partly through the further development of chaplaincy. Firstly, chaplaincy has been seen in many universities as a key part of student personal support. At one level, this has been about providing worship and pastoral care for the students who are a part of a particular religion. This is an extension of consumer care. Secondly, some universities recognise a broader function for chaplains which relates to key problems on campus, not least student death or bereavement. This recognises that chaplains will be able to provide a level of inclusive pastoral care, which goes beyond their faith constituencies. Some universities actually pay for full-time chaplains, relating to them like National Health Service chaplains, as providers of broad spiritual and pastoral care. Others are still paid for by the faith communities and develop a contract, such as a Services Level Agreement (SLA) with the University. The development of SLAs is in itself significant in that they actually detail the specific role of the chaplain and thus have to begin to define and negotiate what part the chaplaincy plays on campus.[375] The very notion of negotiation is a way of different parties relating to each other in terms of valuing role and presence. An example of the practice of inclusive spiritual and pastoral care developed by such chaplaincies is the development of co-created student memorial services. These bring together the different students or student groups of which the deceased student may have been a part and enable them to create together the order of service. The resulting service tends to enable real intertextual dialogue, i.e. dialogue between the different groups including the underlying values of the groups.[376] All of this sees religious functionaries as having a much wider role than previously able to pursue, a role which enables the student to develop their own views rather than attempting to impose a religious faith upon them. This approach is by definition non-directive and empowering.

Increasingly then religion is returning to the university campus but in a very different incarnation. Previously it involved many different groups who had competing claims to truth and competing claims to university resources. Now, denominational and faith groupings are increasingly collaborating around pastoral and doctrinal matters, accepting differences but also a common concern for the well being of all students and the development of a creative pluralism on campus. In this light the university does not have to hold religion at arm's length, for fear of offending one or other of the faiths, but can actively work with the different religions. Indeed, the university can actively play a part in the greater development of inter-faith collaboration, not least through the development of inter-faith working in chaplaincies. All of this contributes to healthy pluralism, an inclusive community and collegiality.

This has moved the debate swiftly beyond the development of codes of practice to deal with extreme religious groups or tolerance of religious beliefs to practice based sharing and creative dialogue that can enable religions to contribute both practice and ideas to the development of the university community. Religion can contribute to such developments without having to be confessional, without trying to pressurise students or university into believing and practising a particular religious faith. The university can then enable an awareness and appreciation of and respect for the different faiths and their distinct ideas around practical collaboration, without demanding allegiance to any particular one. None of this excludes a response of faith by any person involved, it simply does not demand it. Moreover, this is not simply a tolerance of different religious presence and perspectives. Tolerance in that 'thin' sense involves an unquestioning acceptance of a faith and the right to practise it, without any engagement or appreciation of it. However, working together for a wider good provides a basis from which different religious faiths can be appreciated in practice. This inevitably deepens trust between the groups concerned and allows a deeper testing and challenging of the faiths, which far from endangering faith can develop it.

Such developments as outlined above are not uniform across higher education. However, they are increasingly happening and they do point to a relationship between faith communities and the university which is coming of age and which is deepening reflections on values in higher education.

Spirituality

Alongside concern for skills development in university education there has been increasing work on the spiritual dimension of higher education. This reflects the increasing independence of spirituality from formal religion. Writers such as Hay argue that spirituality is a human universal. He argues that it can be defined in terms of 'relational awareness' and that it has a biological base.[377] Others argue that spirituality is more than relational awareness.[378] It includes the drive to find significant meaning in relationships with the self, other people and groups, the environment and any deity. A working definition might be:

• Awareness and appreciation of the other (including the self, other person, group, environment or deity)
• Capacity to respond to the other
• The development of significant life meaning based upon these relationships.[379]

Such meaning involves the development of faith and hope, both in a generic sense,[380] life purpose and reconciliation. Spirituality per se can thus be differentiated from religion. Religion involves a particular, systematic practice of spirituality, with shared doctrine which focuses on the Divine. Spirituality is broader than religion and can simply involve the individual's response to and development of life meaning and related world views focused on significant relationships.

This opening up of spirituality as an element in the development of the person is well reflected in primary and secondary education even to the extent of being enshrined in legalisation and codes. The 1988 *Education Reform Act*, for instance, requires schools to promote 'the spiritual, moral, cultural, mental and physical development of pupils'.[381] The 1944 *Education Act* extends the idea to the community:

> ...and it shall be the duty of the local education authority for every area, as far as their powers extend, to contribute to the spiritual, moral mental and physical development of the community by securing that efficient education...be available to meet the needs of the population of their area.[382]

These extracts point to both a sense of spiritual development that is a part of the development of the person and to the sense of the spirituality of a community, both of which education can contribute to. Whilst this stresses the inclusiveness of such spirituality there are still problems even in primary and secondary education. Religions often still want to define the spirituality purely in their terms. Beck charts the way in some religious thinkers simply identify religion, spirituality and morality, and thus seek increased attention to formal religion in the curriculum.[383] Such a view, however, simply assumes clear connections between spirituality, religion and morality, something which is contentious even within theological circles. Worst of all, it works against a genuinely student-centred development of spirituality, or an appreciation of diverse spiritual perspectives.

In a very different way other researchers, such as Peter Doble and Chris Meehan at the University of Leeds, are looking to develop a spirituality in education that would be essentially school-centred, with staff and pupils developing a reflective spiritual framework for their school.[384]

For higher education, spirituality and religion have tended to be equated and to be placed simply in the realm of religious rights and respect for them. However, there are increasing signs of spirituality being explored as a genuine dimension of higher education, quite apart from any specific religious approach. Part of this is reflected in research and development to do with professional practice and part in terms of the broader view of spirituality and personal and professional development.

Spirituality and the professions

Perhaps the most dominant profession which has been researching spirituality in terms of professional practice is nursing. There are different emphases in this. O'Brien and Bradshaw, for instance, stress a 'Nightingale' view, i.e. one that relates directly to a Christian tradition.[385] A number of others see a view which is both patient and profession-centred.[386] The patient-centred view recognises that the experience of significant illness may in some way radically affect the belief system that the patient has up to this point. By belief system is broadly meant the significant life meaning, in terms of faith and hope, arising from key relationships. Both faith and hope here are used in a generic sense.[387]

Such a view of spirituality can be developed as part of virtually any discipline and links into reflective activities common now amongst personal development planning. This has led to the development of a number of modules throughout UK universities which directly relate spirituality to the curriculum. Good examples of this are in both Medicine and Healthcare. Medical schools, for instance, distinguish between the core curriculum and Special Study Modules (SSM). The core curriculum deals with 'the central kernel of competence which each and every medical student is expected to acquire by the time they leave medical school'.[388] The SSM has knowledge objectives which are 'deeper' and 'broader' than the core curriculum, including:

- To equip students for a future of self-directed learning;
- To develop essential transferable skills such as information gathering; communication and presentation skills, problem solving and critical reasoning;
- To develop appropriate attitudes of self-motivation, and self-evaluation, together with an understanding of the importance of active learning;
- To allow students to extend their knowledge and understanding in subject areas of their choice.[389]

The modules target specific skills and attitudes rather than simply facts. Perhaps most importantly they stress learning as an active experience and the development of the reflective practitioner. Hence, through reflection, a great deal of time is spent on the purposes and underlying values of the profession. Reflection on spirituality naturally fits into this whole area and has led in some universities to the development of modules in spirituality and medicine and the development of several different research topics on that theme. Such modules include:

- Definitions of spirituality and how they relate to health
- How spirituality relates to mental health in particular
- Spirituality and therapy
- Spirituality and trauma
- Spirituality, dying, death and bereavement
- Spirituality and the identity of the healthcare professions
- Assessment of spiritual need.

Research topics include examination of the 'stages of dying' in terms of different faith stages, the development of patient-centred views of spirituality and the development of different approaches to assessing the spirituality of the patient.[390]

Spirituality and personal development

Parallel to such developments in medicine and healthcare are developments in general skills-centred modules open to all students. These modules aim to focus on vocational skills as part of the curriculum. Once more then the driver is work application, opening up modules run by agencies as diverse as careers offices and student counselling. One such course is run by Student Action, a student community volunteer society, in coordination with the department of Continuing Education. It includes the theories, values and issues underlying the process of volunteering, the skills necessary for voluntary work, the stages of volunteer development and the effect of voluntary work on the community.

Into such a market place of elective modules, spirituality naturally takes its place, both in relation to any reflection on vocation and in relation the skills development agenda. One example of what can be done is the Lifeskills and Spirituality module at the University of Leeds:

Lifeskills and Spirituality module includes:

Defining spirituality

This invites wide-ranging reflection on the meaning of spirituality, arriving at a working definition which is tested throughout the course.

Spirituality is then distinguished from religion, psychology and ethics, and students are invited to reflect (confidentially) on their own spirituality through working out a life map or values history. Narrative as the vehicle of spirituality is explored through personal and literary stories.

Spirituality and Health

The relationship of spirituality to health and well-being is explored. This leads to an examination of the part spirituality can play in the healing process, and an identification of the key skills involved. Focus is on empathy as a spiritual skill and the underlying attitude of unconditional care, especially in terms of agape.

This is developed in relating to hope, faith, purpose and reconciliation and forgiveness, culminating in the idea of shalom.

All this is applied to death, dying and bereavement.

Conflict Resolution

The dynamics of forgiveness and reconciliation are developed in relation to the skills of conflict resolution, including contexts such as the family.

Work

The nature of work in terms of purpose, vocation, hope and faith is examined. How this ties in with professional decision making and management is then examined, along with and the underlying skills.

This includes work culture and whistle blowing.
Community
Different kinds of community, how they learn and develop identity and meaning, are examined. The different meanings of these communities are tested and the underlying skills of community development in a postmodern age articulated.
Global Issues
Spirituality and how awareness of global issues, especially poverty and the care of the environment, is developed and connected to everyday life, including issues about multi-national and state responsibility.
The Divine
Because a significant part of the course is seminars where the different spiritual narratives of the students are shared the Divine is not absent up to this point. However, thoughts about the transcendent other are drawn together at the end, not least issues about how we can know such an 'other', or even talk about him.

All such modules are student and practice-centred, enabling reflection on the 'other' (be that self, other person, group, environment or the divine), on how we respond to the other, and on how we generate significant life meaning for ourselves and others through those relationships. Precisely because such reflection does not shirk the conflicts in ideas and feelings that might arise, it enables dialogue which works through to criteria for challenging different spiritualities, not least as to whether they are healthy or not. Assessment is carried out through long essay, reflective journal and analytical review of a novel.

Such initiatives then begin to show some ways in which focus on spirituality is changing the previous religious agendas within the university. Firstly they show the practical application of spirituality. Secondly they introduce a strong person-centred sense of the term in which the individual is responsible for working out their spirituality in relation to their significant relationships. Thirdly, this provides a basis for systematic sharing of significant narratives around reflection on practice, what van der Ven refers to as intertextual dialogue. [391] Such intertextuality is the basis of moral and spiritual development. It enables many different views on significant life meaning to be articulated and appreciated. At one level this enables appreciation of different significant concepts offered by different religions and spiritualities. In the area of business and global concerns, for example, students can examine concepts such as the Judeo-Christian *shalom* (justice and peace), or the Confucian *kyosei* (harmony), both of which have been used in different ways by industries and business ethics.[392] At the same time the focus on shared reflection of practice and life meaning enables a mutual testing of that meaning and on occasion a mutual respectful challenge. All of this values the different religious and spiritual traditions, old and new, as part of a much wider reflection, and provides a safe and creative way in which to test then and any other spiritual meanings. In turn this enables the development of inclusive, affective and holistic thinking in practice. In all this, connections between belief systems and value systems are worked out.

Conclusions

Higher education is beginning to relate much more effectively to the religion and spirituality. After the initial domination of education by the churches, higher education institutions clearly were suspicious. They are now finding that religion, not least through chaplaincy, does have an important part to play on campus, in the development of inclusive community, the provision of spiritual and pastoral care, and in ensuring the widest possible religious and spiritual dialogue. Alongside the emancipation from religious dominance this has allowed religion and its values to relate through conversation, collaboration, mutual challenge and co-creation.[393] Perhaps even more important is the development of an approach towards spirituality which can recognise that values are not simply about ethical concepts or the capacity to make rational decisions but about underlying beliefs systems and belief relationships. These are the values which underlie values, stressed by the Muslim student at the start of this chapter. The importance of belief systems and their relationship to practice are, in turn, being increasingly researched in professions such as nursing and even in relation to work in general.[394]

17

The integrity of the university

Simon Robinson and Clement Katulushi

In this chapter we aim to pull together some of the questions and issues raised in the previous chapters and place them in an overall analysis of values in higher education.

We first examine the crisis experienced by UK higher education in the late-twentieth century, noting four different aspects of it. We then question the nature of this crisis. This is then put into the context of one university's mission and value statements. In analysing this we suggest that there are four different kinds of values which the university has to handle: academic, learning, social and management. We analyse these in turn. A definition of integrity applied to the university will emerge which is not simply about an aggregate of the virtues, but rather involves reflectivity, dialogue, and process.

The university in crisis

Like a good many institutions the university seems to have been in crisis over the past three decades.[395] Some would tell us that the very idea of the university has been under threat. Mary Warnock, at a higher education chaplains' conference, for instance, voiced her regret at voting for the change of polytechnics to universities in the House of Lords, precisely because she felt that the idea of a university had gone, 'We no longer know what a university is'.[396] This, however, is to assume that there ever was a clear, agreed idea of the university. In fact, two things do seem clear historically: first that the 'university' has been constantly evolving and second that it has evolved in response to different groups in society and to the underlying values of the many stakeholders.

Oxford and Cambridge were, in origin, universities which provided education for the professional classes, focussing on Theology and Law. They, like Newman's vision of the university, had little sense of research. The modern university began to emerge in the late-seventeenth century in Halle, reaching its peak in Berlin in the first decade of the nineteenth century. This was a very different institution, defined by Gordon Graham as 'a non-denominational institution in which natural science played a significant part and where theology and history were subject to critical scrutiny'.[397] That very critical attitude and desire for objectivity and freedom from religion ushered in new values and began to move towards a wider view of utility.

Over time the purpose and values of the university then have been tested and developed in different ways. As Peter Scott notes above, the purposes and values of the university have continued to be developed in relation to the needs and views of the local and wider communities, including industry.

In the light of all this there have been no ideal embodiments of the university. Those who disagree might turn to the Oxbridge vision as the outstanding view of a university. The tutorial system is the envy of all, enabling a strong sense of student autonomy and real collegial learning. The college system is a model of community, with proximity providing the basis for student well-being, through discipline, pastoral care and learning. There is a deep sense of community, which naturally communicates values within the institution of care, respect, responsibility and commitment, as well as the pursuit of excellence.

However, what such a view had and still has, in terms of close community, it lacked in terms of equality and inclusivity. As noted in the last chapter, the Anglican church dominated Oxbridge in nineteenth-century Britain.[398] Looking back now it seems astonishing that the church could have exhibited such an attempt to dominate higher education, and much of the subsequent history of the sector is about widening participation in every sense. Ironically, with the abolition of religious testing, in 1852 and 1854, there were many who felt that the universities were at that point in crisis. Even the editor of the Roman Catholic *Month*, Richard Clarke, warned of an inevitable decline in morals, because of the loss of the religious perspective, saying 'the abolition of tests, the admission of all forms of Dissent, Judaism and Paganism tend to establish that sort of truce which men are almost compelled to make who differ in first principles' leading to 'a common consent to exclude religion from their life more and more'.[399]

Today the crisis would seem to be of a different kind, one which many view as apocalyptic. Suitably we might discern the four riders of the apocalypse who have challenged the seemingly 'settled values' of the university.

The first of these 'riders' is the sheer magnitude of the enterprise, with the aim of involving half the 18–30 population in higher education by 2010. With the increase in numbers comes greater distance in teaching, with less and less tutorials and seminars, more distance learning and a fragmentation of the learning experience. Inevitably pastoral support from tutors is lessened, leading to greater reliance on the central student support services, and the inevitable uncoupling of pastoral and teaching functions.[400] Hence, the great drive to equality seems to cut a swathe through the vision of the learning *community*. O'Neill also argues that the greater equality also is internally incoherent, not least because it is not clear how academic standards can be maintained with what must be a wider range of ability.[401]

The second rider is increased professionalization, in search of efficiency and accountability. Never before has the lecturer had to be so efficient, with a concomitant rise in administrative tasks. Never before has the academic had to be so clearly accountable. This includes accountability to students, who have the chance to evaluate the modules. The old system of external examiners guiding the development of modules is now replaced with teaching quality assessment and an audit culture. All this is accompanied by increased attention to criteria of assessment, evidence based development and performance indicators, and targets. O'Neill suggests that this leads to several problems. The first is an erosion of trust. Trust of the academic, like other professions, begins to depend upon paperwork, outcomes and so on. She suggests that if professionalization is to be judged on its outcomes, this should include whether it generates trust. She finds little evidence of such an outcome. The second problem is teleopathy – a confusion of ends or purposes and focus on secondary purposes.[402] O'Neill argues that the emphasis on accountability leads to a 'distorting of the proper aims of professional practice'.[403] This becomes inevitable when targets are set centrally and are connected to finance, and consequently the flourishing or survival of an academic department. In that case it is the survival that becomes the major end and the quality of the teaching or research becomes only a means to that end. Even that quality can be eroded, with lecturers, for instance, publishing too early in order to meet RAE targets.

In the wider context O'Neill sees this as a part of the impossible search for perfect accountability. Of course, none of this is new or unique to higher education. Campbell noted similar issues in the healthcare professions in the 1980s, suggesting that one of the major problems of professionalization was task orientation which took away from the essential relational elements of care.[404]

Closely related to the issues of accountability and targets comes the third rider, involving contract, market and choice. With great accountability comes more transparency and clearer contract relationships internally and externally. The development of an internal contract culture with schools and departments becoming cost centres, and thus more financially accountable, was a shock to many universities. For many academics and support staff there was a feeling that this led to a breakdown of purpose and community.[405]

Part of the contract culture is a focus on the rights of the student as consumer. This means more student say in the running of modules, through staff/student committees, more accessible complaints procedures and more student choice with respect to modules. Optional modules are now in a thriving market place, with departments looking to attract students and so make money. One physics department produced what became known as the 'physics for poets' module, i.e. physics without mathematics or 'serious science'. It attracted several hundred students, providing a tidy income for the department. This is not to frown upon such entrepreneurship. It is to suggest that education can easily become in that light a consumable. If we add to that the pressure to retain students, then satisfying the educational client can soon become the prime end. It is precisely in this area that Bauman's concerns become very clear.[406] Education becomes packaged and fragmented, with little sense of the nature of learning or the need to be committed to a learning relationship whose outcome cannot be predicted. In all this there is the attendant temptation to get rid of the risk of learning.

The fourth rider is the commercialization of higher education. This involves two aspects, the business world setting the agenda for research and teaching, and the university becoming more and more like business in its practice. There is strong pressure from business and Government to stress the development of skills which make the graduate employable, and also to develop the economic utility of the higher education. The increase of business practice can again be a matter of teleopathy. It is also reinforced by the ways in which government set targets in retention and research connected to finance, and respond to different students 'markets'. The 'international student' recruitment market, for instance, promises high income from full fees. Hence, most universities target key international regions. Bok argues that such commercialization runs the danger of lowering academic standards and adversely affecting the reputation, and the integrity, of the university.[407]

It is tempting then to see a straightforward crisis which is eroding core values such as trust, commitment, community, equality, freedom, with the assumption that these core values are being replaced by other more instrumental values. However, the 'crisis' is far more complex than this, and further reflection reveals several strong positive values which have emerged in the past two decades:

• Despite some uncertainty about the exact effects of widening participation strategies there is evidence of greater equality and inclusiveness.[408]

• In the UK, prior to the 1980s, there was little appreciation amongst academics, and the community in general, of the cost of higher education. As this was borne more and more by central government so universities and their faculties had to accept greater constraints and greater accountability. Far from being a bad thing this can help to develop a strong sense of common responsibility and realistic view of resources. The view that money was never an issue before the 1980s is not entirely correct. Finances have always been critical. It is simply that these were provided by those with powerful resources for a limited number. The cost of widening participation is inevitably high.

• Some values are being explored and developed in different contexts. The value of community, for instance, has always been assumed to require proximity. However, institutions such as the Open University and the University of the Highlands and Islands are exploring ways in which community can be developed through IT, different media and summer schools. The OU refers to itself as 'everyone's local university'.[409] This reaches a further level through the development of work-based universities, as in Unipart and the National Health Service.[410] Both of these examples also further the widening participation agenda and the connection of higher education to work.

• Alongside community there is increasingly an acceptance of the need for collaboration and partnership, something reinforced by Government and European funding schemes. In turn collaboration leads to greater interdisciplinary creativity.

• Values are also emerging in remarkable ways. For instance, the stress on a duty of care for students with mental health problems, noted by Humphrys, takes one beyond a simple idea of customer care.[411] It is beyond the scope of this chapter but the way in which customer care has led to a broader duty of care and how these two relate to each other would repay more detailed analysis.

• As David notes, alongside financial constraints there have also been major developments in creative pedagogy which have stressed the whole person and moved beyond the simplistic idea of skills development for economic utility. As we shall note below this takes the question of values into the curriculum, and the student teacher relationship.

The development of such values as these paints a more positive picture alongside the crisis view. Undoubtedly trust can be the victim of hyper-accountability. However, trust is also the function of negotiation and the best sense of positive contract. Contract and negotiation can be liberating.

In the light of such complexity we will now examine and analyse, as an example of practice, a working document from the University of Leeds on Mission and Values.[412] Part of the strategic plan, this document states the basic values.

University of Leeds: Mission and Values
Mission
The University
• secures internationally recognised excellence in research whilst simultaneously providing a first class, innovative and flexible learning and teaching environment for students of all ages and backgrounds
• is committed to the dissemination, transfer and application of knowledge for the benefit of all sections of society
• is an international institution which also serves the nation and local and regional communities

• strives always to provide value for money and to be accountable to the communities which it serves.

The University's distinctive strengths are:
• that it is able to maintain all the core disciplines in strength and on that platform to provide special opportunities for interdisciplinary study and research
• its capacity to be flexible and adaptable, especially in the provision of learning and teaching and for research.

Values
The work of the University is shaped by its commitment to the following values and principles:
• **Critical independence and academic freedom**: the University encourages objective, analytical and disinterested study and seeks, for example, to provide an environment in which its members can test and question received wisdom and put forward new and potentially controversial ideas.
• **Lifelong learning**: valuing learning for its own sake as well as for the social and individual benefits it can bring, the University seeks to provide opportunities for higher and continuing education at all stages of adult life.
• **Inclusion**: the University is proud to be a multi-cultural and diverse community, and is determined to ensure that it treats all individuals fairly, with dignity and respect; that all the opportunities are open to all; and that it provides a safe, supportive and welcoming environment for staff students and visitors.
• **Responsiveness**: the University is committed to being responsive to the needs of the communities which it serves
• **Openness and transparency**: the University is committed to the highest standards of corporate governance (as exemplified in its Code of Practice on Corporate Governance) and in particular to conducting its affairs with integrity, honesty and transparency.

We would suggest that this statement involves four different kinds of value. First are academic values, which relate to the profession of teaching and research, including the responsibility for the profession to maintain standards, and relate to the different stakeholders. Second are what might be termed learning values. These relate to the nature and end of learning, as a life long and developmental process. Third there are social values. These are general social values which nonetheless relate to the education enterprise, not least the principles of equality, democracy or community. Fourth are management values, embodied in the code of practice for Corporate Governance. Again these are values which are not unique to the university, but are relevant to any large corporate body.

Academic values

Academic values are really part of the values of the academic profession. Like other professions we can see the development of specialised knowledge and skills and a concern with standards, freedom and autonomy, relation to the client and relation to the wider community and environment.[413] Central to these concerns are the values of: independence; impartiality; responsibility; and competence.

The academic has to retain independence from any interest group pressure. This is to ensure in research and teaching that judgement is neither partial nor distorted. Disinterestedness is essential if the academic is to reach a judgment as far as possible based on the available data and critical analysis. Of course this does not mean that the researcher should not be fired by their own interest in the sense of their passion for discovery. As Campbell notes of healthcare professionals this is essential to professional motivation.[414] However, it always important to have a transparent system which enables reflection and testing. The authority and integrity of the academic and her institution is questionable if this is not maintained in a very open way. Such autonomy can lead to controversial conclusions which, as the Leeds statement notes, test received wisdom. Testing this can be risky, hence the need to maintain an environment which supports such research and teaching and clearly signals to the outside world the importance of this support.

This is not a simple open-ended view of academic freedom, asserting the academic's right to be free from constraints as she pursues her own interest. On the contrary the academic's interest may itself be partial, and needs to be tested internally both against interest and against constraints. This is an ongoing debate which is part of the nature of the academic community. The commitment and faith that Williams writes about very much undergirds this approach, enabling both a positive freedom to research and maintain critical dialogue, and a negative freedom, freedom from coercion and constraints.[415] These two kinds of freedom are familiar from Berlin's distinction.[416] Michael Novak suggests a further form of freedom, the freedom to do one's duty.[417] This does not prescribe the content of duty but rather stresses the importance of examining different duties and responsibilities.

Such a concern is precisely common to all professions. This is usually focused on the client, but also includes other stakeholders. For the academic, the client will vary from student, to funding body and so on. She will also have responsibilities to her university and possibly to a wider profession, such as medicine or engineering. Precise responsibility is not something that can be predetermined. Its content needs to be negotiated in each situation. Robinson suggests that responsibility is in fact more a virtue, demonstrating an attitude of concern or service.[418] The university in this sense can be seen as serving both its clients and society as a whole, through teaching and research.

Competence undergirds all this, and this demands shared criteria and transparency. In turn it demands a commitment to professional development, one of the key values which has been developed in higher education in the late-twentieth century. Importantly, the modern academic is also asked to demonstrate competence in administration and awareness in pastoral care. Administration takes its place alongside research and teaching as evidence for salary increments or promotion. Pastoral care is also being rewarded more clearly by some universities.

Learning values

Dearing saw the purpose of learning as complex, with higher education as instrumental both in terms of developing the capacity and enabling the well-being of the student, and also in terms of the contribution of the person to society. Held in tension here is the value of fitness for work, and personal interest, and also service to society. Beneath such values can be seen a view of humanity as interdependent, with personal ambition operating alongside contribution to the common good.[419] As it stands this acts as a well-balanced basis for higher education practice which will encourage skills development and reflection on values. However, the end of learning, and the underlying values are more contentious.

Ronald Barnett argues that higher education is in essence emancipatory and holistic.[420] In effect, it liberates the student from the narrow focus of the disciplines, enabling reflective thinking which can critique the assumptions of the discipline and look beyond to relations with other areas. Products of this process are 'self understanding and self empowerment', enabling students to 'come into themselves'.[421] Philosophy and sociology are important tools in this reflection, 'because they make possible self-understanding and self-empowerment in a particularly striking way'.[422] This process of emancipation is something that is implicit in the nature of higher education. Hence, argues Barnett, unless someone is coming to university with a limited view of training then students of any discipline will have to go through this process.

Barnett justifies this argument in two ways: philosophical and historical. The first of these builds on R.S. Peters' view of education in general. Peters argues that many of the arguments about the purpose of education are in fact 'disputes about principles of procedure'.[423] A key principle, for instance, is that in education the student should be treated with respect for her autonomy. This in turn involves enabling the student to develop analytical and critical skills, and the capacity to think holistically and synoptically, i.e. across disciplines. In effect Peters takes this view to emerge from the logic of the concept of education.

In extending a similar argument to higher education Barnett focuses especially on the concept of *higher*. He argues that 'higher' education requires higher order thinking, and this involves the development of 'analysis, evaluation, criticism and even imagination'.[424] This level of thinking transcends the simple acquisition of work-centred skills, developing an awareness of the wider context and the capacity to learn about learning. Inevitably this affects the way the whole person reflects and learns.

Barnett's appeal to history is simply that the emancipatory concept of has undergirded much of the last 150 years of higher education in the writings of such as Newman, Huxley, Mill, Jaspers and Leavis.

John White argues forcefully against such a view on three grounds.[425] Firstly, it is not clear why higher education per se should demand such higher thinking. The same aim could be appropriate to all levels of education. Secondly, Barnett's choice of historical thinkers is arbitrary, and in any case cannot determine how we should think in the future. Thirdly, and perhaps most fundamentally, accepting the emancipation as the central task of higher education is in effect forcing a particular view on the student. Appealing to the freedom of the student he argues that the emancipatory aim of higher education cannot be made compulsory.[426] It is reasonable to pursue it with certain students, such as those with an interest in a wider perspective and those training for professions such as nursing, where reflection on 'the larger social horizons of their calling and their role within it' are important.

In effect White takes this argument down to one about freedom and the inability to impose a single major aim on higher education. In one sense he is right. As David Jenkins argues there are several aims in higher education one cannot be stressed at the expense of others.[427] Moreover, the issue of the freedom of the student is critical, and ultimately any student may determine that he does not want to 'be empowered'. However, several arguments suggest that the issue is more complex:

• Rowan Williams bases an argument for holistic learning on the nature of humanity.[428] What marks us out is our capacity to reflect, learn about learning, and in effect transcend ourselves and begin to try to make sense of our world. The skills to do with this are what we are about not simply as members of a community or workforce but as human beings. The process is fundamentally dialogic and part of putting faith in the university is about enabling that dialogue. It is of course a dialogue freely entered into, but the dialogue is fundamental to learning, and hence the means of enabling this should be in place.

• A more utilitarian approach stresses the importance of holistic learning to the optimum functioning of the professional. In developing a taxonomy of learning for the professional engineer, for instance, Carter notes the critical connection of knowledge and skills to personal qualities.[429] The personal qualities include traditional virtues, but also what he refers to as 'spiritual qualities'. The latter involves awareness and appreciation of the other and the capacity to respond to the other. Carter argues that such a holistic approach is important to effective decision making and therefore the best functioning of the professional.

• It is a short move from this to argue, with Fryer, for the importance of broader learning in order to enable students to be effective citizens.[430] This invites us to view the student not as some atomistic individual but as a part of the community, with responsibilities as well as rights. Katulushi goes further to view the student as global citizen, and the university as a global community being informed by as well as informing a global ethic.[431] This has led Gwen Collins, for example, to develop a global teaching network, to encourage the global perspective as part of most modules.[432] All this approach invites us to question the atomistic liberal view of the person which lies at the base of White's position. We would rather argue that the person is part of a wider community of interdependence and that learning should enable the person to function in that context.

• Other arguments extend this to the need for values to be overtly involved in the learning relationship. Again this can be partly utilitarian, with the Council for Industry and Higher Education, for instance, arguing that all students should have some education in applied ethics.[433] This is not, as some have suggested, about universities prescribing values, but rather about the development of ethical imagination and awareness, and the skills of ethical decision making. An acquaintance with ethics and values, it is argued, makes the student a more effective practitioner at work. Connecting values to work is also carried out by some university careers services. Several careers modules invite the student to reflect on their values in relation to vocation. A great deal of this is about encouraging reflection and making connections, as both David and Cowan observe.[434] Hence, this is not a skills-versus-virtues debate but about developing both. This recognises that the affective domain is involved in any learning as much as the cognitive, and stresses the need for holistic critical reflection. Once again such learning takes one beyond narrow definitions of disciplines.

Underlying all this are some core values of the learning relationship, autonomy, collegiality and justice, values which underlie Bauman's chapter. Respect for the autonomy of the learner is central to the learning relationship. Important in this is the student taking responsibility for her own learning, learning how to learn rather than uncritically accepting the view of the teacher. Autonomy in such a relationship cannot be summed up in the liberal view of simply respecting the choice of the individual, not least because the traditional student is developing emotionally and intellectually, and because the student does not know as much about the area of learning as the lecturer.

It could be argued that autonomy as the capacity to reflect and make decisions therefore is actually developed through the learning relationship. The learning experience is therefore about enabling that development. It can be risky, given the need to take responsibility for learning. Hence, as the Leeds vision statement notes the need is for an environment which will enable those risks to be taken. In Cowan's terms this means an environment which will provide core instrumental values of empathy, congruence, and unconditional positive regard.

Learning in Higher Education, however, takes one beyond the simple Rogerian view to, as Cowan notes, a more collegial stance. In the light of this it is not appropriate to see the student as customer, or even client, but more as apprentice relating to master.[435] This is a relationship that has a high degree of mutuality to it, albeit asymmetrical. The more the student is taking responsibility for learning the more she moves to a research mode and thus becomes a co-learner with the lecturer. It is all the more important then for the lecturer to enable the student to take risks, and constructively learn from any mistakes. The stress here is as much on formative assessment as summative, and moves the focus in learning away from the commodification of learning to learning as a life long search or journey. It also acts as a balance to the exclusive focus on individual academic success.[436]

All this points to a community of learning which is characterised by collegiality and, in Megone's and Newman's terms, the familial.[437] In the light of such a community the student and staff can accept their limitations, become used to mutual challenge and become reflective partners in learning. Such learning requires contract, of verbal or written kind, in order to clarify expectations. The contract, however, is an instrument to facilitate learning, not the end of learning. The student is not so much customer, with service provided by the institution, as a member of a community, with all the rights and responsibilities this brings with it. The university as institution, i.e. as managed corporation, is there to facilitate this community.

The nature and task of collegiality is important to explore a little further. Quoting Randall Collins, David Ford suggests that at the heart of collegiality is 'intensive, disciplined face-to-face conversation and debate between contemporaries and across generations.'[438] It is this form of community which enables the transmission of good practice and shared values across generations. Secondly, such community enables the formation and development of persons.[439] Thirdly, such a community enables research and teaching to be united. More than that, Ford suggests that both research and teaching be seen as essentially part of the learning process. Fourthly, it sets the character of any governance. As shall seen below good governance is critical for any large organisation. Higher education demands that governance sustain collegiality and a 'long term vision in the interests of future generations'.

Alongside autonomy and collegiality is justice. This is important in three different ways. First, if respect for autonomy is about the development of the particular person then justice demands equitable response to different groups of students. Second, justice demands that all students are subject to the same criteria of judgement and discipline, and based on these students should be rewarded according to merit. This is expressed in the many different rules of the community. Thirdly, justice can also be based upon need, ensuring the needs of students are met. Disability and equality and diversity offices are good examples of this in action. All of these aspects of justice are important to the learning process and relationship.

Respect for autonomy and justice and related values, then, go beyond the development of disinterested and critical thinking. Hence, far from being value free, or simply leaving the student to determine her own values, learning seeks to communicate these values in and through the learning relationship. Learning which includes understanding as well as training, itself depends on these values. Freedom in the learning is discovered through the development of these values and the related virtues. As Megone notes there is need for a community which actually embodies such virtues and communicates them to the members, and enables their practice. Such a community provides the long-term basis of faith and trust which enables the student to take the risks of learning, which as Bauman notes, includes the capacity to wait, to take the long view.

Social values

The university is related to the local and global community. As such it is inevitably involved in values which are a part of education but also transcend it, as part of values which the wider society is committed to. A key example of that is equality.

At one level this is about ensuring equal opportunities within the institution. At another level it is about going beyond that to a vision of greater equality in society. R.H. Tawney saw 'the kingdom of ideas' as bringing the classes together and changing society.[440] Here equality in higher education is actually affecting the wider community.

This introduces us to the possibility of the university not simply sharing values with the rest of society but also helping to shape society. The Robbins report writes of, 'The transmission of a common culture and common standards of citizenship'.[441] Dearing, perhaps less confident of the content of such common standards looked to the university to 'shape a democratic, civilized and inclusive society'.[442]

At one level Dearing sees these as expressing respect and liberal tolerance. Yet all three concepts have difficulties in terms of practical meaning. Democracy can have a very broad meaning. The idea of civilization is historically relative. The aim of inclusivity is an ideal. Moreover, what does it mean to shape a society? It is one of the key questions as to how this might be done, and if there are any more fundamental values behind this. In all this, should the university be passively tolerant and impartial, or should it be committed to key values?

It would be easy in the concern for freedom of speech and belief to settle for a passive tolerance of all values. David Jenkins, however, argues for something more.[443] He suggests that the university should try to hold together many different purposes and their underlying values. However, alongside research, learning and training the university should be both an 'essentially critical place', and a place of betterment. The critical stance demands that universities can achieve a degree of self-transcendence or distance such that they can subject all the other purposes and related organisations in and outside the university to critical scrutiny. This demands that universities stand out against reductionism or any attempts to limit the openness and plurality of the university. Jenkins' point about betterment is individual, corporate and political. Universities are for the betterment of human beings, but they are also about contributing towards a bigger picture, about contributing to the moral imagination of the wider community. Similarly Dan Hardy sees the university as in some sense the self-transcendence of society. Its role as reflective and learning organization enables it to transcend society and thus act as questioner, and even conscience.[444] The idea of transcendence is important. Whilst it might be a little fanciful to some to see the university as standing above society there is no doubt that a transcending of the situation is a critical part of the reflective, learning process. Hence it is reasonable to say that the university should embody such transcendence.

This critical stance and move for betterment takes the university beyond the simply objective or impartial. Here, it would seem, are values which are worth fighting for. It is a short step from this, in certain contexts, to a vision of the university which sees itself, in collaboration with other institutions, as prophetic, that is standing out for justice and peace in society.[445] Ignacio Ellacuria's speech on receiving an honorary doctorate illustrates this well:[446]

> The starting point of our conception of what a university should be consists of two considerations. The first and most obvious is that the university has to do with culture, knowledge and a particular exercise of intellectual reason. The second consideration, which is not so obvious and commonplace, is that the university is a social reality and a social force, historically marked by what the society is like in which it lives and in which it should live...
>
> Our intellectual analysis finds that our historic reality, the reality of El Salvador, the reality of the third world, that is, the reality of most of this world, the most universal historical reality, is fundamentally characterised by the effective predominance of falsehood over truth, injustice over justice, oppression over freedom, poverty over abundance, in sum evil over good...
>
> This is the reality with which we live and have to cope and we ask ourselves what to do about it in a university way. We answer, firstly, from an ethical standpoint: we must transform it, do all we can to ensure that good predominates over evil, freedom over oppression, justice over injustice, truth over falsehood and love over hatred. If a university does not decide to make this commitment, we do not understand what validity it has as a university...
>
> The university should become incarnate amongst the poor, it should become science for those who have no science, the clear voice for those who have no voice, the intellectual support of those whose very reality makes them true and right and reasonable, even though this sometimes takes the form of having nothing, but who cannot call upon academic reasons to justify themselves.
>
> For this work we have been severely persecuted... If our university had suffered nothing during these years of passion and death for the Salvadorian people, it would mean it had not fulfilled its mission as a university, never mind displaying its Christian inspiration. In a world where falsehood, injustice and oppression reign, a university that fights for truth, justice and freedom cannot fail to be persecuted.

These are powerful words, betraying a Christian liberation theology. Nonetheless, Ellacuria sees this as the role of the university regardless of his Christian inspiration. Some will find difficulties with this approach, not least the negative view of politics and society, and a strong underlying Marxist analysis. However, regardless of these points, Ellacuria locates the university in the realities of his society, which at that time did involve injustice and terror. He argues that the university cannot divorce itself from that reality and that it has a prophetic role, to transform, to change.

All this sees the university as a moral agent which is involved in the issues of its society and which contributes to the development of significant values within that society. This takes justice beyond the realms of learning and into society. This is not to argue for a simplistic anti-capitalist stance, but rather for explicit articulation of values and continued dialogue about them with all stakeholders.

Management values

The modern university is a major corporate body, albeit a public one. Whilst universities characterise themselves as a community of scholars, it is a community with a high financial turnover which has to be managed. Hence, there are few Vice-Chancellors now who do not have the skills of management. Management demands the values of good governance. The range of values in the management of a corporation can be seen in the University of Leeds Corporate Governance Code of Practice, including: efficiency, accountability, democracy, collegiality, transparency and the promotion of integrity. All this is underpinned in that document by the Nolan principles of public life:

- *Selflessness*, involving a focus on the public interest.
- *Integrity*. This includes ensuring no conflicts of interest.
- *Objectivity*. From a management perspective this reinforces the academic imperative to be disinterested, making judgments on the merits of the situation.
- *Accountability*, including submission to 'Whatever scrutiny is appropriate'.
- *Openness*, especially in policy development and decision making.
- *Honesty*, including declaration of interests.
- *Leadership*. These principles should be promoted by leadership and example.

These principles are increasingly called upon to inform Corporate Governance documents, but are particularly appropriate to the public nature of the university. Behind this can be seen a philosophy of stewardship and service, with an acceptance of realism about resources and the need for creativity. Resource realism accepts both limitations of resources and acknowledges and appreciates their different provenances. This acknowledges no single ownership of the higher education enterprise and an obligation to use the resources for the greater, public, good.

Mention of the public good raises the issue of the social responsibility of the university as a corporation. The social responsibility debate in wider business and professional ethics falls broadly into two arguments, the liberal and the stakeholder. The first, as set out by writers such as Friedman and Sternberg, suggests that the proper business of business is to maximise profits for the shareholders, and to stay within the law.[447] This means that no business should be forced to be involved in community, political or charitable activities unless they wanted to. Such work is primarily that of those elected to local and national government. Hence, it is argued, there is no social obligation or responsibility. Similarly it might be argued that the proper business of higher education is to teach and research, all within the framework of the law, not to concern itself with social concerns and the like. The contrasting argument is that any business has many different stakeholders to whom in different ways the business has some responsibility.[448] The precise content of that responsibility is a matter of discussion and negotiation in relation to the stakeholders and may differ according to particular context. The important point is that the corporation and its flourishing is inextricably linked with the different groups or communities in society.

It would be very difficult to fit the university into the individualistic liberal position. Firstly, the university's public nature has the element of service for the greater good. Secondly the university through its research in science, medicine and social science is constantly affecting society, hopefully for the better. Thirdly, the university does depend upon many different stakeholders, who both provide resources and also have a view on the purpose of the university. In fact, the university itself is a complex network of many different groups and organisations, each of which may have different value perspectives. Deciding a 'university view' is difficult without taking these into account. Stakeholders, external and internal include:

- National and local government
- Community organizations
- Other funding bodies
- Industry and professions
- Undergraduates and postgraduates
- Teachers and researchers
- Student support services
- Student Union
- Trade unions.
- Society as a whole

An illustration of the issue of social responsibility is the case of BAT and Nottingham University:

'The smoking gun'?

In 2000 British American Tobacco sponsored the Centre for Social Responsibility at Nottingham University to the tune of £3.8 million. Colin Campbell, the Vice-Chancellor of Nottingham University, gave several reasons in defence of this:

- All the proper process had been adhered to in terms of research funding.
- The funding was not objected to at significant points in the process. In the Nottingham University senate, for instance, only two from 400 objected.
- There are few funding arrangements in that area that are not affected by tobacco money.
- The entire nation benefits from excise on tobacco.
- Had Nottingham not taken this money, some other institution would.

These arguments are problematic. The fact that due process was followed does not necessarily make the action right. The fact that certain key institutions did not criticise the decision until after the grant had been awarded does not make the action right, nor the fact that others in the Nottingham area benefit from BAT's generosity. Money gained from tax, moreover, cannot be equated with money derived directly from the sale of tobacco. Moreover, there were particular issues at the time which raised questions about the wisdom of accepting the money. BAT was under investigation from the Department of Trade and Industry for allegations that it exploited smuggling around the world. Smoking is the biggest preventable cause of cancer in Britain, leading to the deaths of over 120,000 people a year. The tobacco industry is not objective in this matter. It actively seeks to affect people's judgement and to encourage habitual use of tobacco, increasingly targeting the third world. The University of Nottingham is not objective in this matter either, having a strict no-smoking policy.

In all this the University was justifying its actions with an appeal to the narrow view of social responsibility. All process had been attended to, few objections had been raised. Even the Cancer Research Council had apparently not raised any objections in that initial process, though who in the organisation the University spoke to there was at issue. The question raised of such a process is 'Did it genuinely submit the issue to critical scrutiny?' To which the answer has to be, no. The broader view of social responsibility looks at and tests wider responsibilities than simply adherence to law and procedures. This would take into account a wide range of moral views, including all the stakeholders, and seek to find ways of ensuring that the values in the situation were clarified and that value conflicts were properly addressed. In the Nottingham case, there was serial consultation, with the specific point of finding out if there were any objections to the project. Reflection was thus fragmented, involving little opportunity for explicit and detailed dialogue about underlying values and possible major conflicts. It is true that the Senate is a centre of critical reflection. However, it is not clear that having such an issue as part of a busy agenda can facilitate genuine stakeholder dialogue.

In contrast a broader approach would have aimed to bring together the stakeholders and discuss all aspects of the decision at a major meeting. Importantly, it would have aimed to clarify the values of all the stakeholders within the institution and beyond and consider how different options might affect or fulfil those values.

We might consider how differing groups might have responded as part of that dialogue:

• The school of medicine, not least cancer researchers, might have noted that an important role of research at universities was to save lives. How does that role square with receiving money from a group who are linked with major health and social problems, and a major drain on the National Health Service?

• The centre for Business and Professional Ethics might note that all business is concerned to establish and maintain its ethical reputation. How far would this move affect the perceived integrity of the university?

• The University Student Union would doubtless have noted that their premises were smoke-free and that they in collaboration with the university support services were issuing health and well-being leaflets which noted the effects of tobacco on the smoker and those around him, encouraging students to give up smoking, and suggesting ways of stopping. The Union's position is quite complex, not least because it stresses the value of freedom of choice for students, and does not want to prescribe behaviour. The Union would also have a high financial turnover, part of which might be connected to tobacco. Nonetheless, most Unions do actively campaign for students to stop smoking.

• The student medical practice would have noted the increase in student smoking and related effects on conditions such as asthma.

• Philosophers might have asked questions about integrity, such as 'would you encourage your sixteen-year-old child to smoke, and if not why should the university be party to an industry which encourages your sixteen-year-old child to smoke?' Such questions look to the connection between personal, public and professional values, and suggest there may, in some situations, be important connections. This leads to questions about the relationship between social responsibility and the role of the university to help shape a civilized society. It could be argued that it is part of the university's responsibility to look to build a society that does not encourage behaviour that leads to illness and death.

• The university legal advisor might note that universities have increasingly accepted a duty of care and this might be deemed to go against such a policy.

• Administrators might ask questions about how the reputation of the university night be affected. In turn how might that affect, for instance, student intake, or other research monies.

All of this suggests three conclusions for the university as corporation. Firstly, the university in pragmatic terms needs to work closely with its stakeholders and to be part of a value dialogue. The outcome of this will affect perceived integrity, and the university's role in society rests on integrity. Secondly, the university has a responsibility to society which includes working for public good. In practice, the greater good can only be articulated in context and in dialogue, hence the need to work this through with stakeholders. Social responsibility in this context might be seen in terms of either encouraging positive goods (beneficence) or avoiding harm (non-maleficence). There seems little doubt that working against smoking and its effects falls into either of these two categories. Thirdly, working through social responsibility demands negotiation of how that responsibility might be fulfilled amongst the stakeholders. Reflection on values then does not simply stay in the seminar room but moves into practice, and thus into creative collaboration to enable the practice that will reflect values and responsibility.

Integrity

Reflection on these different value areas perhaps then helps us to come to some idea of what integrity might involve for the university. Robert Solomon suggests that integrity is actually no single thing but rather 'a complex of virtues, working together to form a coherent character, an identifiable and trustworthy personality'.[449]

However, integrity is perhaps something a little more dynamic than this. Coherence and consistency require a continual reflective process which can both remain true to a complex of values and also respond to new challenges and constraints. This involves: commitment to core values, careful handling of some very diverse values, and creative collaboration which ensures that values are embodied and not simply paid lip-service to.

Firstly, what Bauman refers to as the invariant values remain central. These include: autonomy, critical reflection, dialogue, disinterestedness, mutuality, collegiality, community, equality, a shared concern for the common good, and a commitment to the ongoing, long-term learning relationship. It is important therefore to keep articulating these values as part of the story of higher education.

Secondly the relationship between different values and kinds of values can be complex, and demands constant reflection. This can involve several tasks:

• Different kinds of values may have to be held in tension, despite the pressure to polarize them. The push for social values such as equality, for instance, has to be held in tension with good stewardship which enables more people to benefit from higher education. At the same time the core value of community expressed in collegiality has to be asserted alongside massification, that is if real learning is to be experienced.

• At other times subtly different meaning between the value areas will reinforce each other. A good example of this is community. Community as collegiality lies at the heart of the learning process and inclusive community is central to social values. Another example is the stress on accountability and transparency. Both of these are at the heart of good governance *and* democracy. They are also at the heart of collegiality and learning. Corporate social responsibility demands the corporation look outwards to the needs of all stakeholders, and this is further sharpened by the responsibility of the university, along with others, to shape society. This relation to society is picked up in the learning process itself, with connections to citizenship, local and global. The learning experience of the student then begins to parallel the learning organization.

• The many different values which emerge from this reflection themselves affect the meaning of the different concepts. The term autonomy is affected by the nature of learning, moving away from a simple liberal view. The term community is affected by the stress on equality, moving to an inclusive meaning. This leads to a view of community which stresses the quality of relationships, and the capacity to hold together different views, rather than simply solidarity or common identity. Equality in turn looks not simply to numbers of student places filled or students retained but to the learning and developmental experience of the student.

Hence, there is need for constant dialogue both holding together the different values and enabling appreciation how that dialogue affects the meaning. Such reflection is not simply academic or abstract. It does demand decisions, and there will be values that cannot be held in tension. We have suggested, for instance, that certain forms of commercial activity do actually contradict core principles, not least through the commodification of education or through the pursuit of ends that are against the common good. We have also suggested that ensuring an honest reflection on values demands a process that involves the major stakeholders. Here, democracy and transparency are key to integrity, and also key to an openness and awareness of the values of other significant groups and how they relate to higher education.

Universities will also have to look carefully at the concept of customer and customer care. At one level customer care is laudable, and as noted above it has led to greater reflection on a broader duty of care. The problem is rather that exclusive focus on the customer model can lead to an erosion of collegiality. It can stress satisfaction of individual rights and needs and not an awareness and appreciation of the community, or responsibility to the community. It can also lead to competition for the customer. Such competition in halls of residence, for instance, might lead to a focus more on the provision of email facilities than on the provision of sub-wardens, with responsibility for pastoral care and community. With limited budgets, and choices to be made, which is more important?

This raises critical questions of the decision-making processes in the university. Is collegiality spelled out clearly in the values statements? Perhaps more importantly do such values statements stay on the agenda at school and department decision making?

It would be wrong to suggest that commercialization is new. Perkin notes a 600-year history of just that, with Bernard of Clairvaux reporting avarice and ambition motivating scholars.[450] It has always been important to achieve balance. However, with massification the dangers are more manifest. Quality Assurance, for instance, is important but finds it hard to cope with interdisciplinary work. Modularisation increases student autonomy but fragments the learning experience.

The challenge to higher education in the twenty-first century then is to hold values in tension – not allow one or other to dominate – but also to stand out against whatever will dehumanize management, the learning experience, professional standards and social principles. The university has to ensure processes that will enable this. Inevitably, this will lead to an evolution of values in practice much as Wilson describes. There are questions about the Habermas view of dialogue in all this, not least the importance of commitment to dialogue, and therefore of shared values which precede it, but we cannot address them in this chapter.

Reflection on values also explores the values underlying values, the world views and belief systems that give value. Again this is an ongoing dialogue, allowing the university community to see something of the need for learning and research as good in themselves, but also good because of the wide service they give to society. Mcleish takes this even further, inviting us to see a creative and even healing relationship between academia and the social and natural environment.[451] Collins invites us to see the academic enterprise in the global perspective.[452] Nafstad reminds us that we may be endorsing problematical values through research practice that takes for granted underlying views of humanity.[453]

Building on the core values and on the process that can handle very different values, all of which excites the moral imagination, the third element in the process of integrity is the stimulation of collaborative creativity. If clarification of values involves dialogue then how value might be embodied needs a continuation of that dialogue into practice. This is a world that Tawney would have rejoiced in, with his stress on developing living experiments in democracy in industry and education.[454]

As McNay notes, sustaining community in an age of mass education demands great imagination.[455] Community within the department demands greater active involvement from the students. A good example of this is the proctoring scheme in the department of Philosophy at the University of Leeds, involving students in teaching and reflecting that brings the different modules together. Focus on learning journals, progress files and careers modules enables common reflection on the purpose, context and value of learning. As Cowan reminds us this is where closer attention to the experience of Alverno College could pay dividends.[456] E-learning and summer schools can develop a sense of community for distance learning.

The university as a whole can develop events and reflection that celebrate the wider view of community, local and global. Indeed the modern university can be seen as a community of communities, or a plurivocal community, or network of learning.[457]

How can equality really be developed when half the 18–30 year old population will *not* be in higher education? The answer might be found in stressing further the theme of life-long learning, looking to bring higher education and further education even more closely together, and looking to develop university in the work place.[458] Mary Warnock might, perhaps, find the identity of the university even harder to grasp with such developments. However, perhaps the identity and consistency of the university is precisely found in the values noted above and the capacity to handle all of these, and not in any one function or purpose. Such developments demand that higher education in its various forms be a learning organisation, i.e. an organisation that learns.[459] It also demands a wide collaboration with all stakeholders that will increase the possible options.

Given the increasingly important role of central government in higher education these reflections offer some comfort and much challenge to them. The greater egalitarian thrust is commendable but demands more resources for and research into the provision of community that will enable learning and development. The greater concern for accountability, transparency and consumer care has to be tempered by a stress on collegiality and the shared responsibility of membership

The integrity of the university in all this is not simply about consistency and congruence, nor simply about the integration of several key virtues. It is also itself about honest and open reflection and learning, and enabling others to reflect actively. This process takes higher education beyond a stance of simple disinterestedness or liberal tolerance to one which is proactively helping to articulate and shape values in society. This is perhaps the idea of civilization behind the Dearing report, involving reflection, dialogue, mutual challenge, awareness and appreciation of the other, and as Ford suggests the development of wisdom, at a personal and corporate level.[460] In all this higher education is not simply recognising and responding to major values, it is actively contributing to and developing the meaning and practice of values in society. The university could then be seen to be a key part of the development of justice and peace in any society.

It is perhaps fitting that we should end this chapter and book with some of the thoughts of one of the first PVCs at the University of Leeds. The values we have reflected on in this book and the need to hold many in tension are not new. By 1906 Arthur Smithells had realised that the argument about the responsibilities of a university to its social and economic environment was partly bound up with the search for a separate and coherent identity for the civic universities distinct from the Oxbridge model. The strengths included 'freedom from luxurious idlers' (somehow associated with Oxbridge!), and more positively, 'the representation of all classes of the community, of all sects, and of many nations', and the 'co-education of the sexes'.[461] Arguing against Newman's contention that a 'university cannot intellectualize its neighbourhood', he wrote: 'I can see nothing but mutual advantage in their contact with great towns, and I look confidently to their close association for the destruction of a barrier that has been both artificial and mischievous'.[462] He believed academics should reach out to help shape the surrounding society. Smithells believed that for Leeds to develop as a university it should aspire to have as many students as possible in residence, and that this was vital for building a diverse, cosmopolitan, and more than merely local institution. This was an enterprise that saw the university as responsive partner in society and rewriting the values of community, inclusivity and equality within and outside the university. Leeds has tried to keep faith with this vision and these values for its first century. As it begins its second century, in collaboration with the rest of higher education and its stakeholders, it must maintain that faith in the university and in all its diverse embodiments and values.

Contributors

Zygmunt Bauman is Emeritus Professor of Sociology at the Universities of Leeds and Warsaw. He is one of the most notable social theorists of this and the last century and the world's foremost sociologist of modernity. His many important books include: *Modernity and the Holocaust* (1989), *Post Modern Ethics* (1992), *Liquid Modernity* (2000), *Thinking Sociologically* (2001), *Liquid Love: On the frailty of human bonds* (2003), *Wasted Lives: Modernity and its outcasts* (2003), *Identity* (2004).

Thomas Bender is Professor of History at New York University, and Director of the International Center for Advanced Studies. An authority on nineteenth-century American culture and the comparative study of cities he also writes on the history of academic disciplines and historiography. A Fellow of the American Academy of Arts and Sciences his many publications include: *Community and Social Change in America* (1978), *New York Intellect: A history of intellectual life in New York, from 1750 to the beginnings of our own times* (1987), *The Anti-Slavery Debate* (1992), *Intellect and Public Life* (1993), *Budapest and New York* (1994), *The Transformation of American Culture* (1998), *The Unfinished City: New York and the metropolitan idea* (2002), *Rethinking American history in a global age* (2002 edn).

Melvyn Bragg, author/broadcaster, was born in Wigton and educated locally and at Oxford where he read Modern History. His first novel, *For Want of a Nail,* was published in 1965 and his latest, *Crossing the Lines,* in June 2003. He has written over a dozen books, mostly novels but also a biography of Richard Burton, and an Oral History of England – *Speak for England* and *The Adventure of English: The Biography of a Language.* He has worked in broadcasting since 1961 and is currently Controller of Arts and Features at LWT, editor and presenter of *The South Bank Show* and *The Adventure of*

English and executive producer of several other arts strands. He writes for various publications. He is President of the National Campaign for the Arts, a governor of the LSE and Chancellor of the University of Leeds. He writes and presents *In Our Time* on Radio 4 on Thursday mornings. In 1998 he was made a Life Peer, Lord Bragg of Wigton. He has won several awards for television including the RTS Gold Medal and Richard Dimbleby award; for radio, including two Sony awards; the Ivor Novello Award for Best Musical and several awards for his novels including the WH Smith Literary Award for *The Soldier's Return*.

Gwen Collins is a full-time chaplain in the ecumenical team that serves Leeds Metropolitan University and the University of Leeds. She is a minister of the United Reformed Church, which sponsors her post. With a background of a first degree in Geography from Oxford and sixteen years of church-based development work in the highlands of Papua New Guinea, Gwen has a strong interest in critiquing academic analyses in the light of the perspectives and needs of the majority world. Her research project reflects this interest.

John Cowan is the author of *On Becoming an Innovative University Teacher*. He began working life as a structural engineer, before entering academia. Increasingly he was drawn into staff development, educational development work in the UK and in Third World countries (in which he tried to serve without fee for a few weeks each year) and educational research. As a result, he was appointed to the first chair of engineering education in the UK. Ten years with the Open University as Scottish Director, and then Professor of Learning Development, gave him the chance to encourage action researching by his staff, and to see enhancement of learning ensuing in consequence. He has co-authored a well-regarded text on formative evaluation, and contributed numerous chapters to books on higher education. He has been honoured in Britain, Europe and Latin America for various aspects of his work. Now officially long retired, he remains an active teacher, mainly engaged in e-learning and workshop activities, and mostly supporting undergraduate learning – to which his main commitment has always been.

Miriam David is Research Dean for the Faculty of Humanities and Social Sciences and Professor of Policy Studies in Education at Keele University and half-time Associate Director of the ESRC's Teaching and Learning Research Programme (TLRP) responsible for research in and of Higher Education and lifelong learning, based at Cambridge University's Department of Education. She is an executive editor of the *British Journal of Sociology of Education* and former editor of *The Journal of Social Policy*. She has an international reputation for her research on families, gender, education and public policies, including recent work on professional and doctoral education. Her publications include: *Personal and Political: Feminisms, sociology and family lives* (2003), and *Closing the Gender Gap: Post-war education and social change* (with Madeleine Arnot and Gaby Weiner 1999).

Bob Fryer was the Assistant Vice-Chancellor of the University of Southampton and Director of New College before becoming the Chief Executive of the National Health Service University in 2002. He is a former chair of the National Advisory Group for Continuing Education and Lifelong Learning. He chairs the National Learning and Skills Council's Distributed and Electronic Learning Group. He was awarded a CBE for services to community education in 2003. Professor Fryer's publications include *Sociological Perspectives* (with Paul Corrigan 1982), *Leadership and Democracy: The history of the National Union of Public Employees: 1928–1993*, Vol. 2 (with Steve Williams 1997).

Nigel Humphrys has worked in University Student Services for the past eighteen years. For four years he was an International Student Advisor at the University of Herefordshire. During this period Nigel founded the Association for International Student Advisors, which is a special interest group within UKCOSA, the Council for International Education. Nigel has been a counsellor of the University of Southern Maine, USA, London Guildhall University and for the past ten years the Head of the Student Counselling Service at the University of Leeds, which he founded in 1995. Nigel was formerly chair of the national group of Heads of University Counselling Services.

Clement Katulushi is Administrative Officer for the Chaplaincy to the Universities in Leeds as well as Training Consultant for Barnardos' Castle Project in Leeds. He chairs the African Communities Trust and is a member of the Adrian Hastings Scholarship Committee and a part-time tutor in Religious Studies at the University of Leeds. Before coming to Leeds, Dr Katulushi was Head of Religious Education and a Senior Lecturer at Nkrumah Teachers' College in Kabwe, Zambia. He has also served as Head of the RE Department at Chikankata Secondary School in Zambia, and was Chair of the Zambia Association of RE Teachers for several years. His writings include 'I am because we are: community in Africa' (*Shap Journal in World Religions in Education*, 2001/2002) and 'Teaching traditional African religions and gender issues in Zambia' (*British Journal of Religious Education*, 1999, vol. 21(2)).

Tom Mcleish is Professor of Polymer Physics at the University of Leeds and Director of the IRC in Polymer Science and Technology, Director of the White Rose Life Science Interface DTC, a member of the steering committee of the Isaac Newton Institute for the Mathematical Sciences and a member of EPSRC's TOP committee. He was awarded the Dutch National Polymer Science Prize and the Annual Award of the British Society of Rheology (2003). He was elected a Fellow of the Institute of Physics in 2003. His work on the fundamental dynamics of entangled, branched polymers led to the formulation of the pom-pom constitutive equation with Ron Larson, for which they were awarded the Society of Rheology Publication Prize. His publications are many and wide-ranging, from rheology to theology.

Chris Megone is Senior Lecturer in Philosophy and Director of the Centre for Business and Professional Ethics at the University of Leeds. He teaches Ethics, Applied Ethics and Ancient Philosophy. Recent publications include *Aristotelian Ethics* (1997), *European Neonatal Research: Consent, ethics, committees and law* (2001), *Case Studies in Business Ethics* (2002).

Hilde Eileen Nafstad is Associate Professor in Social and Developmental Psychology at the University of Oslo, Norway. She is affiliated with the Ethics Programme of the University of Oslo as supervisor and in undertaking research on ethics in the professions as well as developing area ethics of psychology and the social sciences. Her research profile is both applied and basic, including books and articles on quality of life and public policies; society's ideologies and value systems; minorities; and human development of empathy and altruism. Her most recent publications include *The Caring Human Being* (2004 edn); 'Positive psychology: historical, philosophical and epistemological perspectives' (2004); 'Ideological shifts in society and assumptions in psychology: a challenge for positive psychology' (2004); 'The neo-liberal ideology and the self-interest paradigm as resistance to change' (2003).

Simon Robinson was Senior Anglican Chaplain and Hon. Fellow in Theology at the University of Leeds until November 2004. He is now Professor of Applied and Professional Ethics at the Leeds Metropolitan University. Previous publications include: *Serving Society: The social responsibility of business* (1992); *The Decision Makers: Ethics and engineers* (with James Armstrong and Ross Dixon, 1999); *Agape, Moral Meaning and Pastoral Counselling* (2001); *Case Studies in Business Ethics* (ed. with Chris Megone 2002); *Their Rights: Advance directives and living wills explored* (with Kevin Kendrick 2002); *Spirituality and the Practice of Healthcare* (with Kevin Kendrick and Alan Brown, 2003); *Ministry Amongst Students* (2004).

Peter Scott is Vice-Chancellor of Kingston University. Prior to this he was Pro-Vice-Chancellor, Professor of Education and Director of the Centre for Policy Studies in Education at the University of Leeds. Before moving to Leeds he was, for sixteen years, editor of the *Times Higher Education Supplement*. His research interests are the governance and mangement of universties and colleges, and non-standard access to higher education. His most recent publications are: *The Meaning of Mass Higher Education* (1995), *Governing Universities* (1996), *The Globalization of Higher Education* (1998), *Higher Education Re-formed* (2000), *University Leadership: The role of the Chief Executive* (2000), *Ten Years On: Higher Education in Central and Eastern Europe* (2000), and *Re-thinking Science: Knowledge production in an age of uncertainties* (2001).

Mike Sells produced the print for the front cover. He has lived in Headingley on and off for nearly thirty years and has always been fascinated by the wonderful architecture in Leeds. He began making screen prints many years ago but now uses a lot of digital techniques as well. This print is one of a series on the University. Mike is a graduate of the University and lives

in Headingley with his wife and three children.
Some of the prints are available at the alumni office in the University of Leeds or see *www.leedsprints.com*.

Sue Vickerman gained a BA and an M.Phil in the Theology Department of the University of Leeds. She began writing in earnest after moving around the world as a peace activist and teacher. Her poetry and short stories have appeared in many magazines and anthologies. She has received two Arts Council writers' awards. Publications include a poetry pamphlet *SHAG* (Arrowhead Press, 2003) and a full-length collection *The Social Decline of the Oystercatcher* (Biscuit Publishing, 2005). Sue Vickerman's webpage is *www.arrowheadpress.co.uk*.

Rowan Williams taught at Mirfield Theological College before teaching Theology at Cambridge and then Oxford, as Lady Margaret Professor of Theology. In 1992 he was consecrated Bishop of Monmouth, and was then made Archbishop of Wales in 1999. In 2002 he was made Archbishop of Canterbury. His many books include: *The Wound of Knowledge* (1990), *On Christian Theology* (1999), *Lost Icons* (2000), *Arius* (2001), *Darkness Yielding* (2001), *Resurrection* (2004).

Alan Wilson graduated in Mathematics from Cambridge. He converted to the social sciences through research on cities. His latest book, *Complex Spatial Systems*, was published in 2000. He was appointed Professor of Urban and Regional Geography in the University of Leeds in 1970, and was Vice-Chancellor from 1991 to 2004. He was the co-founder in the early 1980s of GMAP Ltd. He was a member of the Economic and Social Research Council from 2000 to 2004. He was elected as FBA in 1994, an AcSS in 2000 and knighted for services to higher education in 2001. He holds Honorary Fellowships with University College, London (2003) and Corpus Christi College, Cambridge (2004). In February 2004, he took up the post of Director-General for Higher Education in the DfES in London.

Notes

Notes to introduction

1. NCIHE, Chairman Sir Ron Dearing CB, *Higher Education in the Learning Society*, London: HMSO, July 1997.

2. In the conception of this book, the editors were concerned with the question of how values inform higher education, and how in turn higher education informs values.

Notes to chapter 1: The university and civic values   *Peter Scott*

3. Michael Shattock (ed.), *Making a University: A celebration of Warwick's first twenty-five years*, Coventry: University of Warwick, 1991.

4. Negley Harte and John North, *The World of UCL 1828–1990*, London: University College London, 1991.

5. Peter Searby, *A History of the University of Cambridge,* vol. III: *1750-1870*, Cambridge: Cambridge University Press, 1997.

6. Thomas Bender, 'The cultures of intellectual life: the city and the professions', in *Intellect and Public Life: Essays on the social history of academic intellectuals in the United States*, Baltimore and London: Johns Hopkins University Press, 1993.

7. Thomas Kelly, *For the Advancement of Learning: The University of Liverpool 1881–1981*, Liverpool: Liverpool University Press, 1981.

8. Christine Shin, *Paying the Piper: The development of the University Grants Committee 1919–46*, London: Falmer, 1986. Michael Shattock, *The UGC and the Management of Universities*, Buckingham: Open University Press, 1994.

9. Philip Larkin, *Required Writing: Miscellaneous pieces 1955–1982*, London: Faber, 1983.

10. Michael Beloff, *The Plateglass University*, London: Secker and Warburg, 1968.

11. Walter Bagehot, *The English Constitution*, Cambridge: Cambridge University Press (Cambridge Texts in the History of Political Thought), 2001, originally published 1867.

12. Peter Scott, 'Higher Education', in Dennis Kavanagh and Anthony Seldon *The Thatcher Effect: A decade of change*, Oxford: Oxford University Press, 1989. Peter Scott, 'Education policy', in Dennis Kavanagh and Anthony Seldon, *The Major Effect*, London: Macmillan, 1994.

13. Chris Skelcer, *The Appointed State: Quasi-governmental organisations and democracy*, Buckingham: Open University Press, 1998.

14. Bender 1993.

15. Harold Perkin, *The Rise of Professional Society: England since 1880*, London: Routledge, 1989. Harold Perkin, *The Third Revolution: Professional élites in the modern world*, London: Routledge, 1996.

16. Peter Baggen, Agnes Tellings and Wouter van Haaften (eds.) *The University and the Knowledge Society*, Bemmel (The Netherlands): Concorde Publishing House, 1998.

17. David Harvey, *The Condition of Postmodernity*, Oxford: Blackwell, 1990.

18. Walter Benjamin, *The Arcades Project* (translated by Howard Eiland and Kevin McLaughlin), Cambridge Mass., and London: Belknap Press, 1999.

19. Michael Gibbons, Camille Limoges, Helga Nowotny, Simon Schwartzman, Peter Scott, Peter and Martin Trow, *The New Production of Knowledge: The dynamics of science and research in contemporary societies*, London: Sage, 1994. Helga Nowotny, Peter Scott and Michael Gibbons, *Re-thinking Science: Knowledge and the public in an age of uncertainty*, Cambridge: Polity, 2001.

20. Philip Bobbitt, *The Shield of Achilles: War, peace and the course of history*, London: Allen Lane, 2002.

Notes to chapter 2: Faith in the university   *Rowan Williams*

21. J.H. Newman, 'Knowledge viewed in relation to professional skill, discourse VII', *The Idea of a University*, London 1899; in V.F. Blehl (ed.) *The Essential Newman*, New York, 1963, pp. 190–1.

22. Anthony O'Hear, 'Why our ivory towers must never surrender', *Daily Telegraph*, 20 December 1988, p. 12.

Notes to chapter 3: The liquid-modern challenges to education

Zygmunt Bauman

23. Oliver Burkman, 'My dad is a living deterrent…', *Guardian*, 21 March 2001.

24. Richard Sennett, *The Corrosion of Character*, New York: W.W. Norton & Co., 1998, p. 25.

25. Edward D. Myers, *Education in the Perspective of History*, New York: Harper, 1960, p. 262.

26. John Kotter, *The New Rules*, New York: Dutton, 1995, p. 159.

27. Sennett 1998, p. 25.

28. Italo Calvino, *Invisible Cities* (translated by William Weaver), London: Picador, 1971, p. 91.

29. Compare Werner Jaeger, *Paidea, Die Formung des griechischen Menschen*, Berlin, Walter de Gruyter, 1958.

30. Nigel Thrift, 'The rise of soft capitalism', in *Cultural Values*, April 1997, p. 52.

31. Dany-Robert Dufour, 'Malaise dans l'éducation', *Le Monde diplomatique*, November 2001, p. 11.

32. Luc Boltanski and Ève Chiapello, *Le nouvel esprit du capitalisme*, Paris: Gallimard, 1999, p. 171.

33. 'From modernism to hypermodernism and beyond', in John Armitage (ed.) *Virilio Live: Selected interviews*, London: Sage, 2001, p. 40.

34. Interview with Jérôme Sans, in Armitage (ed.) 2001, p. 118.

Notes to chapter 4: From academic knowledge to democratic knowledge *Thomas Bender*

35. Louis Menand, 'The demise of disciplinary authority', in Alvin Kernan, *What's Happened to the Humanities*, 1997, pp. 201–19.

36. Some of the confusion derives, as John Guillory has pointed out, from failure to distinguish literary politics of the syllabus reading list from larger social politics of exclusion. There is a connection of course, but they are not really coordinate issues or structures of politics, and it is easier to make the syllabus representative than it is to make the student body so. There is, he writes, 'a confusion between representation in the political sense – the relation of a representative to a constituency – and representation in the rather different sense of the relation between an image and what the image represents. The collapse of the latter sense into the former has had the unfortunate effect of allowing the participants in the "symbolic struggle" over representation in the canon to overestimate the political effects of this struggle, at the same time that the participants have remained relatively blind to the social and institutional conditions of symbolic struggles.' The real issue, therefore, is the distribution of the cultural capital of literacy. See John Guillory, *Cultural Capital: The problem of literacy canon formation*, Chicago: University of Chicago Press, 1993, p. viii. See also p. 7.

37. Clifford Geertz, *Local Knowledge*, New York: Basic, 1983, chap. 1; David Hollinger, 'The disciplines and the identity debates', in Thomas Bender and Carl E. Schorske (eds.) *American Academic Culture in Transformation*, Princeton: Princeton University Press, 1998, pp. 333–6.

38. The high degree of specialization and autonomy in the U.S. is sustained in part by American egalitarianism and wealth, both of which encourage and enable avoidance of judgement of relative value. See John Higham, 'The matrix of specialization', in Alexandra Oleson and John Voss (eds.) *The Organization of Knowledge in Modern America*, Baltimore: Johns Hopkins University Press, 1979, pp. 3–18.

39. Thomas Bender and Carl E. Schorske (eds.) *American Academic Culture in Transformation*.

40. Hannah Arendt, 'Truth and politics', in Peter Laslett and W.C. Runciman (eds.) *Philosophy, Politics and Society*, 3rd series, New York: Barnes & Noble, 1967, pp. 104–33.

41. John Dewey, *Experience and Nature*, Lasalle, IL: Open Court, 1929, pp. 9–10.

42. See Helene Silverberg (ed.) *Gender and American Social Science*, Princeton: Princeton University Press, 1998.

43. Thomas Bender, *New York Intellect*, New York: Alfred A. Knopf, 1987, pp. 277–8.

44. Robert Kohler, *Partners in Science: Foundations and natural sciences, 1900–1945*, Chicago: University of Chicago Press, 1991.

45. Mary Poovey, *A History of the Modern Fact: Problems of knowledge in the science of wealth and society*, Chicago: University of Chicago Press, 1998.

46. My confidence on this point is bolstered by Thomas L. Haskell, *Objectivity is Not Neutrality: Explanatory schemes in history*, Baltimore: Johns Hopkins University Press, 1998, esp. chaps. 5–7.

47. Carl E. Schorske, 'The new rigorism in the human sciences', in Bender and Schorske (eds.) *American Academic Culture in Transformation*, pp. 309–29.

48. On Greenberg's theories in the 1940s, see especially, 'Towards a newer Laocoon', in John O'Brian (ed.) *Clement Greenberg: The collected essays and criticism*, vol. I; Chicago: University of Chicago Press, 1986, pp. 23–38.

49. Here see Andreas Huyssen, *After the Great Divide: Modernism, mass culture, post-modernism*, Bloomington: Indiana University Press, 1986, pp. vii–xii; Thomas Bender, *Intellect and Public Life*, Baltimore: Johns Hopkins University Press, 1993, chap. 7; Clement Greenberg, 'Avant garde and kitsch', in O'Brian (ed.) *Clement Greenberg*, pp. 5–22.

50. After 1968, for somewhat different reasons, both the left and the right, especially in the social sciences, retreated to the academy. And the economist Robert Lucas won the Nobel Prize for theorizing this.

51. For this discussion, I am relying heavily upon the essays, including my own, in Bender and Schorske (eds.) *American Academic Culture in Transformation*.

52. Bruce Kuklick, *The Rise of American Philosophy*, New Haven: Yale University Press, 1977; Robert Westbrook, *John Dewey and American Democracy*, Ithaca: Cornell University Press, 1991, p. 538.

53. See Mary Poovey, 'Beyond the current impasse in literary studies', in *American Literary History*, II, 1999, pp. 354–77; John Guillory, panel presentation on the 'Crisis in literary studies', NYU, 21 February 1999.

54. I distinguish Lindblom from Dewey because Lindblom finds Dewey not sufficiently democratic, misreading Dewey in my view. See Charles Lindblom, *Inquiry and Change: The troubled attempt to understand and shape society*, New Haven: Yale University Press, 1990, and Charles Lindblom and David K. Cohen, *Usable Knowledge: Social science and social problem solving*, New Haven: Yale University Press, 1979.

55. David Bromwich, *Politics by Other Means: Higher education and group thinking*, New Haven: Yale University Press, 1992.

56. See Poovey 1999, p. 370.

57. Haskell, *Objectivity*, chap. 6.

58. Besides Karl Mannheim, *Ideology and Utopia*, translated by Louis Wirth and Edward Shils, New York: Harcourt, Brace, 1936, I would note Jürgen Habermas, *Knowledge and Human Interests*, Boston: Beacon Press, 1971. Both of these writers see the incorporation of interest reaching a consensus. What follows departs from the assumption, again proposing a 'weak' position.

59. W.E.B. Dubois, 'The Negro College', *Crisis*, 1933, in Nathan Huggins (ed.) *W.E.B. Dubois: Writings*, New York, Library of America, 1996, p. 1010.

60. William James, 'The social value of the college bred', *McClure's*, 30, 1908, p. 420.

61. This point is made by Mannheim, *Ideology and Utopia*, p. 168.

62. See the recent remarks on this issue in Linda Gordon, 'The trouble with difference', *Dissent.*, 46, 1999, pp. 41–7.

63. See Thomas L. Haskell, *The Emergence of Professional Social Science*, Urbana: University of Illinois Press, 1977.

64. John Dewey, 'Philosophy and Democracy', in Jo Ann Boydston (ed.) *The Middle Works, 1889–1924*, 14 vols.; Carbondale: University of Southern Illinois Press, 1982, pp. 11–52, 50.

65. See R. Jackson Wilson, *The Quest for Community: Social philosophy in the United States, 1860–1920*, New York: Oxford University Press, 1970, chap. 2, esp. pp. 44–5; Thomas L. Haskell, 'Professionalism *versus* capitalism'; R.H. Tawney, Emile Durkheim, and C.S. Peirce 'On the disinterestedness of professional communities', in Thomas L. Haskell (ed.) *The Authority of Experts*, Bloomington: Indiana University Press, 1984, pp. 180–225, esp. 203–20.

66. Haskell, *Objectivity is Not Neutrality*, chap. 6; James Kloppenberg, 'Objectivity and historicism: a century of American historical writing', *American Historical Review*, 94, 1989, pp. 1010–30. See also Thomas Bender, 'The social sciences, objectivity, and pragmatism', *Annals of Scholarship*, 9, 1992, pp. 183–97.

67. This is also a major point of John Guillory's important book, *Cultural Capital.*

68. John Dewey, *Experience and Nature*, p. 101.

Notes to chapter 5: Values in higher education: a social and evolutionary perspective *Alan Wilson*

69. This chapter is an expanded version of a talk given in the University of Leeds Chaplaincy Seminar Series in October 1999.

70. Newman: '[The University] is a place of teaching universal knowledge'.

71. Ake Andersson in A.E. Andersson, D.F. Batten, K. Kobayashi, and K. Yoshikawa (eds.) *The Cosmo-Creative Society: Logistical networks in a dynamic economy*, Berlin: Springer-Verlag, 1993.

72. University of Leeds, 2002, *Strategic Plan: 2002–03 to 2006–07.*

73. A.H. Halsey, *The Decline of Donnish Dominion: The British academic professions in the twentieth century*, Oxford: Oxford University Press, 1992.

74. A. Marshall, 'The future of the working classes', in A.C. Pigou (ed.) *Memorials of Alfred Marshall*, London, 1925.

75. J. Habermas, *Theory and Practice*, London: Heinemann, 1974.

76. Richard J. Bernstein, *The Restructuring of Social and Political Theory*, Oxford: Blackwell, 1976.

77. *Times Literary Supplement*, September 1999.

78. I. Berlin, 'The hedgehog and the fox', in H. Hardy and R. Hausher (eds.) *Isaiah Berlin: The proper study of mankind*, London: Chatto and Windus, 1978.

79. It was Newman who argued passionately for a 'liberal' as distinct from a vocational education – interestingly as a better training of the mind for the future. Allen (1988) captures the appropriate sentences: 'Through this kind of education "a habit of mind is formed which lasts through life, of which the attributes are freedom, equitableness, calmness, moderation and wisdom." Newman claimed that individuals who have been educated in this way will be able to "fill their respective posts in life better" and be "more intelligent, capable, active members of society".' From M. Allen, *The Goals of Universities*, Milton Keynes: Open University Press, 1988.

80. *Times Literary Supplement*, September 1999.

81. This is the universities' version of the agency-structure problem.

82. *www.leeds.ac.uk/vkp/*.

83. The breadth argument is put very well by Peter T. Flawn, *A Primer for University Presidents: Managing the modern university*, Austin, Texas: University of Texas Press, Texas, p. 86.

84. Shils' first two sentences are: 'Universities have a distinctive task. It is the methodical discovery and teaching about serious and important things.' E. Shills, *The Calling of Education*, Chicago: University of Chicago Press, 1997.

85. John Horgan, *The End of Science*, New York, Broadway Books, 1997.

86. For an interesting discussion in the university context, see D. Bok, *Higher Learning*, Cambridge Mass., Harvard University Press, 1987, p. 163.

87. Note the Business School dilemma: are these schools there to do research *on* business, or *for* business?!

88. Bok 1987.

89. See the discussion in D. Kennedy, 'University and government, university and industry', in K.J. Arrow, R.W. Cottler, B.C. Eaves and I. Olkin (eds.) *Education in a Research University*, Stanford Calif.: Stanford University Press, 1996.

90. Clark Kerr, *The Uses of the University*, Cambridge, Mass., Harvard University Press, 1995, p. 115.

91. Phillips quoted George Bugliarello, President of Brooklyn Polytechnic University, as saying: 'The university has become adept at survival, to the point that it is not always clear whether the great range of activities in which universities are engaged today represents a deep ideological commitment or simply a manifestation of the need to survive.' D. Phillips, 'The research mission and research manpower', in *Universities in the Twenty-First Century*, London: National Commission on Education and the Council for Industry and Higher Education, 1994.

92. The following argument is based on the conclusion of A.G. Wilson, 'Strategy and development for university management', chap. 2 in P. Scott (ed.) *Higher Education Re-formed*, London: Falmer Press, 2000.

93. Though the type of mathematics may be very different!

Notes to chapter 6: Universities and citizenship: the forgotten dimension? *Bob Fryer*

94. Throughout this chapter, I deliberately draw no distinction between the general category of 'higher education' and the more specific notion of 'the university'. There is indeed an important debate to be had about the possible distinctions between these two and whether any traditional distinction still holds good under contemporary conditions. But this debate is not relevant for the concerns of this chapter. As a consequence, I largely make reference to universities, but occasionally have resort to the more general term 'higher education'.

95. NCIHE, Chairman Sir Ron Dearing CB, *Higher Education in the Learning Society*, London: HMSO, July 1997, para. 5.11 ff., pp. 72–81. In this chapter I refer to the committee's main report as *Main Report*.

96. See J-F. Lyotard, *The Postmodern Condition*, Minneapolis, University of Minnesota Press, 1984; S. Seidman (ed.) *The Postmodern Turn*, Cambridge: The University Press, 1994. For critiques of postmodernism see C. Norris, *What's Wrong with Postmodernism?*, London: Harvester Wheatsheaf, 1990 and, from the viewpoint of Marxism, A. Callinicos, *Against Postmodernism*, Cambridge: Polity, 1989.

97. *Main Report*, p. 80.

98. *Main Report*, pp. 80–1.

99. NCIHE, *Report 1: Report on national consultation*, p. 22. In this chapter, I refer to this as *Consultation Report*.

100. *Consultation Report*, p. 22.

101. *Consultation Report*, p. 21.

102. *Consultation Report*, p. 23.

103. *Higher Education Report*, Chairman Lionel Robbins, London: HMSO, 1963.

104. Karl Jaspers, *The Idea of a University*, London: Peter Owen, 1960, quoted in R. Barnett, *The Idea of Higher Education*, Milton Keynes: Open University Press, 1990.

105. See Charles E. Glassick, M. Taylor, and G.I. Mareoff, *Scholarship Reassessed*, Carnegie Foundation for the Advancement of Teaching, San Francisco Calif.: Jossey Bass, 1997. I am indebted to my friend and colleague Professor Phil Candy for this reference.

106. *The Future of Higher Education*, London: HMSO, January 2003, para. 1.44, p. 21.

107. *The Future of Higher Education*, para. 1.45, pp. 21–2.

108. *Main Report*.

109. *Consultation Report*, p. 23.

110. *Consultation Report*, p. 23.

111. *Main Report*, p. 79.

112. Martin J. Salvic (ed.): John Henry Newman, *The Idea of a University*, New York: Holt, Rheinhart and Wilson, 1960.

113. This has long been seen as one of the key moral responsibilities of so-called 'public intellectuals', of which constituency university scholars are but one element.

114. D. Held, *Democracy and the Global Order*, Cambridge: Polity, 1995, p. 11.

115. J.G.A. Pocock, 'The ideal of citizenship since classical times', in Gershon Shafir (ed.) *The Citizenship Debates*, Minneapolis: University of Minnesota Press, 1998, p. 33.

116. For an excellent and accessible review of the various meanings and uses of 'social capital', see J. Field, *Social Capital*, London: Routledge, 2003.

117. R.D. Putnam, *Making Democracy Work: Civic traditions in modern Italy*, Princeton: Princeton University Press, 1993, p. 167.

118. R.D. Putnam, *Bowling Alone*, New York: Simon and Schuster, 2000, pp. 338–9.

119. Putnam 2000, p. 341.

120. T.H. Marshall, *Citizenship and Social Class and Other Essays*, Cambridge: Cambridge University Press.

121. Cited by Richard Hoggart in *The Uses of Literacy*, Harmondsworth: Penguin Books, 1958, p. 247.

122. In Shafir 1998.

123. J. Smith and A. Spurling, *Lifelong Learning: Riding the tiger*, London: Cassell, 1999, p. 62.

124. M. Ignatieff, 'Citizenship and moral narcissism', in G. Andrews (ed.) *Citizenship*, London: Lawrence and Wishart, 1991, p. 30.

125. W. Carr and A. Hartnett, *Education and the Struggle for Democracy: The politics of educational ideas*, Buckingham: Open University Press, 1996.

126. M. Slowey, 'Higher education and civil society', in M. Slowey and D. Watson, *Higher Education and the Lifecourse*, Maidenhead: SRHE/Open University Press, 2003.

127. R. Fieldhouse, 'Tradition in British University adult education and the WEA', in C. Duke (ed.) *Liberal Adult Education: Perspectives and projects*, Warwick: Continuing Education Centre, 1992, p. 11.

128. L. Bown, *Learning, Liberty and Social Purpose: A reminder of our radical liberal inheritance in adult education and some thoughts on its future*. Fifteenth Albert Mansbridge memorial lecture, University of Leeds: Department of Adult Continuing Education, 1995.

129. For a useful, although sometimes slightly hagiographic, account of the development of the WEA, see Stephen K. Roberts, *A Ministry of Enthusiasm*, London: Pluto, 2003.

130. For a thorough history and analysis of 20th-century adult education in this country, see Roger Fieldhouse and associates, *A History of Modern British Adult Education*, Leicester: NIACE, 1996.

131. Bown 1995, p. 7.

132. E.P. Thompson, *The Making of the English Working Class*, Harmondsworth: Penguin Books, 1964.

133. For still the best detailed history of these domains of learning see Brian Simon, *Education and the Labour Movement 1870–1920*, London: Lawrence and Wishart, 1965.

134. Jonathan Rose, *The Intellectual Life of the British Working Classes*, London: Yale University Press, 2001, p. 278.

135. A. Giddens, *Modernity and Self-Identity: Self and society in the late modern age*, Cambridge: Polity, 1991, p. 212.

136. This momentous event and its complex and turbulent sequel is all well rehearsed in Roger Fieldhouse's *A History of Modern British Adult Education*, Leicester: NIACE, 1996.

137. See, for example, the excellent studies by Roger Fieldhouse, 'The ideology of English adult teaching 1925–1950', *Studies in Adult Education*, 15, September 1983, and 'Conformity and contradiction in English responsible body adult education 1925–1950', *Studies in Adult Education*, 17, October 1985.

138. Rose 2001, p. 276.

139. Department of Education and Science, *Adult Education: A plan for development*, (Report of a Committee of Inquiry appointed by the Secretary of State for Education and Science under the Chairmanship of Sir Lionel Russell CBE), London: HMSO, 1973, p. 12.

140. J. Holford, *Union Education in Britain: A TUC activity*, Nottingham: Department of Adult Education, 1994.

141. J. McIlroy, 'The triumph of technical training?' and 'Trade Union education for a change', both in Brian Simon (ed.) *The Search for Enlightenment: The working class and adult education in the twentieth century*, London: Lawrence and Wishart, 1990.

142. R. Johnston, 'Adult learning for citizenship: toward a reconstruction of the social purpose tradition', *International Journal of Lifelong Education*, 18(3), May-June 1999, p. 176.

143. The most balanced critique of the strengths, weaknesses and opportunities of lifelong learning is in John Field, *Lifelong Learning and the New Educational Order*, Stoke-on-Trent; Trentham, 2000 and 2002.

144. S. Ranson, *Towards the Learning Society*, London: Cassell, 1994, p. 102.

145. Ranson 1994, p. 106.

146. D. Watson and R. Taylor, *Lifelong Learning and the University: A post-Dearing agenda*, London: Falmer Press, 1998.

147. Watson and Taylor 1998, p. 138.

148. Watson and Taylor 1998, p. 119.

149. R. Hoggart, *An Imagined Life: Life and times 1959–1991*, Oxford: Oxford University Press, 1993, p. 124.

150. R. Hoggart, *The Uses of Literacy*, Harmondsworth: Penguin, 1958, p. 267.

151. Hoggart 1958, p. 189.

152. Ronald Barnett, *Higher Education: A critical business*, Buckingham: Open University Press, 1997; *The Idea of Higher Education*, Milton Keynes: Open University Press, 1990; and *Facilitating Reflective Learning in Higher Education*, Buckingham: SRHE/Open University, 1998.

153. J. Delors et al, *Learning: The treasure within*, 1996, pp. 61–2.

154. Delors et al. 1996, p. 134.

155. Delors et al. 1996, p. 4.

Notes to chapter 7: Feminist values and feminist sociology as contributions to higher education pedagogies and practices *Miriam David*

156. D. Leonard, *A Woman's Guide to Doctoral Studies*, Buckingham: Open University Press, 2001. L. Morley, *Quality and Power in Higher Education*, Buckingham: Open University Press, 2003.

157. M.E. David, *Personal and Political: Feminism, sociology and family lives*, Stoke-on-Trent: Trentham Books, 2003.

158. M. Peters, 'National education policy constructions of the "knowledge economy": towards a critique', *Journal of Educational Enquiry*, 2(1), 2001. J. Blackmore, 'Is it only "what works" that "counts" in new knowledge economies? Evidence-based practice, educational research and teacher education in Australia', *Social Policy and Society*, 1(3), 2002, pp. 257–67.

159. Morley 2003.

160. M.E. David and D. Woodward, *Negotiating the Glass Ceiling: Senior women in the academic world*, London: Falmer Press, 1998. D. Woodward and K. Ross, *Managing Equal Opportunities in Higher Education*, London: SRHE and Open University Press, 2002.

161. David 2003.

162. David 2003.

163. D. Schön, *Educating the Reflective Practitioner*, San Francisco: Jossey-Bass, 1987. D. Schön, *The Reflective Turn: How professionals think in action*, London: Teachers' College Press, 1991. P. Denicolo and M. Popeeds, *Sharing Understanding and Practice*, Farnborough: EPCA Publications, 1997. P. Denicolo and M. Pope, *Transformative Professional Practice: Personal construct approaches to education and research*, London: Whurr Publishers, 2001.

164. K. Jones, *Education in Britain since 1944*, Cambridge: Polity Press, 2003. P. Chamberlayne, J. Bornat and T. Wengraf (eds.) *The Biographical Turn in the Social Sciences*, London: Routledge, 2000.

165. N. Rose, *Governing the Soul*, London: Routledge, 1998. E. Stanley, *The Auto/ biographical I*, Manchester: Manchester University Press, 1992.

166. A. Giddens, *The Transformation of Intimacy*, Cambridge: Polity Press, 1992.

167. A. Oakley, *Experiments in Knowing*, Cambridge: Polity Press, 2000.

168. M. Fine and L. Weis, *Silenced Voices and Extraordinary Conversations: Re-imagining schooling*, New York: Teachers College Press, 2003. P. Drake and P. Owen (eds.) *Gender and Management Issues in Education: An international perspective*, Stoke-on-Trent: Trentham Books, 1998. E.A. St Pierre and W. Pillow (eds.) *Working the Ruins: Feminist post-structuralist theory and methods in education*, New York and London: Routledge, 2000.

169. P. Bourdieu, *Reflexive Sociology*, Cambridge: Polity Press, 1992. A. Giddens, *The Consequences of Modernity*, Cambridge: Polity Press, 1990. A. Giddens, *The Transformation of Intimacy*, Cambridge: Polity Press, 1992. U. Beck, A. Giddens and S. Lash, *Reflexive Modernisation*, Cambridge: Polity Press, 1996.

170. Drake and Owen 1998. St Pierre and Pillow (eds.) 2000. B. Kamler, *Relocating the Personal: A critical writing pedagogy*, State University of New York: SUNY Press, 2001.

171. R. Deem, 'Border territories: a journey through sociology, education and women's studies', *British Journal of Sociology of Education*, 17(2), 1996, pp. 5–19. M.E. David and D. Woodward, *Negotiating the Glass Ceiling: Senior women in the academic world*, London: Falmer Press, 1998. V. Walkerdine, *Daddy's Girl*, London: Macmillan, 1997. G. Weiner, *Feminisms in Education*, Buckingham: Open University Press, 1994. F. Williams, 'Good enough principles for welfare' *Journal of Social Policy*, 24(4), 1999, pp. 667–89.

172. Oakley 2000.

173. A. Curthoys, 'Adventures in Feminism: Simone de Beauvoir's autobiographies, women's liberation and self-fashioning', *Feminist Review*, 64, 2000, pp. 3–18. J. Blackmore, *Troubling Women*, Buckingham: Open University Press, 1999. S. Middleton, *Disciplining Sexuality: Foucault, life histories and education*, New York: Teachers' College Press, 1998. D. Britzman, *After-Education: Anna Freud, Melanie Klein and psychoanalytic histories of learning*, Albany N.Y.: State University of New York Press, 2002. W. Luttrell, *Pregnant Bodies; Fertile Minds*, London and New York: Routledge, 2003.

174. C. Ramazanoglu with J. Holland, *Feminist Methodology: Challenges and choices*, London: Sage, 2002.

175. Kamler 2001.

176. J. Blackmore, 'Is it only "what works" that "counts" in new knowledge economies? Evidence-based practice, educational research and teacher education in Australia', *Social Policy and Society*, 1(3), 2002 pp. 257–67. M.E. David, *Personal and Political: Feminism, sociology and family lives*, Stoke-on-Trent: Trentham Books, 2003.

177. Z. Eisenstein, *The Radical Future of Liberal Feminism*, New York: Longmans, 1981.

178. M. Arnot, M.E. David and G. Weiner, *Closing the Gender Gap: Post-war education and social change*, Cambridge: Polity Press, 1999.

179. N. Fraser, *Justice Interruptus*, London: Routledge, 1997.

180. A. Giddens, *The Third Way*, Cambridge: Polity Press, 1998.

181. Morley 2003.

182. Blackmore 2002.

183. M.E. David, 'Feminist sociology and feminist knowledges: contributions to higher education pedagogies and professional practices in the knowledge economy', in *International Studies in the Sociology of Education*, 2004 forthcoming.

184. D. Reay, M.E. David and S.J. Ball, *Degrees of Choice: Class, gender and race in choices of higher education*, Stoke-on-Trent: Trentham Books, 2005 forthcoming.

Notes to chapter 8: Virtue and the virtual university   *Chris Megone*

185. In this paragraph I am assuming a distinction between ethical virtues and intellectual virtues, but claiming that the achievement of intellectual excellence or virtue requires a community whose members exhibit ethical virtue. (Some now write

as if ethical and intellectual virtues are all of a piece, but I am following Aristotle in distinguishing the two kinds of virtue. See Aristotle, *Nicomachean Ethics*, II–VI; Linda Zagzebski and Michael de Paul (eds.) *Intellectual virtue: Perspectives from ethics and epistemology*, Oxford: Clarendon, 2003. Michael Brady, 'Virtuous motives and the "value problem"', unpublished MS.

186. Stephen Burwood, *Journal of Applied Philosophy*, 20, 2003, p. 300. I have inserted the term 'shared' here, but in context it seems clear that that is what is meant.

187. Gordon Graham, *Universities: The recovery of an idea*, Thorveton, Devon: Imprint Academic, 2002, p. 125.

188. Once such flesh has been put upon the bones, it might be possible to revisit the issue whether a university sector should really include all these types in order to fulfil its wider role in the wider community, but that is not a concern of this paper.

189. Sir Walter Moberly, *The Crisis in the University*, London: SCM Press, 1949, chap. 2. Moberly's own terms are Christian-Hellenic, Liberal, and Technological and Democratic, but I use the term 'liberal' in a different way below, and my terminology points to the affinities between the first two.

190. Moberly, p. 31.

191. Such a view would cohere with an Aristotelian conception of the human good according to which intellectual excellence is at least a component of *eudaimonia*, or the final good. Aristotle, *Nichomachean Ethics*, I, 5, 7 and X, 7–10.

192. Owen Chadwick, *Newman*, Oxford: Oxford University Press, 1983, pp. 52–3.

193. Newman, *The Idea of a University*, Notre Dame: University of Notre Dame Press edition, 1982, preface, pp. xxxix–xli. I owe this point to Mark Nelson.

194. I owe this suggestion to Jean Porter.

195. Chadwick, *Newman*, p. 53.

196. Moberly, p. 32.

197. Moberly, pp. 32–3, Chadwick, *Newman*, pp. 52–5.

198. Moberly, p. 33.

199. Newman, *The Idea of a University*, p. 109. It was in virtue of its inability to do that that the University of London was, in his terms, a virtual university.

200. Moberly, p. 36.

201. Moberly, pp. 36–42. The description of this conception follows Moberly's account, although there are several distinct strands to the understanding of freedom or autonomy here, and they are not necessarily interrelated.

202. Moberly, p. 42. In the second quote he is citing Friedrich Paulsen, *The German Universities and University Study*, translated by F. Tilly and W.W. Elwang, New York: C. Scribner and Sons, 1906, p. 1.

203. The notion of autonomy here is that of liberal political theory, where autonomy lies in being allowed to pursue one's own course, free from interference by others.

204. In the UK see the recent Schwartz Committee report, *Fair Admissions to Higher Education: Draft recommendations for consultation*, 2004, Executive Summary, section 2, for an articulation of this conception.

205. Moberly, pp. 43–9.

206. It is plausible that many UK universities, such as the University of Leeds, might take themselves to conform to this model, even if as they evolve in response to particular demands and opportunities, it may be hard for them to adhere consistently to its principles.

207. For a political expression of the view, see William Galston, *Liberal Pluralism*, Cambridge: Cambridge University Press, 2002.

208. J.S. Mill, *On Liberty*, London: John Parker and Son, 1859.

209. This report was given by Aleksandr Filonenko, of Kharkiv State University, Ukraine, at the conference, 'Religious voices and the public sphere', held at the University of Leeds in June 2003, so was contemporary at that time. What is given here is my understanding of the report, so any errors in interpretation are mine not Professor Filonenko's.

210. The liberal might at this point suggest that his position can be supplemented to meet this challenge by simply adding one more value, namely the requirement that members of the academic community have a commitment to finding the truth or, in Aristotelian terms, that they have the desire to understand. Since this is an intellectual value, not an ethical value, its addition allows the criticism to be met without posing any challenge to the liberal position. In reply to this I do not deny the importance of the desire to understand. The argument that follows simply holds that other ethical virtues must be manifested in order to sustain the sort of community that is necessary for the fulfilment of that desire. I am grateful to Mark Nelson for discussion of this point. The issue is discussed further in the main text below.

211. Aristotle, *Nicomachean Ethics*, I, 7, and *Politics*, I, 1–3. The position in the text represents an interpretation of these passages. See also C. Megone, 'Aristotle's Ethics', in R. Chadwick (ed.) *The Encyclopaedia of Applied Ethics*, San Diego: Academic Press, 1998, vol. 1. Two points might help the reader unacquainted with Aristotle. First the claim that humans are essentially rational refers to the essential powers or potentialities that each human instantiates – of course these powers are only ever actualised by each human to some degree. In other words, Aristotle's position does not commit him to the view that any human (let alone all) is actually fully rational. Second Aristotle does not understand rationality in a narrow sense, as involving purely intellectual reasoning, let alone purely formal powers of reasoning. Humans can be more or less rational in their desires and emotions as well as in their beliefs. The powers that constitute our rational powers must be understood as broad and complex.

212. In putting these ideas together I am not claiming that Newman's notion of a family is Aristotle's notion of a *polis*. (Aristotle recognised the family as a necessary sub-community within a *polis*.) The essential overlap here is the idea that human rational potentialities must be developed in a community of some sort. The familial community is a necessary condition for the development of some powers (but not sufficient, only a good familial community is sufficient). The familial nature of the community in question is developed in what follows, noting in particular the significance of trust.

213. Aristotle, *Nicomachean Ethics*, IV, 6, 1126b10 ff.

214. Aristotle, *Nicomachean Ethics*, IV, 7, 1127a12 ff.

215. And, in a similar way, to see the community itself as an instrumental means to satisfying the desire to understand would again undermine the existence of such a community. The community is valuable for its own sake as part of the actualisation of human nature. But actualizing that aspect of human nature coheres with achieving intellectual excellence.

216. See p. 25 above.

217. 'Knowing oneself to be an object of love and friendship is a central way of acquiring the capacity to trust...' as Williams also observes, p. 25.

218. p. 25 above

219. Others may also object that talk of the university as an *alma mater* may sometimes be adopted as a cloak to disguise failures to respect other virtues, such as justice. Thus it may well be that the size of many modern universities precludes management structures operating in anything like a familial way, so that what matters here is not an unrealistic appeal to friendliness to disguise exploitation, but a scrupulous adherence to a more impartial conception of justice. However I have focused here on the importance of a familial relationship within the university's intellectual life, rather than within its management. And I have tried to indicate the substantive activities that are required to give content to the notion of a familial community as an ideal. Of course claims can be made about university life as familial or collegial when in fact none of the structures (or virtues) are in place to give that content. But the inappropriate use of the familial or collegial conception is a topic for a different paper. I thank Jean Porter for drawing my attention to these issues.

220. I am grateful to David Charles, Mark Nelson, Jean Porter, Simon Robinson, Tim Williamson and audiences at the Café Humanite in Ilkley, and the Oriel Philosophy society, for comments on earlier drafts of this chapter.

Note to chapter 9: The rise of the rock dove   *Sue Vickerman*

221. Written for the University of Leeds Centenary Service, April 2004.

Notes to chapter 10: Values and scientific research   *Tom McLeish*

222. D.B. Resnik, *The Ethics of Science*, London: Routledge 1998.

223. J. Turney, *Frankenstein's Footsteps*, Yale: Yale University Press 1998.

224. T. Peters, *Science, Theology and Ethics*, Aldershot: Ashgate 2003.

225. Gregory of Nyssa, *On the Soul and the Resurrection*, translation from Nicene and Post-Nicene Fathers, Series II, vol. V, Christian Classics Ethereal Library, Calvin College, 1999.

226. W.C.K. Poon and T.C.B. McLeish, 'Real Absences in the Sciences: Scientists' response to George Steiner's *Real Presences*', *Theology*, 2, 1999.

227. 2 Cor 5:18, 19.

228. G. Steiner, *Real Presences*, London: Faber, 1989.

229. N. Lash, 'Contemplation, metaphor and real knowledge', in *The Beginning and End of Religion*, Cambridge: Cambridge University Press, 1996.

230. See p. 26 above.
231. J. Barzun, *Science, the Glorious Entertainment*, London: Secker and Warburg 1964.
232. M. Polanyi, *Personal Knowledge: Towards a post-critical philosophy*, New York: Harper and Row, 1964.
233. e.g. Committee on the Conduct of Science, *On Being a Scientist*, 2nd edn, Washington D.C.: National Academy Press, 1994.
234. O. O'Neill, *A Question of Trust: The BBC Reith lectures 2002*, Cambridge: Cambridge University Press, 2003. *www.bbc.co.uk/radio4/reith2002/*.
235. Turney 1998.
236. A. Tilby, *Science and the Soul*, London: SPCK, 1992.
237. D. Burke, 'Assessing Risk: Science or Art?', *Science and Christian Belief*, 2004.
238. T.C.B. McLeish and W.C.K. Poon, 'How many cultures? "Real presences" and the healing of the academy', *Interdisciplinary Science Review* 26, 2001, pp. 167–72.
239. See chapter 4 above.
240. See chapter 2 above.
241. This chapter is based on a paper presented to the International Conference on 'Teaching applied ethics in higher education', Roehampton Univeristy, 2–4 September 2003.

Notes to chapter 11: Assumptions and values in the production of knowledge *Hilde Eileen Nafstad*

242. D. Føllesdal, *The Norwegian Research Council's Ethics Program*, Stencil: University of Oslo, 2001.
243. L. Krasner and A. Houts, 'A study of the "value" systems of behavioral scientists', *American Psychologist*, 39, 1984, pp. 840–50.
244. K.J. Gergen, 'Social psychology as history', *Journal of Personality and Social Psychology*, 26, 1973, pp. 309–20.
245. A.R. Mahrer, 'Philosophy of science and the foundations of psychotherapy', *American Psychologist*, 55, 2000, pp. 1117–25.
246. G.S. Howard, 'The role of values in the science of psychology', *American Psychologist*, 40, 1985, pp. 255–65.
247. W. James, *A Pluralistic Universe*, Cambridge Mass.: Harvard University Press, 1979 edn.
248. G.G. Noam and K.W. Fisher, 'Introduction: The foundational role of relationships in human development', in G.G. Noam and K.W. Fisher (eds.) *Development and vulnerability in close relationships*, Mahwah, N.J.: Lawrence Erlbaum Associates, 1996, pp. ix–xx.
249. A.P. Fiske, 'The four elementary forms of sociality: Framework for a unified theory of social relations', *Psychological Review*, 99, 1992, pp. 689–723. R.J. Herrnstein, 'Rational choice theory: necessary but not sufficient', *American Psychologist*, 45, 1990, pp. 356–67. H.E. Nafstad, 'The neo-liberal ideology and the self-interest paradigm as resistance to change', *Radical Psychology*, 3(1), 2002, pp. 3–21. P.A.M. van Lange,

'Beyond self-interest: a set of propositions relevant to interpersonal orientations', in W. Stroebe and M. Hewstone (eds.) *European Review of Social Psychology*, 11, 2000, pp. 297–331.

250. Fiske 1992, p. 689.

251. van Lange 2000.

252. van Lange 2000, p. 299.

253. Fiske 1992. Nafstad 2002.

254. I.S. Jørgensen and H.E. Nafstad (in press), 'Human strengths – philosophical and historical roots' in P. Lindley and S. Joseph (eds.) *Handbook in Positive Psychology*, New York: Wiley.

255. Howard 1985, p. 264.

256. W. McDougall, *An Introduction to Social Psychology*, London: Methuen, 1908.

257. M.L. Hoffman, 'Developmental synthesis of affect and cognition and its implications for altruistic motivation', *Developmental Psychology*, 11, 1975, pp. 607–22. M.L. Hoffman, *Empathy and Moral Development: Implications for caring and justice*, Cambridge: Cambridge University Press, 2000. C.D. Batson, *The Altruism Question: Toward a social-psychological answer*, Hillsdale, N.J.: Lawrence Erlbaum, 1991. M.E.P. Seligman and M. Csikszentmihalyi (eds.) 'Positive psychology', *American Psychologist*, 55(1) (special issue), 2000.

258. D.T. Miller, 'The norm of self-interest', *American Psychologist*, 54, 1999, pp. 1053–60.

259. Miller 1999, p. 1053.

260. Miller 1999.

Notes to chapter 12: The atrophy of the affect   *John Cowan*

261. D. Goleman, *Emotional Intelligence*, London: Bloomsbury Publishing, 1996.

262. B.S. Bloom, M.D. Engelhart, E.J. Furst, W.H. Hill and D.R. Krathwohl, *Taxonomy of Educational Objectives* – Handbook I: *Cognitive domain*, London: Longmans Green, 1956.

263. J. Heywood, *Assessment in Higher Education*, London: Jessica Kingsley Publishers, 2000.

264. D. Krathwohl, B.S. Bloom and D.B. Mersia, *Taxonomy of Educational Objectives*, Handbook 2: *Affective domain*, London: Longmans Green, 1964.

265. J.H. Newman, *Letter to Mrs William Froude*, cited in *The Oxford Dictionary of Phrase, Saying and Quotation*, Oxford: Oxford University Press, 1997.

266. P. Ramsden, *Learning to Teach in Higher Education*, London and New York: Routledge, 1992. J. Biggs, *Teaching for Quality Learning at University*, Buckingham: Open University Press, 1999. S. Ketteridge, S. Marshall, and H. Fry, *The Effective Academic*, London: Kogan Page, 2002. D. Bligh, *What's the Use of Lectures?* Exeter: Intellect, 1998. S.D. Brookfield, *Understanding and Facilitating Adult Learning*, Buckingham: Open University Press, 1986. S. Rowland, *The Enquiring University Teacher*, Buckingham: Open University Press, 2000. P.T. Knight, *Being a Teacher in Higher Education*, Buckingham: Open University Press, 2000.

267. P.J. MacDonald, 'Selection of health problems for a problem-based curriculum', in D. Boud and G. Feletti (eds.) *The Challenge of Problem-Based Learning* (2nd edn), London: Kogan Page, 1997.

268. Heywood, 2000. L. Kaplan, *Developing Objectives in the Affective Domain*, San Diego: Collegiate Publishing, 1978.

269. M. Mentkowski and associates, *Learning that Lasts*, San Francisco: Jossey-Bass, 2000.

270. J.H. Newman, *The Idea of a University*, London: Longman Green, 1847 edn.

271. R. Gardner, J. Cairns and D. Lawton (eds.) *Education for Values*, London: Kogan Page, 2000.

272. G. Collier, 'Learning moral commitment in higher education', *Studies in Higher Education*, 26(1), 1997, pp. 73–83.

273. R. Barnett, *Beyond All Reason: Living with ideology in the university*, Buckingham: Open University Press, 2003, chapter 9.

274. Krathwihl et al. 1964.

275. *Education for Capability Manifesto*, London: Royal Society of Arts, 1980.

276. L. Kaplan, *Developing Objectives in the Affective Domain*, San Diego: Collegiate Publishing, 1978.

277. L. Carroll, *Through the Looking Glass – and what Alice found there*, London: MacMillan and Co. Ltd., 1935.

278. J. Dowie and A. Elstein, *Professional Judgment: A reader in clinical decision making*, Cambridge: Cambridge University Press, 1988.

279. A.J. Romiszowski, *Designing Instructional Systems: Decision-making in course planning and curriculum design*, London: Kogan Page, 1981.

280. D.A. Kolb, *Experiential Learning: Experience as a source of learning and development*, Englewood Cliffs, New Jersey: Prentice Hall, 1984.

281. J. Cowan *Education for Capability in Engineering Education*, unpublished D. Eng. thesis, Heriot-Watt University, Edinburgh, 1986.

282. J.V. Wertsch, *Vygotsky and the Social Formation of Mind*, Cambridge, Mass.: Harvard University Press, 1985.

283. J. Cowan, *On Becoming an Innovative University Teacher*, Buckingham: Open University Press, 1998.

284. Bligh 1998.

285. C.R. Rogers, *Freedom to Learn – A view of what education might become*, Columbus, Ohio: Merrill, 1964.

286. B.F. Skinner and C.R. Rogers, *Dialogue on Education and the Control of Human Behaviour*, 1962, unpublished until printed in H. Kirschenbaum and V.L. Henderson (eds.) *Carl Rogers Dialogues*, London: Constable, 1990.

287. C.R. Rogers, *Freedom to Learn – for the 80's*, Columbus, Ohio: Merrill, 1983.

288. Collier 1997.

289. C.R. Rogers, *A Way of Being*, Boston: Houghton Mifflin Co, 1980, p. 271.

290. C.R. Rogers, *On Becoming a Person*, Constable: London, 1967. Rogers 1983.

291. I. McGill and L. Beaty, *Action Learning*, London: Kogan Page, 2001.

292. C.R. Rogers, 'Empathic: unappreciated way of being', *The Counseling Psychologist*, 5, 1975 pp. 2, 4.
293. McGill and Beaty 2001.
294. Rogers 1975.
295. Rogers 1980.

Notes to chapter 13. Values and student support   *Nigel Humphrys*

296. C. Lago and N. Humphreys, 'Issues of difference in further and higher education', in J. Lees and A. Vaspe (eds.) *Clinical Counselling in Higher Education and Further Education*, London: Routledge, 1999.
297. Student Services: *Effective approaches to retaining students in higher education*. London: UUK, 2002.
298. *Responding to Mental Health Issues: Duty of care responsibilities for student services in higher education*, AMOSSHE/UUK, December 2001.
299. J. Fley, 'Student personnel pioneers: those who developed our profession', *NASPA Journal*, 17(1), pp. 23–9.
300. D. Lanhom, *Student affairs: a profession's heritage*, American College Personnel Association Media Publication No. 40, University Press of America, 1949.
301. Robert Young, 'Guiding values and philosophy', in R. Young (ed.) *Student Services: A handbook for the profession*, 3rd edn., London: Jossey-Bass, 1996, pp. 83–105.
302. M.B. Fisher and J.L. Noble, *College as Personal Development*, Englewood Cliffs, NJ: Prentice Hall, 1960.
303. Frank Furedi, 'Get rid of those professional stabilisers', *Times Higher Education Supplement*, 17 October 2003.
304. Simon Robinson, *A Very Peculiar Practice: Services for students and staff at the University of Leeds*. Occasional Paper for the Centenary of the University of Leeds, 2004.
305. A. Grant, 'Where is the Evidence?', *Association for University and College Journal*, Winter 2003.
306. See Ahead4health website: *www.leeds.ac.uk/ahead4health*. See also *Guidelines on Student Mental Health Policies and Procedures for Higher Education*, London: UUK, 2000.
307. Student Personal Development website: *www.leeds.ac.uk/spd/*.
308. The Mental Health of Students in HE. London: Royal College of Psychiatrists, January 2003.
309. S.D. McNair, 'Getting the most out of HE: supporting learner autonomy'. Department for Education and Employment, 1997.

Notes to chapter 14: Values and the global community   *Clement Katulushi*

310. See *www.unesco.org/iau/he/globalization-intro.html*, accessed on 9 June 2004.
311. Diana Warwick, 'Globalization: the challenges and opportunities for UK higher

education', March 1999. See *www.universitiesuk.ac.uk/speeches*, accessed on 23 June 2003.

312. Donald Macleod, '1,000 academics to lose research funding', in *Guardian*, 24 February 2003 and also 'Research funding at risk', *Guardian*, 11 February 2003.

313. Accessed *www.manchester.ac.uk* on 2 March. Note that this website subsumes the earlier websites of the founding universities: *www.umist.ac.uk* and *www.man.ac.uk*.

314. Duran Seddon *Immigration, Nationality and Refugee Law Handbook*, Joint Council for the Welfare of Immigrants, London: 2002, p. 300.

315. Seddon 2002, p. 4.

316. *Towards A Policy on International Students Education*, London: UKCOSA, 1986, 1, p. 4.

317. Gordon Graham, *Universities: The recovery of an idea*, Imprint Academic, 2002, p. 67.

318. Adrian Furnham, 'Foreign students – education and culture shock', in *The Psychologist*, 17(1), 2004, pp. 16–19.

319. See R.H. Fryer in chapter 6 above.

320. Jane Elliot et al., *Communities and their Universities: The challenge of lifelong learning*, London: Lawrence & Wishart, 1996, p. xv.

321. It is the case sometimes that there is tension between the communities in the universities and the communities in which they are located. Such tension may lead to overseas students being unwelcome. A case in point is the ongoing discussions between the University of Leeds and Leeds Metropolitan University and the local residents of Headingley in Leeds who attribute the general degradation of Headingley to high student population in the area. Leeds City Council is exploring ways to restrict houses of multiple occupants to stem what is seen as the student influx. The *Independent* made a comment about this saying, 'Students, as any parent knows are a mixed blessing. They bring many benefits – money, ideas and cultural activity – but they also bring noise, litter and a rootlessness that is antithetical to a stable, prosperous community.' From article: 'Comment: Universities must reach out', *Independent*, 21 October 2004.

322. Marjorie Reeves, *The Crisis in Higher Education: Competence, delight and the common good*, Milton Keynes: Open University Press, 1988, pp. 46 ff. Reeves gives a useful, detailed discussion of the university along the guild model. She argues that all scholarly activities by their nature share certain intrinsic values, such as openness in the quest, persistence in following the clues and integrity in recording and communicating their findings.

323. John Mohan, 'Re-connecting the academy? Community involvement in American and British universities', in Jane Elliot et al., 1996. pp. 93–106. Mohan advances the case for collaborations between universities and the various sectors of the communities in which they are located, such as partnerships, voluntary work and placements, etc.

324. Olga Wojtas, 'Partners master rough seas to win £20 million', *Times Higher Education Supplement*, 10 September 2004.

325. Robert Stevens, *University to Uni: The politics of higher education in England since 1944*, London: Politico's, 2004. Stevens explains how Norman Tebbit threatened to demote universities which failed to toe government policies to polytechnics.

326. Marjorie Reeves, *The Crisis in Higher Education: Competence, delight and the common good*, Open University Press, 1988, p. 45.

327. John Hall et al., *Insitutional Support for Overseas Students in Scotland*, Scottish Council for Research in Edinburgh, 1998, p. 38.

328. James B.M.N. Rugiireheh-Runaku, *The Humble Beginnings of Makerere University*, Spot Publications, 1995, pp. 9–10.

329. Michael J. Kelly, *The Origins and Development of Education in Zambia – from pre-colonial times to 1996*, Lusaka: Image Publishers, 1999, p. 124.

330. National Committee of Inquiry into Higher Education, *Higher Education in the Learning Society*, Stationery Office, 1977.

331. UKCOSA 1998, p. 12.

332. Paul Filmer, 'Disinterestedness and the modern university', in Anthony Smith and Frank Webster, *The Postmodern University? Contested visions of higher education in society*, Buckingham: SRHE and Open University Press, 1997.

333. Carolyn Baylies and Janet Bujra, *AIDS, Sexuality and Gender in Africa: Collective strategies and struggles*, 2000.

334. J. Whitehead, 'Transforming embodied values of humanity into educational standards of judgement for use in creating a new disciplines approach to educational theory', University of Bath Department of Education, 2002, p. 5.

335. An example of this is the document released by the ACU 'HIV/AIDS: towards a strategy for Commonwealth universities' as reported in the *Bulletin*, May 2002 and available on *www.acu.ac.uk/bulletin*.

336. A.N. Shimmin, *The University of Leeds: the first half-century*, Cambridge: Cambridge University Press, 1954, p. 98.

337. M. Escobar, A.L. Fernandez, G. Guevara-Niebla, with Paulo Freire, *Paulo Freire on Higher Education – a dialogue at the National University of Mexico*, Albany: State University of New York, 1994.

338. J. Whitehead, 'Transforming embodied values of humanity into educational standards of judgement for use in creating a new disciplines approach to educational theory', University of Bath Department of Education, 2002.

339. Ignacio Ellacuria is quoted by Jon Sobrino in *Companions of Jesus: The murder and martyrdom of the Salvadorean Jesuits*, London: Cafod/CIIR, 1989.

340. Diana Warwick, 'Globalization: the challenges and opportunities for UK higher education', March 1999. See *www.universitiesuk.ac.uk/speeches*, accessed on 23 June 2003.

341. Jonathan Sacks, *The Dignity of Difference: How to avoid the clash of civilizations*, Continuum, 2002, pp. 26, 27.

342. D. Held, A. McGrew, D. Goldblatt and J. Perraton et al., *Global Transformation: Politics, economies and culture*, Cambridge: Polity Press, 1999.

343. Roger King, 'Globalization and the national context: finding a balance', *The Bulletin*, May 2003, p. 6.

344. Michael Gibbons, 'Competition, globalization and the future of higher education', in *The Bulletin*, May 2003, p. 8.

345. In her keynote speech to the Association of Commonwealth Universities, Mary Robinson, former President of Ireland and UN High Commissioner for Human Rights, argued that a key task of universities is in teaching the skills which students need to be responsible citizens, drawing on common values, a common framework that applies to all people and a common set of tools that all academic disciplines can use as a guide in addressing new challenges. See 'Who is your community in a globalising world?' in *The Bulletin*, May 2002, on *www.acu.ac.uk/bulletin* and *www.acu.ac.uk/2003*.

346. See discussion by David Palfreyman in Warner and Palfreyman 2001, pp. 14–15).

347. It is estimated that the total revenue for higher education in the UK is around £12.8 billion with about 60 per cent coming from UK or EU Governments. See 'The nature of higher education', accessed January 2004 from *www.hefce.ac.uk*. The Higher Education Funding Council for England estimates that of the over 1.8 million HE students in UK universities, there are about 200,000 overseas students from over 200 countries representing almost 12 per cent of the student population.

348. Lucy Hodges, 'Students no longer welcome', in the *Independent*, Thursday 21 October 2004, pp. 6–7. See my earlier comments about the tension between communities in the university and the community surrounding the university.

349. Phil Baty, 'Lambert offers cash for code', *Times Higher Education Supplement*, 5 December 2003, p. 1.

350. Duke Maskell and Ian Robinson, *The New Idea of a University*, Thoverton, Imprint Academic, 2002.

351. *Times Higher Education Supplement*, 23 September 2004, p. 3.

Notes to chapter 15: Only connect   *Gwen Collins*

352. The text was produced in an interactive process between myself and thirty-two other people. I worked with them in an interactive, co-operative way, exercising restraint in terms of my own input once the interview was underway, but being ready to comment honestly on the purpose of the research, or other related matters, when appropriate. Unwittingly I was employing feminist interviewing ethic...[that] transforms interviewer and respondent into co-equals who are carrying on a conversation about mutually relevant, often biographically critical, issues. This narrative, storytelling framework challenges the informed consent and deception models of inquiry... Indeed, according to Denzin and Lincoln, all interviews are negotiated texts. For further discussion of negotiated texts see N.Z. Denzin and Y.S. Lincoln (eds.) *Handbook of Qualitative Research*, second edn, Sage Publications, 2000, pp. 633 f.

353. This research is to be submitted to the University of Birmingham in 2004/5 as a doctoral thesis.

354. This and each of the following quotes are from the transcriptions of interviews.

355. This refers to a degree course dealing with the consequences of gross violations of human rights.

356. Tables 1 and 2 were compiled in the following manner: Up to two entries were made for each person on each table. In deciding where to put an entry I combined a holistic and an analytical approach. A holistic approach involved keeping the overall content of the interview clearly in mind. An analytical approach involved breaking the text down into elements by compiling for every interview a series of statements that were either quotes or summaries of quotes of relevant sections. These were used as column headings for a mapping exercise that made it possible to re-connect quickly with the salient points of each text whilst keeping the whole picture in mind. This detailed examination of the texts enabled me to make sense of the data and construct these tables in order to present it in broad categories.

357. S.A. Khan, *Environmental responsibility: A review of the Toyne Report*, DfEE, Welsh Office, Dept. of the Environment, referring to Further and Higher Education, 1996. 'Key recommendation 1: Responsible global citizenship should be recognised as a desired core learning outcome; "Enabling responsible citizenship" should be recognised as a core business of learning institutions and a legitimate purpose of lifetime learning.'

358. R. Barnett, *Realizing the University in an Age of Supercomplexity*, SRHE and Open University Press, 2000, pp. 171 f.

359. Essay by N. Maxwell in T. Bentley and D.S. Jones (eds.) *The Moral Universe*, Demos Collection 16/2001, p. 156.

360. G.G. Brundtland in F. Dodds, *Earth Summit 2002: A new deal*, Earthscan, 2000, p. 253.

361. Report of the UN Commission for the Nutrition Challenges of the 21st Century, 20 March 2000, cited by I.J. Mohan Razu, the *Expository Times*, vol. 114, 10 July 2003, p. 336.

362. See chapter 14 of this book.

363. I have been involved, with others, in setting up Global Perspectives Networks in two universities. In both cases the network has brought together academics from a wide range of disciplines. Energy is generated by meeting others with deep concerns about global issues, and by working together to find ways to integrate values and academic practice. Good practice is shared in terms of helping students to be prepared to meet the challenges of the global future creatively and with confidence. Both universities are participating in this work at an institutional level. The new Academy for the Advancement of Learning and Teaching (AALT) is supporting a team from one of these universities working on furthering global perspectives across the curriculum, through its pilot Change Academy programme. These two universities were also recently engaged in a project to design, deliver and compare 'global perspectives' modules in different subject areas within four universities, under the direction of the Development Education Association (DEA). The results of this project have been published in the DEA's 'Improving Practice' series as *Global Perspectives in Higher Education*, DEA, Nov. 2003, to which I refer readers who are interested in a fuller understanding of this

approach. *www.dea.org.uk/higher*; Email: dea@org.uk; Tel: 020 7490 8108. Table 2 from that publication (reproduced with permission) lists the common elements that emerged in these modules.

Notes to chapter 16: Values, spirituality and higher education *Simon Robinson*

364. D. Bebbington, 'The secularization of British universities since the mid-nineteenth century', in B. Longfield and G. Marsden (eds.) *The Secularization of the Academy*, Oxford: Oxford University Press, 1992, pp. 259–77.

365. S. Robinson, *Ministry Among Students*, Norwich: Canterbury, 2004, pp. 216 ff.

366. S. Gilliat-Ray, *Religion in Higher Education*, Aldershot: Ashgate, 2000, p. 96.

367. John Reader, *Beyond All Reason*, Cardiff: Aureus, 1997.

368. M. Perry, *Gods Within*, London: SPCK, 1992.

369. *Employment Equality (Religion or Belief) Regulations*, Statutory Instrument No. 1660, 2003, London: HMSO.

370. *Employment Equality (Religion or Belief) Regulations*, section 20.

371. E. Barker, *New Religious Movements*, London: HMSO, 1995.

372. *Extremism and Intolerance on Campus*, CVCP, 1998.

373. Gilliat-Ray, p. 171.

374. Gilliat-Ray, pp. 58 ff.

375. Robinson 2004.

376. S. Robinson, 'Thanks for the memory…death of a student, memorials, mourning and postmodernity', *Contact*, 138, 2002, pp. 16–25.

377. D. Hay with R. Nye, *The Spirit of the Child*, London: Harper Collins, 1998.

378. S. Robinson, K. Kendrick, and A. Brown, *Spirituality and the Practice of Healthcare*, Basingstoke: Palgrave, 2003.

379. Robinson, Kendrick and Brown 2003, p. 23.

380. J. Fowler, *Faithful Change*, Nashville: Abingdon, 1996.

381. C. Alves, 'Not just a matter of words? The religious education debate in the House of Lords', *British Journal of Religious Education*, 13(3), 1991.

382. HM Government (England and Wales) (1944), *Education Act 1944*, London: HMSO, p. 4.

383. J. Beck, 'Spiritual and moral development and religious education', in A. Thatcher (ed.) *Spirituality and the Curriculum*, London: Cassell, 1999, p. 153.

384. C. Meehan, *Spiritual Development and Developing Spirituality in Relation to the Distinctiveness of Catholic Sixth Form Schools*, unpublished Ph.D. thesis, University of Leeds, 1999.

385. M. O'Brien, *Spirituality in Nursing*, Boston: Jones and Bartlett, 1998. A. Bradshaw, *Lighting the Lamp: The spiritual dimension of nursing care*, London: Scutari Press, 1994.

386. Robinson et al. 2003.

387. Fowler 1996. J.H. Westerhoff III, *Will our Children have Faith?*, New York: Seabury, 1976.

388. SSM Student Manual, University of Leeds, p. 5.

389. SSM Student Manual.

390. Robinson et al., 2003.

391. J. van der Ven, *Formation of the Moral Self*, Grand Rapids: Eerdmans, 1998.

392. L. Newton, 'Corporate codes from Borg Warner to the Caux principles', in R. Fredericks (ed.) *A Companion to Business Ethics*, Oxford: Blackwell, pp. 374–85.

393. Robinson 2004, pp. 50 ff.

394. Robinson et al. 2003, pp. 67 ff. D. Randolph-Horn and K. Paslawska, *Spirituality at Work*, Leeds: Leeds Church Institute, 2002.

Notes to chapter 17: The integrity of the university *Robinson and Katulushi*

395. M. Reeves, *The Crisis In Higher Education*, Milton Keynes: Open University Press, 1988. W. Moberly, *The Crisis in the University*, London: SCM, 1949.

396. Mary Warnock, Anglican Chaplains' Conference, High Lea, Hoddesden, September, 1996.

397. Gordon Graham, *Universities: The recovery of an idea*, Thorverton: Imprint Academic, 2002, p. 7.

398. D. Bebbington, 'The secularization of British universities since the mid-nineteenth century', in B. Longfield and G. Marsden (eds.) *The Secularization of the Academy*, Oxford: Oxford University Press, 1992, pp. 259–77.

399. Quoted in S. Gillat-Ray, *Religion in Higher Education*, Aldershot: Ashgate, 2000, p. 22.

400. S. Robinson, *Ministry Amongst Students*, Norwich: Canterbury Press, 2004, pp. 214–15.

401. O. O'Neill, *A Question of Trust: The BBC Reith lectures 2002*, Cambridge: Cambridge University Press, 2003.

402. Elaine Sternberg, *Just Business*, Oxford: Oxford University Press, 2000.

403. O'Neill 2003, chapter 2.

404. A. Campbell, *Paid to Care?*, London: SPCK, 1985.

405. D. Randolph-Horn and K. Paslawska, *Spirituality at Work*, Leeds: Leeds Church Institute, 2002.

406. See chapter 3 above.

407. Derek Bok, *Universities in the Marketplace*, Princeton: Princeton University Press, 2003.

408. Robinson 2004, p. 9.

409. Robinson 2004, p. 208.

410. Chris Megone and Simon Robinson (eds.) *Case Studies in Business Ethics*, London: Routledge, 2002.

411. Robinson 2004, p. 216.

412. *www.leeds.ac.uk/*.

413. J. Armstrong, J. Dixon and S. Robinson, *The Decision Makers: Engineers and ethics*, London: Thomas Telford, 1999, pp. 29 ff.

414. A. Campbell, *Moderated Love*, London: SPCK, 1984.

415. Chapter 2 above.

416. I. Berlin, 'Two concepts of liberty' in A. Quinton (ed.) *Political Philosophy*, Oxford: Oxford University Press, 1969, pp. 141–53.

417. M. Novak, *Morality, Capitalism and Democracy*, London, IEA, 1990.

418. S. Robinson, *Serving Society: The social responsibility of business*, Nottingham: Grove Ethics, 1992.

419. Reeves 1988, pp. 74 ff.

420. R. Barnett, *The Idea of Higher Education*, Milton Keynes: Open University Press, 1990.

421. Barnett 1990.

422. Barnett 1990.

423. R.S. Peters, *Authority, Responsibility and Education*, London: Allen and Unwin, 1959, p. 90.

424. Barnett 1994, p. 85. This is noted by John White, 'Philosophy and the aim of higher education', in *Studies in Higher Education*, 22(1), 1997, pp. 7–19.

425. White 1997.

426. White 1997, p. 13.

427. D. Jenkins, 'What is the purpose of a university – and what light does Christian faith shed on this question?', *Studies in Higher Education*, 13(3), 1988.

428. p. 28–31 above.

429. R. Carter, 'A taxonomy of objectives for professional education', *Studies in Higher Education*, 10(2), 1985, pp. 135–49.

430. Chapter 6 above.

431. Chapter 11 above.

432. Gwen Collins, *Going Global at Leeds Metropolitan University*, a discussion document for the Global Network at Leeds Metropolitan University, 2003.

433. *Higher Education and the Public Good*, The Council for Industry and Higher Education, 2004.

434. Chapters 7 and 12 above.

435. Reeves 1988, pp. 76 ff.

436. G. Legood, 'Universities', in G. Legood (ed.) *Chaplaincy*, London: Cassell, 1999, pp. 132–43.

437. pp. 127–9 above.

438. D. Ford, *Knowledge, Meaning and the World's Great Challenges: Reinventing Cambridge University in the twenty-first century*, Cambridge: Cambridge University Press, 2003, p. 23.

439. D. Ford, 'Responsibilities of universities', *Studies in Christian Ethics*, 17(1), 2004, pp. 22–37, 27.

440. R.H. Tawney, *Equality*, London: Allen and Unwin, 1930.

441. *Higher Education: The report of the committee appointed by the Prime Minster under the chairmanship of Lord Robbins*, 1961, London: HMSO, 1963.

442. *National Committee of Enquiry into Higher Education*, chaired by Lord Dearing, 1997.

443. Jenkins 1988.

444. D. Hardy, 'Theology in the public domain', unpublished paper given in the HE Chaplains' Conference, Hoddesden, 9 September 1992.

445. See chapters 6 and 10 above.

446. Quoted in J. Sobrino, *Companions of Jesus*, CAFOD, SCAF, 1989.

447. M. Friedman, 'The social responsibility of business is to increase profits', in T. Donaldson and P.H. Werhane (eds.) *Ethical Issues in Business*, Englewood Cliffs, N.J.: Prentice-Hall, 1983. Sternberg, 2000.

448. Robinson 1992.

449. R. Solomon, *Ethics and Excellence*, Oxford: Oxford University Press, 1992, p. 168.

450. H. Perkin, 'The historical perspective', in B. Clark (ed.) *Perspectives in Higher Education: Eight disciplinary and comparative views*, Berkeley: University of California Press, 1984.

451. Chapter 10 Above.

452. Chapter 15 Above.

453. Chapter 11 above.

454. Tawney 1930.

455. I. McNay, 'Higher education communities: divided they fail?' A lecture given at the AUA annual conference, Keele University, April 2004.

456. p. 162 above.

457. McNay 2004, p. 6.

458. Robinson 2004, pp. 218–19.

459. P. Hawkins, 'The spiritual dimension of the learning organisation', *Management, Education and Development*, 22(3), 1991, pp. 172–87.

460. Ford 2004, p. 28.

461. A. Smithells, *Papers of Arthur Smithells, Concerning the University of Leeds*, c. 1900–1955, Brotherton Library, Special Collection.

462. Smithells, *Papers*.

Index

professionalization 244
professions 237
Psychology 55, 150–8
public good 259
purpose in higher education 219
Putnam, R. 81

Quality Assurance 265

RAE 245
Ramazanoglu, C. 285
Ramsden, P. 161, 290
Randolph-Horn, D. 298
Ranson, S. 98, 283
Rawls, J. 58
Reay, D. 285
Reeves, M. 200, 293, 294, 299
religion 226–41
religious rights 232
research 66, 69–70, 85–90,
    136–49, 150, 203
Resnik, D.B. 288
responsibility 250
responsiveness 248
rights 82, 197
Robbins Report 13, 76–9, 178,
    180
Roberts, S.K. 282
Robinson, I. 295
Robinson, S. 5, 183, 250, 292,
    297, 298, 299
Rogers, C. 167, 291
Roman Catholic Church vii
Romiszowsky, A.J. 165, 291
Roosevelt, T. 53
Rorty, R. 59
Rose, J. 94, 283
Rowland, S. 161, 291
Royal College of Psychiatrists 186
Rugiireheh-Runaku, J. 294
Russell Report 95–7

Sacks, J. 211, 295
Sans, J. 277
SARS 207
Saudi Arabia 168
Scheherazade 26, 142
Schorske, C. 56
Schön, D. 284
Schwartz, S. 286
scientific enquiry 156–7
Scott, P. 2, 3, 243
Searby, P. 275
Seddon, D. 193, 293
Seidman, S. 281
selflessness 258
Seligman, E.R.A. 54,
Seligman, M.E.P. 156
service level agreement 234
Sennett, R. 38, 40, 276
shalom 4, 139, 241
Shattock, M. 275
Shaw, A. 52
Shi, D. 37
Shills, E. 280
Shimmin, A.N. 294
Shin, C. 275
Silverberg, H. 277
Simkovich, M.K. 54
Simon, B. 282
Skelcer, C. 275
skills 30, 128–9, 225, 252
Skinner, B.F. 154, 291
Slavic, M. 281
Slowey, M. 282
Smith, J. 83, 282
Smithells, A. 6, 267
Sobrino, J. 294
social constructivism 165–6
Social sciences 150–8
Sociology 55, 69
*Special Needs and Disability Act
    2001* 178, 180

307